THE NEW CAMBRIDGE HISTORY OF AMERICAN FOREIGN RELATIONS, VOLUME I

Dimensions of the Early American Empire, 1754–1865

Since their first publication, the four volumes of *The Cambridge History of American Foreign Relations* have served as the definitive source for the topic, from the colonial period to the Cold War. This entirely new first volume narrates the British North American colonists' preexisting desire for expansion, security, and prosperity and argues that these desires are both the essence of American foreign relations and the root cause for the creation of the United States. Expansionism required the colonists to unite politically, because individual colonies could not dominate North America by themselves. Although ingrained localist sentiments persisted, a strong, durable union was required for mutual success, and thus American nationalism was founded on the idea of allegiance to the Union. Continued tension between the desire for expansion and the fragility of the Union eventually resulted in the Union's collapse and the Civil War.

William Earl Weeks is Lecturer in History at San Diego State University. He is the author of *John Quincy Adams and American Global Empire* (1992) and *Building the Continental Empire, 1815–1861* (1996), and co-editor of *American Foreign Relations since 1600: A Guide to the Literature* (2003).

The New Cambridge History of American Foreign Relations

Warren I. Cohen, Editor

THE NEW CAMBRIDGE HISTORY OF AMERICAN FOREIGN RELATIONS, VOLUME I

Dimensions of the Early American Empire,

1754–1865

WILLIAM EARL WEEKS
San Diego State University

CAMBRIDGE
UNIVERSITY PRESS

CAMBRIDGE UNIVERSITY PRESS
Cambridge, New York, Melbourne, Madrid, Cape Town,
Singapore, São Paulo, Delhi, Mexico City

Cambridge University Press
32 Avenue of the Americas, New York, NY 10013-2473, USA

www.cambridge.org
Information on this title: www.cambridge.org/9781107005907

First published 2013

Printed in the United States of America

A catalog record for this publication is available from the British Library.

Library of Congress Cataloging in Publication data
The new Cambridge history of American foreign relations.
p. cm.
Includes bibliographical references and index.
ISBN 978-1-107-03183-8 (hardback set) – ISBN 978-1-107-00590-7 (hardback v. 1) –
ISBN 978-0-521-76752-1 (hardback v. 2) – ISBN 978-0-521-76328-8 (hardback v. 3) –
ISBN 978-0-521-76362-2 (hardback v. 4)
1. United States – Foreign relations. I. Weeks, William Earl, 1957–
II. LaFeber, Walter. III. Iriye, Akira. IV. Cohen, Warren I.
V. Title: New history of American foreign relations.
E183.7.N48 2012
327.73–dc23 2012018193

ISBN 978-1-107-00590-7 Volume 1 Hardback
ISBN 978-0-521-76752-1 Volume 2 Hardback
ISBN 978-0-521-76328-8 Volume 3 Hardback
ISBN 978-0-521-76362-2 Volume 4 Hardback
ISBN 978-1-107-03183-8 Four-Volume Hardback Set

*This book is dedicated to three inspirational teachers:
to Professor Earl Pomeroy and to the memories of
Professors H. Stuart Hughes and Armin Rappaport*

CONTENTS

LIST OF MAPS

GENERAL EDITOR'S
INTRODUCTION

My goal for *The Cambridge History of American Foreign Relations*, published in 1993, was to make the finest scholarship and the best writing in the historical profession available to the general reader. The response of readers and reviewers was gratifying. Then, as now, I had no ideological or methodological agenda. I wanted some of the leading students of diplomatic history, regardless of approach, to join me, and I was delighted to have my invitations accepted by the first three to whom I turned.

When I conceived of the project nearly thirty years ago, I had no idea that the Cold War would end suddenly, that the volumes would conclude with a final epoch as well defined as the first three. The collapse of the Soviet Empire, just as I finished writing Volume 4, astonished me, but allowed for a sense of completion those volumes would have lacked under any other circumstances.

Twenty years have passed since the publication of those volumes. Most obviously, additional chapters were needed to bring the story to the present. In addition, we were aware of the need to incorporate new scholarship, fresh insights into the works. *The New Cambridge History of American Foreign Relations* offers our most recent thoughts.

The first volume of the 1993 series was written by Bradford Perkins, then the preeminent historian of late-eighteenth- and early-nineteenth-century American diplomacy and doyen of active diplomatic historians. Brad's death necessitated a search for a successor to write the initial volume of *The New Cambridge History of American Foreign Relations*. With the concurrence of my colleagues Akira Iriye and Walter LaFeber, I chose William Earl Weeks as this generation's finest student of early American diplomacy.

Weeks has written persuasively, sometimes provocatively, on a broad range of subjects, focused primarily on American expansion. Like Perkins, he stresses the building of an empire and sees a pattern of imperial behavior that existed before the creation of an independent United States. He sees men such as Ben Franklin promoting a vision of a great nation, an empire of freedom that would stretch across the continent. Again, like Perkins, he notes the persistent effort of presidents to dominate policy, contrary to the intent of the participants in the Constitutional Convention. In particular, Weeks raises the stature of James Monroe, portraying him as the first "hidden hand" president, foreshadowing methods Dwight Eisenhower perfected more than a century later. He is equally impressed with the audacity of James Polk as he contributed mightily to the nation's self-declared expansionist mission. He describes how Polk's role in acquiring an empire on the Pacific provided an enormous stimulus to continental expansion. Weeks argues that the concept of Manifest Destiny was applicable to the entire forty years' period preceding the Civil War. He demonstrates that American leaders did not hesitate to eliminate all obstacles to the creation of the early American Empire. He details their brutal treatment of Native Americans as the nation satisfied its lust for land on which various tribes had lived for hundreds of years. And finally, he takes a fresh look at the issue of slavery as a cause of the Civil War.

Walter LaFeber, author of the second volume, is one of the most highly respected of the so-called Wisconsin School of diplomatic historians, men and women who studied with Fred Harvey Harrington and William Appleman Williams and their students, and were identified as "New Left" when they burst on the scene in the 1960s. LaFeber's newly revised volume covers the last third of the nineteenth century and extends into the twentieth, to 1913, through the administration of William Howard Taft. He discusses the link between the growth of American economic power and expansionism, adding the theme of racism, especially as applied to Native Americans and Filipinos. Once again, his rejection of the idea of an American quest for order is striking. He argues that Americans sought opportunities for economic and missionary activities abroad and that they were undaunted by the disruptions they caused in other nations. A revolution in China or Mexico was a small price to pay for advantages accruing to Americans, especially when the local people paid it. His other inescapable theme is the use of foreign affairs to enhance presidential power.

The third volume, which begins on the eve of World War I and carries the story through World War II, is again written by Akira Iriye, past president of the American Historical Association and our generation's most innovative historian of international relations. Japanese-born, educated in American universities, Iriye has been fascinated by the cultural conflicts and accommodations that permeate power politics, particularly as the United States has confronted the nations of East Asia. Iriye opens his book with a quick sketch of the international system as it evolved and was dominated by Europe through the seventeenth, eighteenth, and nineteenth centuries. He analyzes Wilsonianism in war and peace and how it was applied in Asia and Latin America. Most notable is his discussion of what he calls the "cultural aspect" of the 1920s. Iriye sees the era about which he writes as constituting the "globalizing of America" – an age in which the United States supplanted Europe as the world's leader and provided the economic and cultural resources to define and sustain the international order. He notes the awakening of non-Western peoples and their expectations of American support and inspiration. In his conclusion he presages the troubles that would follow from the Americanization of the world.

Much of my work, like Iriye's, has focused on American–East Asian relations. My friend Michael Hunt has placed me in the "realist" school of diplomatic historians. Influenced by association with Perkins, LaFeber, Iriye, Ernest May, and younger friends such as John Lewis Gaddis, Michael Hogan, and Melvyn Leffler, I have studied the domestic roots of American policy, the role of ideas and attitudes as well as economic concerns, the role of nongovernmental organizations including missionaries, and the place of art in international relations. In the final volume of the series, *Challenges to American Primacy, 1945 to the Present,* I also rely heavily on what I have learned from political economists and political scientists.

I begin Part I of the book in the closing months of World War II and end it with the disappearance of the Soviet Union in 1991. I write of the vision American leaders had of a postwar world order and the growing sense that the Soviet Union posed a threat to that vision. The concept of the "security dilemma," the threat each side's defensive actions seemed to pose for the other, looms large in my analysis of the origins of the Cold War. I also emphasize the importance of the two political systems: the paradox of the powerful state and weak government in the United States and the secrecy and brutality of the Stalinist regime. Throughout the volume, I note the importance of the disintegration of prewar colonial empires, the appearance of scores of newly independent states in Africa, Asia, and Latin America, and the turmoil caused by American and Soviet efforts to force them into an international system designed in Washington and Moscow. Finally, I conclude Part I with the reemergence of Germany and Japan as major powers, the collapse of the Soviet Union, and the drift of the United States, its course in world affairs uncertain in the absence of an adversary.

In Part II, two chapters focus on the American role in world affairs since the end of the Cold War. I write of the struggle of political leaders and public intellectuals in the United States to find a new lodestar after the collapse of the Soviet Union rendered containment obsolete. George H. W. Bush and William Jefferson Clinton were hampered by a public tired of efforts to pacify an unruly world, demanding attention to domestic affairs. Not until the al Qaeda attacks on American soil on September 11, 2001, was a new foreign policy goal, articulated by George W. Bush, "the War on Terror," widely accepted – with grim consequences in Iraq and Afghanistan. But in the twenty-first century, it was quickly apparent that the principal challenge to American primacy would be the resurgence of Chinese power. As I write, Barack Obama has disposed of Osama bin Laden, but American troops remain in Afghanistan, Iran and North Korea taunt the American president, and he rebalances his nation's defensive forces across the Pacific.

There are a number of themes that can be followed through these four volumes, however differently the authors approach their subjects. First, there was the relentless national pursuit of wealth and power, described so vividly by Weeks and LaFeber. Iriye demonstrates how Americans used their wealth and power when the United States emerged as the world's leader after World War I. I discuss America's performance as hegemon in the years immediately following World War II, and its response to perceived threats to its dominance through the Cold War – and after.

A second theme of critical importance is the struggle for control of foreign policy. Each author notes tension between the president and

Congress, as institutionalized by the Constitution, and the efforts of various presidents, from 1789 to the present, to circumvent constitutional restraints on their powers. The threat to democratic government is illustrated readily by the Nixon-Kissinger obsessions that led to Watergate, Reagan's Iran-Contra fiasco, and the deceptions of the Bush-Cheney administration that led to the invasion of Iraq.

Finally, we are all concerned with what constitutes American identity on the world scene. Is there a peculiarly American foreign policy that sets the United States off from the rest of the world? We examine the evolution of American values and measure them against the nation's behavior in international affairs. And we worry about the impact of the country's global activity on its domestic order, fearful that Thomas Jefferson's vision of a virtuous republic has been forgotten, boding ill for Americans and for the world they are allegedly "bound to lead."

Warren I. Cohen

INTRODUCTION

We have a record of conquest, colonization, and territorial expansion unequalled by any people of the nineteenth century.

Henry Cabot Lodge, 1895

Who can limit the extent to which the federative principle may operate effectively?

Thomas Jefferson, 1801

American history is longer, larger, more varied, more beautiful, and more terrible than anything anyone has ever said about it.

James Baldwin, October 16, 1963

Dimensions of the Early American Empire, 1754–1865, casts the history of antebellum U.S. foreign relations as fundamentally linked to the creation of an American republican empire. Some readers may be surprised to see use of the term "American Empire" in the title. After all, everyone knows that the United States was founded in opposition to British imperialism; moreover, American leaders have long opposed the creation and spread of other empires.

Yet there are least three reasons "American Empire" is the most accurate term to use in talking about antebellum U.S. foreign relations. First, it was the term the Founders themselves used to describe their creation. George Washington conceived of the United States as a "rising empire," an extensive dominion destined to grow in population, territory, and power. Washington and many others of the revolutionary generation self-consciously saw themselves as part of a historic imperial tradition, especially that of the Roman republic. In their commitment to public service and the public good, in their place names, and in the architectural styles of their public buildings, Americans saw themselves as latter-day Romans destined to export their ways of living to the world.

Washington seemed to be a modern-day Cincinnatus both in his devotion to public service and in the way in which he lightly held power. Thomas Jefferson's "Empire of Liberty" placed imperial expansion within the context of an expanding republican system that he saw as synonymous with progress. Peter Onuf writes, "Jefferson cherished an imperial vision of the new American nation," understanding that only rapid expansion could supply the vast new territories needed to stave off internal crises.[1] In fact, use of the term "empire" in the context of U.S. history fell out of favor only when it took on a negative connotation in the latter part of the nineteenth century as a result of the cruelties associated with the European conquest of Africa and Asia. At least until the Civil War, Americans used the term "empire" in a positive way to describe their civilization.

A second reason for using the term "empire" is to better situate the creation of a transcontinental republic amid the imperial rivalries of the time. Mid-eighteenth-century fears of encirclement by the French and Spanish empires provided the initial impetus to the creation of a colonial unity that could win the imperial struggle for North America. To a considerable degree, the United States was conceived as an entity capable of defeating the European and Native American empires that blocked its expansion. Historians have long puzzled over the seeming contradiction of "the imperialism of antiimperialism" characteristic of American foreign policy during this time, but the anomaly disappears when one realizes that Americans were not opposed to all empires, only to those different from their own. They shared this tendency in common with other European empires that sought to defeat their rivals in the name of their own distinct imperial projects. Americans equated their empire with progress, civilization, and, above all, freedom; they did not see it as a tool of oppression and hence were not reluctant to use the term to describe themselves.

Some historians have argued that when the Founders used "empire" to describe the United States they were using it to refer to what is now called a "nation," thereby making anachronistic its use of the word "empire" today. But this objection fails to consider the fact that nations themselves are often imposed unities on at times unwilling populations.

---

[1] Peter S. Onuf, *Jefferson's Empire: The Language of American Nationhood* (Charlottesville, 2000), 1.

From the Ohio Country westward, the American nation-state was built on the conquest of peoples – Native American, Hispanic, French, and others – incorporated without their consent, who were compelled to give up their traditional ways of life, who often faced removal to new lands further west, and who, in some cases, were threatened with annihilation by acts of violence perpetrated either by frontiersmen or by the U.S. military. Writing the history of American continental expansion requires an excavation of these sorts of basic facts to prevent their being lost to a latter-day version of Manifest Destiny that posits U.S. expansion across an "empty" continent accomplished in a relatively simple fashion. Thus Niall Ferguson is wrong when he states "[O]verland expansion was easy; this is often forgotten."[2] What is often forgotten is the fundamentally imperial nature of the U.S. conquest of a large portion of the North American continent. That expansionist project was neither easy nor cheaply realized; recounting it forms a substantial part of the narrative that follows.

A third reason "American Empire" is an appropriate term is that it encompasses the whole of the territorial domain of the United States, and not only that portion admitted as states at any given moment in history. The western imperial territories functioned as an enormous source of wealth and opportunity to which Americans could remove when conditions turned sour in the states. When economic convulsions such as the Panic of 1837 ruined the prospects of many people in the eastern portions of the country, it created the conditions for an outbreak of "Oregon fever," promising a place to go for a fresh start at realizing the American dream. The development of the states would have been very different without the western imperial territories as a safety valve to defuse and diffuse social and economic crises. Yet the American Empire includes more than the western imperial domain. It also connotes the full cultural, economic, ideological, and maritime reach of a civilization that self-consciously saw itself as the cutting edge of human history. Americans sought not only to trade with the world but also to transform the terms of that commercial intercourse according to the principles of liberal capitalism and to transform the oceans of the world from zones of anarchy to well-ordered highways of commerce. A narrow focus on American "domestic" history – internal

---

[2] Niall Ferguson, *Colossus: The Price of America's Empire* (New York, 2004), 35.

developments within the United States – fails to adequately account for the importance of developments outside the nation's boundaries. A history of the American Empire allows for the foreign policy events crucial to national development to be incorporated into domestic histories and not be artificially separated from them, as often occurs in more traditional national histories. Historians have long understood that the history of American foreign relations is bound up with the history of the American nation-state, but it also must be understood that the history of the American nation-state is to a large extent a function of its foreign relations. More generally it can be said that the boundary between "domestic" and "foreign" is itself an evolving, semipermeable barrier with political, economic, and psychological components. The concept of American Empire allows for a complex transnational, transborder reality to inform the study of both foreign and domestic affairs.

Having established proper terminology the question remains, What is the American Empire composed of? What are its key component parts? How do they fit together to make an imperial entity? This work suggests that the ten key dimensions of the antebellum American Empire are as follows.

First, a preexisting colonial-era desire for expansion and security that could not be met by the individual colonies catalyzed both the creation of the Union and the development of American nationalism. Although the traditional view suggests that a primitive American nationalism led to a union and that this union soon embarked on a program of expansion, *Dimensions of the Early American Empire* argues the reverse: that a preexisting expansionist tendency (and concomitant concerns regarding security) necessitated a union in order to be realized, and that the nation was invented in order to solidify the political union. Historians have demonstrated that concerns over a central government lacking the power to conduct a vigorous foreign policy substantially motivated the creation of the Constitution. This narrative extends that insight, arguing that the idea of union (colonial or otherwise) arose from a desire to execute a foreign policy of expansion and security. Hence, union is the first and most important dimension of the American Empire and of American foreign relations.

A favorable geography forms a second dimension of the American Empire. Although the geographic dimension is often overlooked as a motive force in the creation of the Union, its earliest advocates – such as Benjamin Franklin and George Washington – understood that North America's vast extent, superabundant resources, relatively small native populations, and remoteness from Europe created the conditions for building a prosperous, expansive, and secure society if a political entity could be created capable of taking advantage of them. These favorable circumstances were not the result either of luck (as some would have it) or God's blessing (as it is seen more commonly) but rather a distinct, historic, contingent opportunity that would create the framework for all that would follow. The world's oceans functioned both as highways and as moats, insulating the United States from excessive fear of invasion (and thus the need for continual military preparedness) even as they provided commercial access to the markets of the world. Facing toward both Europe and Asia, the United States represented the keystone country in an emerging global economy, ideally situated to engage the world if it chose to do so and yet relatively impregnable to foreign invasion. To no small degree, geography was destiny in antebellum American history.

The evolution of a distinctive ideology and rhetoric that characterized the United States as a "redeemer nation" constitutes a third dimension of the American Empire. Redeemer nation ideology proved critical in creating a durable American nationalism and in legitimizing American expansionism. It functioned as a lens through which Americans viewed the world, lending a messianic aspect to American foreign relations, an aspect whose importance is often underestimated. It is no exaggeration to say that the redeemer nation ideology is the philosophical foundation of American foreign relations. In parallel to the evolution of the redeemer nation ideology emerged a distinctive rhetoric of American Empire that gave voice to this ideology in the political realm. This rhetoric both framed and defined the political and diplomatic controversies of the era; mastering its use in the public sphere proved the primary way by which power was acquired and directed in the antebellum American Empire.

The Constitution of 1787 represents a fourth dimension of American Empire. Its significance resides chiefly in its role as the centralizing pact that created a federal authority with the power to tax and to borrow, to make national commercial policy, to raise militaries, and to make war. The loose union created under the Articles of Confederation would never have been able to achieve the foreign policy victories made possible by the Constitution. The strong union it created was the essential precondition for a successful imperial foreign policy. The Constitution gave the national government total control over foreign policy, placing virtually no limit on its exercise of powers outside state borders while attempting strictly to limit it within those borders. Inevitably, federal power migrated inward, suggesting the extent to which federal power has historically increased from the outside in. The critical transfer to the central government of responsibility for the western territories (done under the articles government) meant that every act of territorial expansion was a de facto increase of federal responsibility and hence, power. This strong state was achieved while being fundamentally at odds with the popular vision of a decentralized republican state. Richard Van Alstyne trenchantly notes, "[T]he founders of the Republic succeeded in performing a political miracle: they created a Leviathan state, but clad it in the garments of the social compact. It took seventy-five years of controversy and four years of bloody warfare, however, to make good on this paradox."[3]

The fifth dimension of the early American Empire is the essentially popular nature of its imperial expansion. The expansionist tendency, which both predated the creation of the republic and to some extent was the reason for its existence, was a popular phenomenon that received critical support from the federal government but was not initiated by it. American imperial expansion was driven by individual economic motives responding to evolving sources of opportunity. It was not centrally planned or directed, something that both distinguishes it from that of other empires in history and explains much of its success. An ongoing response to contingency informed the evolving limits of the American Empire; its final extent was only one of many possible borders that could have resulted from the fluid international environment of the western hemisphere in the eighteenth and nineteenth centuries.

A strong army and navy along with a prominent martial tradition represents the sixth dimension critical to the construction of the American Empire. Notwithstanding the myth of Americans as a peace-loving folk, the nation's history in the first hundred years of its existence is a record of nearly nonstop conflict with European, Native

[3] Richard W. Van Alstyne, *The Rising American Empire* (New York, 1974; first published 1960), 4.

American, and Mexican foes, both on land and at sea. The impressive record of victories in the name of the American Empire is only part of the story; nearly as important as the tangible gains that victory brought is the role the military tradition plays as the preeminent cultural bonding agent of American nationalism. Every victory reinforced the principle of national unity, even in unpopular wars such as the War of 1812 and the Mexican-American War.

A mostly uncompromising policy of "freedom of the seas" is another key dimension of the early American Empire. Essentially the maritime dimension of the redeemer nation ideology, the project to turn the anarchy of the world's oceans into highways safe for travel and commerce under a U.S. vision of international law was vigorously asserted throughout the period under consideration (except during the Civil War, when the idea of freeing the seas was temporarily abandoned on the grounds of national emergency). The principle of freedom of the seas was affirmed via public pronouncements, by diplomatic agreements, and at times by war, as was the case in the first years of the nineteenth century against the North African states and Great Britain. In peacetime the U.S. navy played a key role as a waterborne sheriff in efforts to end piracy and, less effectively, the struggle to suppress the slave trade. A policy of freedom of the seas, asserted with consistency even in the early days of the nation's history, constituted a de facto expansion of American sovereignty to the global commons of the world's oceans.

The creation and promulgation of an American market empire form another dimension of antebellum foreign relations. Once again, the activities of private citizens drove this aspect of the empire, but the central government provided essential support to international commerce via trade agreements, consular services, and the use of the navy as an avenger of the rights and interests of Americans harmed when doing business abroad. More generally, Americans articulated an ideology of international commerce that defined trade as among "the rights and duties of mankind," as John Quincy Adams put it, and presumed to spread that system throughout the world to those interested in it and impose it on those who were not, most notably Japan. The creation of a global market empire was linked to the growth and development of the domestic economy and in part motivated territorial expansion, as in the case of California, whose access to Asian markets was the initial reason for its acquisition.

Another essential dimension of the growth and development of the antebellum American Empire was the technological innovations of the early nineteenth century, particularly in transportation, communication, production, and war. These technological breakthroughs were linked to the larger Industrial Revolution, which arose simultaneously and not coincidentally (from 1750 onward) with the rise of the United States, a fact whose significance has been largely overlooked. The American Empire would not have happened in the way it did but for the railroad, the telegraph, and the revolver, to name only three key technological innovations of the time.

The tenth dimension of the antebellum American Empire is the profound disagreement that existed over the role and future of slavery. This conflict first arose during the framing of the Constitution, receded for a while, and then reemerged during the Missouri Crisis of 1819–21. From then it slowly but steadily worsened until by the 1850s a de facto split had riven the Union into separate nations. By then a significant and motivated bloc of Americans had deemed slavery to be a moral, economic, and, above all, ideological wrong that had to be abolished if the United States was to realize its destiny as the redeemer nation. The crisis of the Union was manifested in a crisis over the future direction of the Empire: territories that had been conquered but not yet incorporated into the Union. The war began in the mid-1850s on the prairies of Kansas, spreading a few years later to battlegrounds within the Union itself.

The conflict over slavery stands as the central irony of antebellum American history: Americans enthusiastically exported freedom even as they shared no consensus as to its exact meaning and form. This contradiction proved unsustainable. The imposing edifice of union at the center of the empire contained a massive crack in its foundation. A design flaw from the Founders, the crack steadily widened until by the mid-nineteenth century a new generation of Americans demolished the temple of the Union in an apocalyptic war, rebuilding it according to a new plan of freedom.

The narrative that follows combines recent new perspectives on American foreign relations with older but still valuable interpretations, along with the author's own points of view, to create a synthesis that rests on a broad empirical base. A bibliographical essay following the main text seeks to provide a better sense of the scholarly context of its claims. Given the number and complexity of the topics with which it deals and the limited space it has to deal with them, the story must necessarily avoid stepping into the thicket of contrasting interpretations. It proposes a way of conceiving of antebellum American foreign relations but does not presume to be the last word on the matter. Rather, it is hoped that the text stimulates thought, encourages discussion, and suggests possibilities for further study of the antebellum American Empire.

"Are We Rome?" asks Cullen Murphy in a recent thought-provoking book comparing the United States to its Roman predecessor and model.[4] Certainly there are a number of comparisons in this regard that can be made. Yet in the end comparisons to Rome may obscure more than they reveal about the antebellum American Empire. Whatever inspiration and precedent they took from ancient civilizations, especially that of Rome, in the end Americans conceived and accomplished something new and immensely significant at the key transitional moment in world history. This narrative seeks to explain how they did so.

---

[4] Cullen Murphy, *Are We Rome? The Fall of an Empire and the Fate of America* (New York, 2008).

ACKNOWLEDGMENTS

I wish to acknowledge the support and encouragement I have received during the course of writing this book: First, thanks to Warren I. Cohen, Walter LaFeber, and Akira Iriye, my coauthors of *The New Cambridge History of American Foreign Relations,* for asking me to take part in this project. It is an honor to be included in such distinguished company. Special thanks to lead editor Warren Cohen for the help he provided during the writing of the book. Thanks to Eric Crahan, History and Politics editor at Cambridge University Press, for his enthusiasm and guidance in completing the task; thanks also to his assistant Abigail Zorbaugh. Special thanks are due to my two anonymous readers at Cambridge. Their rigorous criticisms and comments on my proposal and draft manuscript greatly improved the project.

Thanks to Regina Paleski, production editor, to her copy editor Betsy Hardinger, and to my indexer, Mary Harper.

Thanks to Christopher Boyce, Elizabeth Cobbs-Hoffman, Ryan Jordan, David La Cross, David Luft, John Marino, Frederic Armstrong (Rick) Nelson, and Ken Serbin for their support in completing this project.

Thanks to Joanne Ferraro and Adriana Putko of San Diego State University; and to Lucy Duvall, formerly of the University of California, San Diego.

All errors in this text are the responsibility of the author.

Some final acknowledgments: first, my thanks to the citizens of California for funding a world-class institution of higher learning that was both accessible and affordable to a young man on his own trying to create a future for himself. May they continue to support the University of California's mission of accessible and affordable excellence in higher education.

This book is dedicated to three teacher/scholars from the University of California, San Diego, who were crucial to my development as a historian. To Earl Pomeroy, a historian's historian, whose careful editing of my work helped me grow as a writer of history and whose arched eyebrows and wry grin made me smile. To the late H. Stuart Hughes, for his inspired teaching and willingness to engage with students. Finally and most especially, this book is dedicated to the late Armin Rappaport. Armin's undergraduate foreign relations class marked the beginning of my career as an historian. His encouragement and example as a teacher, as a scholar, and as a mentor were life changing. He taught me much of what I know about American foreign relations and provided me with the skills and insights to teach myself the rest. Though Armin has been deceased for nearly thirty years, my memory of him remains bright. "I'll see you in New York."

ORIGINS OF THE AMERICAN EMPIRE AND UNION

Empires gave birth to states, and states stood at the heart of empires.

David Armitage, *The Ideological Origins of the British Empire*, 15

Expansion was the essential condition for the growth and prosperity of America.

Gerald Stourzh, *Benjamin Franklin and American Foreign Policy*, 104

Nothing but disunion can hurt our cause.

George Washington, April 15, 1776

JUMONVILLE GLEN, MAY 1754

The world changed profoundly the moment Tanaghrisson's hatchet crashed against the skull of the French officer. After splitting the head of his unresisting captive, the Seneca "half-king" washed his hands in his victim's spilled brains and impaled the head on a pike in a starkly symbolic declaration of hostilities against the French. Tanaghrisson hoped that his provocative act of violence would escalate the brewing clash between France, Britain, and diverse Indian tribes of eastern North America for control of the Ohio Country, a large domain centered on the Ohio River watershed and extending to the Great Lakes. Tanaghrisson aimed to enlist the British in securing his control over at least a part of the territory, both in the name of his tribe and in the name of his own increased power and prestige.

Bearing witness to this shocking act of brutality was twenty-two-year-old colonel George Washington, entrusted by the colonial Virginia legislature to lead a military expedition to the strategically critical Forks of the Ohio, meeting point of the Allegheny, Monongahela, and Ohio Rivers, in order to blunt further French encroachment on lands claimed by Virginia. The expedition had departed from Alexandria, Virginia, in early May 1754, marching through the dense forests of the mountains of western Maryland and Pennsylvania along an Indian path known as Nemacolin's Trail in honor of the Delaware chief said to be its originator. Washington encamped at a clearing in southwestern Pennsylvania known as Great Meadows, a small island of open space in a vast ocean of forest. There he rendezvoused with Tanaghrisson, whom he first had met on an expedition to the Ohio Country the previous November. On that journey Washington had warned the French – who had recently evicted a small British force from the forks of the Ohio and who had begun construction of an outpost on that spot they would name Fort Duquesne – against remaining in the Ohio Country. Returning the following spring, he had enlisted Tanaghrisson – an ambitious Seneca leader of dubious authority – and his followers in a campaign against the French.

On May 6, Tanaghrisson informed Washington of the presence of a French detachment camped for the evening a mere seven miles away. Washington gathered forty men and, along with Tanaghrisson and his band of warriors, marched all night in the rain to arrive at the camp at dawn. From a stone outcropping above a densely wooded glen, Washington's force fell upon the French-Canadians who slumbered below. Those who escaped into the forest fell to the blows of Indian hatchet men positioned behind the trees. About ten French-Canadians perished in the attack; none of Washington's men or his Indian allies died.

Taken captive after the brief and bloody struggle was the young French commander, Lieutenant Joseph Coulon de Villiers de Jumonville, an aristocrat and brother of the commander of French forces at Fort Duquesne, about fifty miles away. Washington, nominally in charge of the attacking force, watched helplessly as Tanaghrisson slaughtered the French commander. News of the attack soon made its way back to the French garrison at the Forks of the Ohio via a sole survivor of the attack who had escaped to tell the tale.

It was only by accident that the young and inexperienced Washington had been named commander of such an important mission. He was to be second-in-command to fifty-four-year-old Joshua Fry, an Oxford scholar who promised to bring some sense of subtlety in confronting the French, aided by Washington's extensive knowledge of the western country gained from his previous two trips to Ohio as a surveyor and explorer. Yet shortly before the expedition departed, Fry was thrown from his horse and killed, thrusting command of a mission critical to both Virginia and the British Empire onto the dashing and rugged Washington. An accomplished horseman, Washington faced no danger of being thrown from his horse.

Washington had a personal as well as patriotic interest in wresting the Ohio Country from the French and their Indian allies. After his brother Lawrence's early death in 1752, Washington had inherited a substantial share of the Ohio Company, a joint stock company of elite Northern Virginia gentry who saw in the western country the next great speculative real estate bonanza. These men, among them Virginia lieutenant governor William Dinwiddie, had been agitating London for some time to assert more strongly Virginia's claim to the Ohio Country, only one part of a more than half-century-long confrontation between Britain and France for imperial control of North America. Washington's own claim to Virginia's western lands, which he had received from his late brother, was itself based on a 1609 document extending the colony's reach westward to the South Sea, and north and west to the Great Lakes and beyond.[1] Washington had mapped and surveyed the Ohio Country for the shareholders at age sixteen, taking care to note for future personal reference what constituted its most valuable lands. As a young and physically robust member of the Virginia gentry, Washington was a natural participant in the imperial thrust west.

Although Washington eagerly sought new wealth in the western lands, he hardly was impoverished before that endeavor. He had inherited approximately two hundred slaves and ten thousand acres of land in Virginia along the Potomac River after his father's death in 1743. Yet the diminished fertility of the soil, exhausted by a century of tobacco cultivation, meant that Washington would need to find new sources of wealth if he hoped to realize his ambition to rise to the top of the Virginia economic and cultural elite. The defeat of the French and Indians in the name of Virginia and the British Empire would redound immensely to

---

[1] Fred Anderson and Andrew Cayton, *The Dominion of War: Empire and Liberty in North America, 1500–2000* (New York, 2005), 14.

his personal benefit. Like his late father and brother, Washington saw military service, notwithstanding its hazards, as the surest path to political and economic success.

Knowing that the attack on Lieutenant Jumonville's force would generate a strong response, Washington and his force dug in at Great Meadows. There he ordered his men to build a small stockade, which he named Fort Necessity, chiefly as protection for his gunpowder supplies. Refusing to assume a position exposed to enemy fire from the surrounding forest, Tanaghrisson and his followers soon departed, leaving Washington and several dozen largely inexperienced Virginia conscripts to confront a few French-Canadians and a much larger number of their Native American allies. On July 3 the enemy attacked, hiding behind the trees as they fired down on Washington's troops, who made easy targets in the shallow rifle pits surrounding the stockade. Making matters worse, rising streams from torrential summer rains soon flooded the low-lying fort and its trenches, making the soldiers' flintlock muskets inoperable and resistance thereby impossible. After the deaths of about thirty of his men, Washington surrendered on July 3, 1754. In the aftermath, the French commander (and brother of the slain Jumonville) graciously spared Washington's life, allowing him and his men to return to Virginia after Washington signed a confession acknowledging his responsibility for the "assassination" of Jumonville and swearing never to return.

George Washington's botched mission to western Pennsylvania provided the spark that reignited the Anglo-French-Indian war in North America, which by 1756 had become a global conflagration known internationally as the Great War for the Empire. By any measure, it was an inauspicious beginning to a military career. Through his experience with Tanaghrisson he had learned of the hazards of entangling alliances. In spite of his failure, Washington emerged from the incident with undiminished confidence in his abilities. In a letter to his brother Jack, he wrote of the assault on Fort Necessity in rapturous terms, noting that he had "heard bulletts [sic] whistle ... and there was something charming in the sound."[2] Paradoxically, Washington's reputation soared in the wake of the failed expedition, thanks in large part to the publication in

[2] Fred Anderson, ed., *George Washington Remembers: Reflections on the French and Indian War* (Lanham, Md., 2004), 74.

Map 1. The Struggle for North America.

June 1754 of a stirring memoir of his trip to the Ohio Country the previous winter. Washington later repudiated his signed confession to the execution of Jumonville, blaming his interpreter for a faulty translation of the French in the original document.

The defeat of the Virginia regiment on the Ohio frontier provoked a strong response from the British government. It had desired to reescalate the ongoing war with France, and yet the humiliation of the Virginians seemed to require a strong response lest the power and prestige of the whole British Empire be called into question. At the instigation of the duke of Cumberland – son of George II and architect of the scorched earth policy that had laid waste to Scotland after the defeat of Bonnie Prince Charlie and his Scots rebels at Culloden in 1742 – an imposing invasion force was gathered. In May 1755, General Edward Braddock and two regiments of the elite Coldstream Guards marched into a newly constructed stockade built on a bluff on the Potomac River near Will's Creek that Braddock named Fort Cumberland, in honor of his patron the duke of Cumberland. There Braddock and his troops, aided by colonial militias and Native American allies, prepared for an assault on the French forces and their Native American allies at Fort Duquesne, about one hundred miles to the west. Brushing off the failures of the Virginia militiamen, British officials confidently expected that a few French soldiers and their Indian allies would be no match for battle-hardened British regular troops.

Washington eagerly embraced another attempt to expand the Anglo-American Empire into the Ohio Country, notwithstanding his signed pledge not to return there. He had a substantial personal stake in the outcome of the battle to control the region. He envisioned an all-water route to Ohio via the Potomac River, conveniently passing by his Virginia estate at Alexandria, which he anticipated would become a key *entrepôt* for goods moving both upriver and down. Later in life he would become a vigorous proponent of the construction of the Chesapeake and Ohio Canal, a waterway running parallel to the Potomac River designed to transport goods upriver in the days before steam power. (Remnants of that canal survive today, repurposed as a hiking and walking trail.) Washington speculated in western lands, eventually owning more than sixty thousand acres west of the mountains, making him one of the largest absentee landowners of his time.[3] He keenly understood that "[l]and is the most permanent estate and the most likely to increase in value."[4]

---

[3] Thomas Slaughter, *The Whiskey Rebellion: Frontier Epilogue to the American Revolution* (New York, 1986), 82.

[4] Richard Norton Smith, *Patriarch: George Washington and the New American Nation* (Boston, 1993), 9.

Thus in 1755 he joined Braddock's expedition as an adjutant and guide, anticipating the advantages a successful expansionist thrust west would give to the British Empire, his home colony of Virginia, and to his own personal reputation and fortune. In this regard, Fred Anderson notes that Washington was "an advocate of empire long before he became the hero of a revolution."[5]

FRANKLIN'S VISION

Joining Washington in Braddock's imperial enterprise was Benjamin Franklin, marking the first time that the trajectories of the two men crossed. Like Washington, Franklin was a zealous imperialist who aimed to remove the Native American and French enemies blocking the migration of Pennsylvanians, Virginians, New Yorkers, and other Anglo-Americans into the seemingly limitless territories west of the Appalachian Mountains. Since the late 1740s Franklin had devoted a substantial portion of his considerable energies to the cause of colonial union, which he believed essential for westward expansion, colonial security, colonial prosperity, and his own speculative success in western lands. The previous summer at Albany he had almost single-handedly turned a congress of northern colonies aimed at strengthening the fraying Anglo-American alliance with the Six Nations of the Iroquois confederacy into a de facto constitutional convention, securing passage of a colonial Plan of Union that created a central governing authority with the power to tax and entrusted with handling expansion and security concerns. The congregants resolved unanimously "[t]hat an [sic] union of the colonies is absolutely necessary for their preservation."[6] Yet the colonial legislatures, lacking the looming threat of Indian attacks that had helped to spur passage of the plan in Albany, were much less eager to join a colonial union. The absence of an immediate security threat, combined with intracolonial rivalries and a zealous determination of local elites not to give up one iota of local autonomy to a distant central government, doomed the plan to defeat. Indeed, in most of the colonies it was never formally considered. In London, where Franklin hoped that Parliament would impose the plan of union on the colonists,

---

[5] Anderson and Cayton, *Dominion of War*, 107.
[6] Leonard Labaree, ed., *The Papers of Benjamin Franklin* (New Haven, 1962), 5:400.

the scheme was received skeptically and quietly shelved. Long-standing British fears of creating a colonial union that might someday slip the leash of imperial control prevented consideration of what might have been a transformative move for the history of the British Empire.

Rejection by both colonial legislatures and by Parliament did not quash Franklin's dream of union. He had first conceived of it in the 1740s. After making himself independently wealthy via his various printing and publishing enterprises, Franklin retired from active participation in private business and devoted himself to two main tasks: first, gaining a better understanding of the mysterious force known as electricity and, second, facilitating the expansion of British North America west of the Appalachian Mountains. In a series of published works, Franklin began to evolve a powerful vision regarding the future both of the North American colonies and of the British Empire. He first gave expression to this vision in "Plain Truth, or Serious Considerations on the Present State of the City of Philadelphia and Province of Pennsylvania" (1747). In it, he voiced concerns that Philadelphia was isolated and vulnerable to attack. The solution was for the colonies to unite for common defense. "At present we are like the separate Filaments of Flax before the Thread is form'd, without Strength, because without Connection; but UNION would make us strong, and even formidable."[7]

A more famous statement of his vision appeared in "Observations Concerning the Increase of Mankind," written in 1751 but not published until 1754. In it, he imagined the British North American colonies formed into one imposing union along a rapidly expanding western frontier. Franklin's awareness of the opportunities available as a result of North America's favorable geography is at the heart of his argument. The abundance of land and other forms of economic opportunity in North America would lead to the proliferation of large families and a consequent doubling of the population approximately every twenty years, something Franklin termed "the American multiplication table." Access to the lands west of the mountains and the limitless opportunity it represented would result in earlier marriages and larger families than was the case in England, where a shortage of tillable soil limited growth. Only with sufficient living room could the prosperity of

---

[7] Gerald Stourzh, *Benjamin Franklin and American Foreign Policy*, 2nd ed. (Chicago, 1969), 44.

the coastal regions be maintained and extended. Franklin conceived a vision of a fast-growing, rapidly expanding domain that would be the embodiment of human freedom, political justice, and material progress. "Observations on the Increase of Mankind" remains, in the words of Gerald Stourzh, "the first conscious and comprehensive formulation of 'Manifest Destiny.'"[8]

Franklin further elaborated his vision regarding the advantages of colonial union in "Plan for Settling Two Western Colonies," written apparently sometime in 1754 and forwarded to the duke of Cumberland in 1756. In it, Franklin described the Ohio Country as being well known as "one of the finest in North America" and absolutely essential for the future prosperity of the colonies in that "our people ... cannot much more increase in number" east of the mountains, a startling claim when one recalls there were only about 2.5 million white colonists at that time. The future was found in Ohio, and if the French were to win it permanently, it would block westward expansion, thereby "preventing our obtaining new subsistence by cultivating new lands ... discourag[ing] our marriages, and keep[ing] our people from increasing; thus (if the expression may be allowed) killing thousands of our children before they are born." He argued, "If two strong colonies of English" were settled in the Ohio Country they would provide security from attack and check the "dreaded junction of the French settlements in Canada, with those in Louisiana ..."[9] In short, Franklin envisioned western expansion as a way for the colonies to escape being encircled by the Gallic menace. As was stated at the Albany Congress, "[I]t seems absolutely necessary that Speedy and Effectual measures be taken to Secure the Colonies from the Slavery they are threatened with."[10] Significant, too, is Franklin's recommendation that the western land claims of the colonies (some of which extended to the Pacific Ocean) be curtailed in the name of practicality: "A single old colony does not seem strong enough to extend itself.... it cannot venture a settlement far distant from the main body, being unable to support it. But if the colonies were united ... they might easily, by their joint force, establish one or more new colonies, whenever they should judge it necessary or advantageous

---

[8] Stourzh, *Franklin and American Foreign Policy,* 59.
[9] Labaree, ed., *Franklin Papers,* 5:458.
[10] Labaree, ed., *Franklin Papers,* 5:373.

to the interests of the whole."[11] As Gerald Stourzh observes regarding the text, "Expansion for defense and expansion for its own sake are merged into one powerful case for the immediate settlement of the western country."[12]

To be realized, Franklin's vision of an expanding British North American empire required a colonial union. This seemed so crystal clear to Franklin that he could not grasp why many colonists resisted it. Such is the fate of the visionary. This sentiment found its most famous expression in a letter he wrote to fellow unionist James Parker in 1751, in which Franklin laments the resistance of the colonists to the idea of union while noting the effectiveness and longevity of the Six Nations Confederacy: "It would be a very strange Thing, if six Nations of ignorant Savages should be capable of forming a Scheme for such an Union, and be able to execute it in such a Manner, as that it has subsisted Ages, and appears indissoluble; and yet that a like Union should be impracticable for ten or a dozen English Colonies, to whom it is more necessary, and must be more advantageous; and who cannot be supposed to want an equal understanding of their Interests."[13] The lesson Franklin learned from the example of the Six Nations Confederacy was not about "democracy," as is sometimes asserted by contemporary scholars, but rather about the importance of union to the establishment of the imperial control of North America.

Perhaps the most radical aspect of Franklin's vision was his conception of an emerging parity between England and the colonies. He proposed that the colonists be treated as equals to citizens of the mother country, candidly admitting in a letter to Peter Collinson in May 1754, "May I presume to whisper my Sentiments in a private Letter? Britain and her Colonies should be considered as one Whole, and not as different States with separate interests."[14] Over time, Franklin saw the colonies not only as a source of raw materials and agricultural products, as had been the case until then, but also as a burgeoning market for British manufactures. In 1760, he wrote to the Scottish philosopher Lord Kames, "I have long been of the opinion that the foundations of

[11] Labaree, ed., *Franklin Papers*, 5:459.
[12] Stourzh, *Franklin and American Foreign Policy*, 73.
[13] Labaree, ed., *Franklin Papers*, 4:119.
[14] Labaree, ed., *Franklin Papers*, 5:332.

the future grandeur and stability of the British Empire lie in America."[15] He would spend nearly twenty years trying to realize this vision of Anglo-American equality, only to find his plea for equality of treatment rejected as it concerned both the colonists and him personally.

Although he was not wholly opposed to the democratic principle, Franklin believed society functioned best when run by an enlightened and wealthy oligarchy, which should make and implement decisions beneficial to the common good. As he wrote concerning the "Plan for the Settlement of Two Western Colonies," "The best public measures therefore are seldom adopted from previous wisdom but forc'd by the occasion." Therefore, even though he refused to acquiesce in an untutored democratic tendency, he actively sought to influence public opinion via the production of letters, articles, pamphlets, and satire appearing in various media. He recognized the need for popular support for major policy initiatives even as he remained skeptical about the efficacy of unmediated democracy.

Educating and guiding public opinion were crucial to gaining that support. One of his most famous efforts in this regard occurred in May 1754, the same month that Washington made his foray into western Pennsylvania. In response to news of the French capture of a British garrison on the Forks of the Ohio, Franklin published in his newspaper the *Pennsylvania Gazette* the woodcut image of a snake, chopped into multiple pieces, each with the name of a colony on it, under the caption "Join or Die." Reputed to be the first political cartoon in American history, it remains one of the most famous. Widely circulated at the time, the image and its pointed caption is one of the first to connect the concept of colonial union with collective security. Some colonial papers suggested another advantage of union by bracketing the motto "Join or Die" with another: "Unite and Conquer."

Washington's and Franklin's efforts to spur unity suggest that the move toward the creation of an American union is best understood as a "grasstips" movement, conceived and implemented by an elite group of patriarchs appropriately known as the Founding Fathers. Franklin and Washington loomed above all others in this group, one a medicine-man prophet, the second a charismatic war chief who reveled in battle and who believed that bullets could not kill him. In Franklin, the incipient

---

[15] Quoted in Stourzh, *Franklin and American Foreign Policy*, 81.

union had a visionary who, struck by lightning once during his kite experiments of 1749, was struck by lightning a second time in the form of a persistent vision of the boundless possibilities represented by colonial union: the creation of a new society unlike any that had preceded it, and of the vast western domain he offered a limitless *lebensraum* for what he anticipated would be the union's rapidly multiplying millions. Franklin grasped better than anyone else that if the enormous energies, enormous wealth, and enormous potential of the thirteen colonies could be harnessed and directed toward a common end by a strong central authority, there would be no foreseeable limit as to what they might accomplish. If Franklin's dream of colonial unity in the name of collective security and collective advantage bore some similarity to a quixotic attempt to catch lightning in a bottle, it also was analogous to a major innovation of its time, the steam engine. For a political union, in a steam engine–like fashion, aimed to harness and direct the enormous potential energies of the British North American colonies, promising to transform the political world in much the same way as the steam engine would transform the economic world. Gerald Stourzh concludes, "Franklin strove for the security, prosperity, and expansion of the British Empire. This was his concept of America's interest."[16] Security, prosperity, and expansion also were the chief motives behind Franklin's subsequent efforts to create a union; indeed, they served as the prime motives for virtually all who came to advocate colonial union. But for most colonists, the costs of autonomy within a union outweighed the practical advantages it offered.

Having been, for the time being, stymied in his push for colonial union, Franklin now sought to facilitate westward expansion by aiding Braddock's expedition. He played an indispensable role in procuring the supply wagons and fifteen hundred horses needed for Braddock's invasion force, as is well known from his *Autobiography*; less well known is that those wagons proved a hindrance to Braddock and his army, demonstrating a tendency to break down on the rock-strewn mountain trail – now called the Braddock Road – that Washington had followed west. Washington, too, played a key part in the expedition, serving as an adjutant and guide to General Braddock. In any case, Franklin and Washington's participation in the expansionist thrust reflected both the

---

[16] Stourzh, *Franklin and American Foreign Policy*, 102.

personal and the public interests each had in acquiring control of the Ohio Country.

Braddock's expedition ended in catastrophic defeat for his forces and in his own death; he was a victim of the Indians and their French allies, his army's inexperience, and his own arrogance. British Redcoats in classic combat formation proved no match for his foes' guerrilla tactics. In a chaotic engagement on July 9, 1755, approximately eight hundred of the twelve hundred soldiers in Braddock's command fell dead or wounded, most of them mistakenly shot by their own side. Braddock's debacle in western Pennsylvania proved to be one of worst defeats in British history in North America. Yet for George Washington the battle proved crucial in establishing his credentials as the warrior-leader of the North American colonies. He was the only British officer – whose obvious symbols of rank made them conspicuous targets – to escape being killed or wounded. Once again he had been exposed to sustained deadly fire at close range and had emerged unscathed, later recounting that he "had one horse killed and two wounded under him – a ball through his hat – and several through his clothes, but escaped unhurt."[17] It was this trial by fire and others to follow that twenty years later would make him the undisputed choice to lead the Continental army. For Franklin, the defeat of a force comprised primarily of British regulars further confirmed the necessity of a centralized colonial government responsible for security and expansion on the western frontier, in particular the making of a uniform Indian policy. For both men, the Braddock disaster marked the beginning and not the end, or, more precisely, the end of the beginning, of their efforts to create a colonial union.

Braddock's defeat set the Pennsylvania and Virginia backcountry aflame. Following the British army's ignominious retreat to the coast, war parties from numerous tribes attacked frontier settlements with devastating effectiveness, burning houses and crops and leaving the mutilated corpses of their tortured captives at strategic points on the roads so as to terrorize any who dared to remain. The historian Matthew Ward estimates that nearly fifteen hundred men, women, and children were killed in the horrific campaign, one thousand more taken captive, and approximately twenty thousand square miles of the

---

[17] Anderson and Cayton, *Dominion of War*, 20.

backcountry laid to waste.[18] Pennsylvania and Virginia proved unable to mount an effective defense against the attacks. Internal political squabbling, the refusal of the large landowners to pay the high taxes needed to mount a credible military force, and poorly trained and led militia combined to make the individual colonies powerless to stop the speedy and stealthy Indian offensive. For a time, even Philadelphia seemed to be at risk of being attacked. In the aftermath of Braddock's shocking defeat and the campaign of terror that followed, many colonists began to fear that the Indian raiding parties and their French allies might drive them into the sea.

Had the colonies adopted the Albany Plan of Union as Franklin urged, the Indian assault might have been blunted. Certainly it offered the hope of a more coordinated colonial response. Only with the arrival of more British regular troops in 1758, and, more importantly, the adoption of a strategy to pacify and divide the Indians of the Ohio Country, was the onslaught stopped. Crafted by General Henry Bouquet, this approach aimed not so much to defeat the Indian resistance as to remove the causes of it. For a while, this brought peace to the frontier, until the blundering policies of Bouquet's successor, Sir Jeffrey Amherst, helped precipitate in 1763 what became known as Pontiac's Conspiracy, a pan-Indian resistance movement aimed at rejecting European ways and trade goods and expelling the British from North America. The movement is named for its war leader, an Ottawa war chief, but it was inspired by Neolin, the Delaware prophet, who, after experiencing a vision of an alternative way of being in 1760, began to call for Indian people to reject the white people's trade goods, firearms, alcohol, and sexual license and return to their traditional ways of living. Neolin's prophecy, inscribed in pictograph form on a hide, soon was carried to tribes all across the Ohio Country, and it was put most dramatically into effect by Pontiac and is followers, who sought to evict the British colonists and the soldiers who protected them.

Within weeks of the beginning of the uprising, all but three British outposts west of the mountains had fallen to Indian attacks. Hundreds of British troops had been killed, and hundreds more settlers killed or taken captive. The Indians had adopted European weapons and to some

---

[18] Matthew C. Ward, *Breaking the Backcountry: The Seven Years War in Virginia and Pennsylvania, 1754–1765* (Pittsburgh, 2003), 2.

extent European tactics, to go with their already impressive warrior skills and extensive knowledge of the terrain. Their capacity to travel light and travel fast meant that a handful of warriors could terrorize an entire frontier region. Although the French had been defeated, both in North America and elsewhere, their erstwhile Indian allies remained unvanquished. Pontiac's resistance, though it eventually resulted in a tentative compromise peace with the British, gave dramatic evidence of the importance of pan-tribal unity in Native Americans' resistance to the European invasion.

By 1763, France had been defeated. The treaty ending the war transferred Canada and all other French claims in North America to Great Britain. But the inability of the British army to secure the area west of the mountains from Indian attacks led to the creation of the Proclamation Line of 1763. Running in a north-south direction roughly along the Appalachian crest (and extended in 1768 to the Ohio River), the Proclamation Line signified the limits of British imperial control if not the limits of their imperial claims. In the name of maintaining peace and security on the frontier, colonists were prohibited from entering the very country over which the war had been started. Yet the British government did not understand that in the name of maintaining peace with their Indian enemies they were kindling a conflict with their own colonists, who were outraged to find their expansionist ambitions now blocked by the Mother Country.

In the wake of the moment of its greatest triumph, the First British Empire began to come apart, a victim in some sense of the same fiscal-military state that had enabled it to build great armies and navies and send them into battle around the world. In the name of victory, this apparatus had produced a war debt of 137 million pounds, much of it incurred in North American operations, a debt that now required repayment with interest. Indeed, the annual interest payments alone of 4.5 million pounds constituted two-thirds of the government's entire budget. It cannot be emphasized too strongly that the conflict between the colonists and Parliament over taxation without representation would not have occurred when and how it did without the costs associated with the Seven Years War and, more fundamentally, the imperial expansionist thrust that caused them.

Given the crucial role the North American colonists had played in the start and conduct of the Seven Years War, it is ironic to consider how intensely some of them denied responsibility for causing the war and for shouldering the cost of posting 10,000 British regulars in North America after the war for colonial defense. Franklin is notable in this regard. With blatant disregard for the facts of history, in 1765 he asserted to the House of Commons that the colonists had lived "in perfect peace with the French and Indians" until Braddock's expedition, undertaken "for the profit of British merchants and manufacturers," had provoked a crisis. Rather disingenuously, Franklin characterized the entire conflict as "really a British war."[19]

THE REVOLUTIONARY CRISIS

British efforts to compel obedience backfired in almost every case. The Quebec Act of 1774 placed the Ohio Country even further out of the reach of Virginia and Pennsylvania speculators by making it a part of Canada. The act also cracked down on smuggling in an attempt to reestablish and reenforce mercantile restrictions and thereby limit the commercial freedom to which the colonists had become accustomed. Given Britain's dire financial condition in the years after the war, and considering the cost of maintaining regular troops in North America for the colonists' protection, from today's perspective, it does not seem outrageous that the Crown would seek to tax them. After all, the colonists had gladly received the protection of the British regulars, notwithstanding their status of being unrepresented in Parliament. Yet rational discussion of the question soon proved impossible, as the rhetoric of rights overshadowed any consideration of responsibilities when it came to colonial defense.

The entire controversy over taxes and representation in the 1760s and 1770s was only a part of the larger issue of the evolving relationship of the colonies to the Crown. Although the colonists played, at best, an auxiliary role in the military victory, the struggle greatly boosted their collective sense of worth and kindled for the first time the emergence of a distinctively American identity and, more importantly, a rising refusal to accept a subordinate role to the Mother Country. The American War of Independence was the culmination of a quarter-century of conflict

[19] Richard Van Alstyne, *Genesis of American Nationalism* (Waltham, Mass., 1970), 98.

between Great Britain and the colonies regarding the nature of their relationship. In the end, the revolutionary faction in the colonies would not accept political subordination or limitations on its territorial and commercial expansionism.

The financial burden of empire created a conflict over the equitable sharing of that burden, a conflict that morphed into a heated debate about the rights of man and, more fundamentally, about the role of the North American colonists in the British Empire. These were true causes of war, although it must be remembered that independence was not the only possible solution nor the one desired by a majority of the people. Yet the radicals – people such as the Adamses, Franklin, and the like – pushed for a formal separation, in the face of moderates such as Joseph Galloway of Pennsylvania, who sought a less drastic solution to the controversy. Amid rising tensions, in November 1775 the Second Continental Congress formed a Committee of Secret Correspondence to communicate with foreign governments. Franklin, John Dickinson of Pennsylvania, John Jay of New York, Thomas Johnson of Maryland, and Benjamin Harrison of Virginia comprised the first diplomatic entity in U.S. history. This marked the beginning of a distinct U.S. foreign policy.

Franklin's exalted place in the pantheon of American patriots some-times obscures his circuitous route to becoming a revolutionary. He had returned to Great Britain in 1758, where he lobbied well-connected friends and members of Parliament for the imposition of a colonial union, possibly with him as its head. For years he agitated for new ways of conceiving of the North American colonies, all the while retain-ing a personal interest in the western lands, including a share of the so-called Walpole Company, a scheme to obtain a royal charter to 20 million acres of land – "one of the biggest land grabs in history," as Gordon Wood terms it.[20] Franklin pushed for a New World colonial union on a par with Great Britain, one imposed by Parliament once it was clear that the colonies were too fractious and too parochial to do it themselves. He went to great lengths to preserve Anglo-American unity during the building crisis, even going so far as to betray the confidence of Thomas Hutchinson, one of his best friends. Franklin was a deter-mined unionist from 1754 onward but within the context of the British

---

[20] Gordon S. Wood, *The Americanization of Benjamin Franklin* (New York, 2004), 136.

Empire. He finally joined the cause of independence in 1774, when he had run out of options and run out of credibility in Great Britain. Only then did he realize that neither he nor any American would ever be treated as equals by British society.

The British government could not control the empire it had constructed on its own and had won from France. It could not prevent Indian attacks on the western frontier except by means of bribery and effusive gift giving, it could not prevent settlers from squatting on lands ceded to Indian tribes by treaty, and it could not compel the colonists to pay taxes, even when those taxes were explicitly set aside for colonial defense. Moreover, it could not enforce mercantile restrictions on colonial trade and ran into stiff resistance when it tried to do so. In essence, it could not control in peace the empire it had won in war.

A sense of being oppressed by a common foe began to drive the colonies closer together. Yet even as late as early 1775, the idea of a formal revolt against the British Crown was unthinkable to most colonists; indeed, it was never accepted by a majority of them. The radical faction pushing for independence – chief among them John Adams – still needed to make their case to a skeptical public, who, though opposed to arbitrary taxation, did not necessarily see a revolutionary struggle as the way to address the problem. One of the most influential voices in building support for this path was Thomas Paine and his bombshell pamphlet "Common Sense." Arriving for the first time in America in 1774 with a letter of introduction from Franklin, whom he had known in London, Paine injected himself into the brewing political controversy with gusto. Throughout his life, he never compromised his ideals in the service of the various causes he joined. Later he would become an outspoken champion of the French Revolution (and at one point its prisoner) and an outspoken critic of organized religion. Like Franklin, Paine was a man of many talents, including the design and construction of the first steel suspension bridge. He also displayed a keen ear for the drift of popular sentiment of the time and had the ability to reflect this sentiment back in what was, for its time, a plainspoken, unadorned style. Within a year of its publication in January 1776, "Common Sense" had sold an estimated 300,000 copies, a massive figure considering that the total white population was only around three million. The pamphlet played well in the taverns and inns that functioned as local outlets in embryonic form of an emerging national news and information network. As much as and perhaps more so than his mentor Franklin, Paine was a powerful shaper of public opinion.

Paine artfully focused the accumulated angers and resentments of colonists on the king and the very idea of monarchy, notwithstanding the fact that the real controversy was their refusal to acknowledge parliamentary, not royal, supremacy. In a phrase designed to resonate in the hearts of a people increasingly concerned not with one's pedigree but one's aptitude, Paine contends, "Of more worth is one honest man to society, and in the sight of God, than all of the crowned ruffians who ever lived." The reference to God in this instance and throughout the text is interesting given Paine's atheistic orientation. Yet he knew that as a pamphleteer, he had to play to the feelings of his Anglo-American audience, most of whom believed in a Christian god and who increasingly began to see God's hand in the development of the British North American colonies. From the start, references to God's guiding hand suffused the rhetoric of American nationalism. Beyond the theological appeals, Paine makes extravagant claims for the possibilities of independence, which he believes offers not only the chance for self-government but also the possibility of ridding the world of its great evils, the first being war. He makes clear the transcendent nature of the struggle: "The sun never shined on a cause of greater worth ... whose impact would be felt 'even to the end of time.'"[21]

Although "Common Sense" is perhaps best remembered for its withering critique of monarchy, Paine's keen understanding of North America's favorable geography informs his support for union, much as it did for his mentor, Franklin. Central to Paine's argument is that a connection to Great Britain had been a drag on America, which "would have flourished as much, if probably much more, had no European power taken any notice of her. The commerce on which she hath enriched herself are the necessaries of life and will always have a market while eating is the custom of Europe." Here Paine has planted the seed for what became a long-term and ultimately problematic American ambition: the role of a neutral carrier of goods in a world at war. Paine belittles the idea that the colonies gain by their

---

[21] Thomas Paine, *Common Sense and other Writings*, with an Introduction and Notes by Joyce Appleby (New York, 2005), 30, 31.

connection to the Mother Country: "I challenge the warmest advocate for reconciliation to show a single advantage that this continent can reap by being connected to Great Britain." Indeed, the connection was little more than an anchor around the colonies' collective necks: Like Franklin before him, Paine frames the British defense of North America as motivated by *"interest* not *attachment"* and asserts that Britain "did not protect us from *our enemies* on *our account*; but from *her enemies* on *her own account*."[22] As Richard Van Alstyne observes, "Here lay the ideological heart of the revolution: the passionate affirmation that America was separate from Europe, that it had fallen prey in the past to European selfishness, and that it would not again permit itself to be exploited."[23]

Paine envisioned the United States building a mighty navy from the abundance of naval stores in North America. "Shipbuilding is America's greatest pride, and in which she will, in time, excel the whole world." Financing for this and other improvements would come from the sale of western lands, which would function as an open-ended source of revenues. Like a salesman pitching a bargain or an evangelical preacher promising salvation, Paine warns that the leap of independence and union that would make it possible must be taken now, while it can be achieved: "We have it in our power to begin the world again ... It might be difficult, if not impossible, to form the continent into one government half a century hence."[24]

In the tradition of Franklin, a major theme in "Common Sense" is the importance of colonial unity: "'Tis not in numbers but in unity that our great strength lies." The colonies had "just arrived at that pitch of strength, in which no single colony is able to support itself, and the whole, when united, is able to do anything." Paine recognizes, however, that this unity can be achieved only by a commitment to a common cause and a common future: "In short, independence is the only bond that can tye [sic] and keep us together."[25]

[22] Paine, *Common Sense*, 32, 35.
[23] Richard Van Alstyne, *Empire and Independence: The International History of the American Revolution* (New York, 1965), 30.
[24] Paine, *Common Sense*, 49, 31, 52.
[25] Paine, *Common Sense*, 46.

DECLARING INDEPENDENCE, AND UNION

The bloody battles at Lexington and Concord in April 1775 marked the beginning of a de facto war of independence for the colonies. Yet reconciliation short of a total break remained a possibility, and moderates such as Joseph Galloway of Pennsylvania worked hard for this outcome. He and others like him were opposed by the radicals, such as Paine, Franklin, and John Adams, who saw efforts at reconciliation as the enemy of their ultimate goal of independence from Great Britain. To them, Lord North's heavy-handed response to the insurgency was a blessing because it encouraged more fence-sitters to join the cause of independence. The formal declaration of an independent "United States of America" in July 1776 was both an announcement to a "candid world" (that is to say, an unbiased one) of the new political entity as well as an internal political triumph over those who opposed a revolutionary break with Britain and a union of the colonies. Certainly the Declaration was a sort of a collective leap off a cliff, a public statement of treason that would now bind into a union the signers and the colonies in whose name they acted if only to avoid the gallows.

The Declaration of Independence, it must be recalled, was not merely a statement of separation but rather an outline for a new epoch of government by the consent of the people based on the principle of human equality. The statement of this universal principle in the preamble refers specifically to "one people" separating from another, although the concluding paragraph suggests that it is actually the peoples of the thirteen individual states/colonies making the statement as one. In any case, by the end of the document, the "one people" of the opening paragraph had been superseded by thirteen "free and independent states" with "full power to levy war, conclude peace, contract alliances, establish commerce" – in short, the power to conduct foreign policy in the international state system. The American Revolution was not caused only or even primarily by grievances about representation and taxation but rather by the desire of the colonists to be an autonomous state with the freedom to do all things that autonomous states can do, especially expand territorially and commercially. In spite of the self-conscious distinctions the American revolutionaries made between themselves and the Mother Country, the United States ultimately represented a new version of the preexisting English imperial model. David Armitage notes this similarity when he writes, "The ideological origins of the British Empire also constituted the ideological origins of the American Revolution."[26]

So the Declaration announced to the world the existence of a new state having the power to make and conduct its own foreign policy. In this respect, historians are right to understand it as the cornerstone document in the history of U.S. foreign relations. However, if originally a foreign policy statement, it also constituted a manifesto of national identity that Americans would feel compelled to live up to in later years or suffer charges of hypocrisy. Its scheme of self-government based on the principle of human equality had revolutionary implications, both at home and abroad. Even before independence was declared, perceptive observers saw through the rebels' supercharged language of liberty. The prominent English Methodist clergyman John Wesley noted this inconsistency in 1775 when he observed, "[T]he Negroes in America are slaves, the whites enjoy liberty ... Is not all this outcry about liberty and slavery mere cant, and playing upon words?"[27]

THE MODEL TREATY

Even as the revolutionaries agitated for independence they drafted plans to engage the world as an independent state, or at least a confederation of states. Chief among these plans was the so-called Plan of Treaties (also known as the Model Treaty), printed in September 1776. Largely the work of John Adams, it represents one of the landmark achievements in his long and illustrious career. As both a foreign policy document and a statement of American nationality, it deserves to be bracketed with "Common Sense" and the Declaration of Independence as the documentary foundations of American foreign relations.

John Adams, though lacking the military experience of Washington or the private sector success or scientific achievement of Franklin, nonetheless is rightfully understood as ranking very high on the list of Founding Fathers of the Union. Like Washington and Franklin, Adams early on became an advocate of colonial union and, unlike Franklin,

---

[26] David Armitage, *The Ideological Origins of the British Empire* (Cambridge, 2000), 10.
[27] Van Alstyne, *Empire and Independence*, 72.

from the start envisioned that union as a fully independent state. In 1755, at age twenty, Adams wrote to a friend that the Puritan migration of the seventeenth century might eventually "transfer the great seat of empire into America ... for if we remove the turbulent Gallicks, our people ... will in another century become more numerous than England itself ... since we have I may say all the naval stores of the nation in our hands, it will be easy to obtain the mastery of the seas, and then the united force of all Europe will not be able to subdue us."[28]

By 1776, Adams was a committed revolutionary, and when the Continental Congress resolved in June that a draft treaty be written to serve as a template for American diplomats in the negotiation of commercial treaties with foreign states, he eagerly agreed to participate in its creation. Nominally the work of a committee of five and modified by the input of the Continental Congress, the Plan of Treaties mostly is attributable to Adams. First, Adams argued for making only commercial connections with other states and avoiding military and political ties, all in the name of avoiding foreign entanglements. Although not a formal part of the Model Treaty and disregarded in the making of the French alliance, Adams's call for the United States to maintain only commercial ties with foreign states became a guiding assumption of American foreign relations until the 1940s. The Model Treaty did not call for "free trade" in the modern sense of removing all barriers to trade but rather aimed to challenge directly the closed mercantile system in the name of opening the markets of the world to all states. Its bold recommendations were based on the idea that the fledgling United States had cards to play in international negotiations, both as a source of raw materials and foodstuffs and as a crucial makeweight in the balance of power. Its most important aspect concerned the vision it had of U.S. commercial interests as a neutral carrier of goods on the high seas. It articulated five basic principles:

- That the United States would pay import duties no higher than those of any other trading partner (later known as the most-favored-nation clause)
- That if one of the signatories was at war and one was neutral, the neutral (i.e., the United States) could trade with the enemies

---

[28] Van Alstyne, *Empire and Independence*, 1.

of the party at war in all noncontraband items, contraband being narrowly defined as arms, munitions, and horses. Food and naval stores – critical items of American export – were specifically exempted as noncontraband.

- That those neutral states could trade not only between ports of nations at war and neutral ports but also between two or more ports of a belligerent state. This would position American merchant vessels to profit immensely from wartime commerce.
- That "free ships shall also give a freedom to goods," that is, noncontraband items of any sort on neutral vessels were not subject to seizure whatever their country of origin. This would make American ships the carriers of choice for all nations at war.
- That neutral goods on ships of nations at war were subject to seizure.[29]

The net effect of these principles would be to give a powerful boost to a neutral trading state, the role Americans envisioned themselves playing. In declaring their independence the colonists, in effect, also declared their union. This, along with the articulation of a foreign policy in the form of the Model Treaty and the establishment of a central government under the Articles of Confederation, constituted the origins of a distinct American political entity.

THE FRENCH ALLIANCE

The French government watched the American quarrel with Great Britain with great interest. Beginning in the 1760s they began to anticipate a colonial rebellion against the Mother Country and assess the benefits it might bring. By April 1776, Charles Gravier de Vergennes, minister of foreign affairs, argued for aiding the Americans in his "Considerations" presented to the king. Like all French diplomats, he burned with a desire for revenge against the British. Supplying the Americans with arms and ammunition seemed to offer the possibility of splitting the British Empire and making its former North American colonies dependent on France. He counseled the king to provide secret aid to the Americans. Finance Minister Turgot, citing France's tenuous

---

[29] The text of the Plan of Treaties can be found in Robert L. Taylor, ed., *Papers of John Adams* (Cambridge, Mass., 1979), 4:290–300.

economic condition, argued against this, but in the end, the desire for revenge trumped the need for fiscal responsibility. The task of coordinating the transfer of this secret aid fell to the famous playwright Caron de Beaumarchais, a prominent champion of the Patriot cause. He soon began to coordinate the transfer of weapons critical to the revolution via a dummy trading company he established as a front. The British, though soon aware of this secret aid to the rebels, did not desire to force the hand of the French by publicly acknowledging it and therefore lodged no formal protest.

In the early days of the war, the French government was not interested in a formal alliance with the rebels. The chances for the failure of the revolution were too great, with potentially negative consequences for those who had aided the insurgents. Thus when the Continental Congress dispatched Franklin in 1777 to secure a treaty of commerce and perhaps an alliance, French diplomats responded coolly and cautiously. France's motives in supplying secret aid were clear: to weaken Great Britain. Yet at the same time, many French aristocrats and intellectuals (often one and the same) held enormous sympathy for the revolutionary cause, a sentiment Franklin artfully played to by appearing to be the archetypal New World natural man. Franklin particularly, and the Americans generally, appeared to be the perfect New World antidote to the corruptions of the ancien regime, a pastoral agricultural people without large cities and the corrosive influence of enervating luxury. Franklin, ever the master of surfaces, famously played to these sympathies by, among other things, wearing a coonskin cap at court and affecting a simplicity of manner quite at odds with the reality of his existence.

Although the American commissioners came as supplicants, they well understood that France's desire for revenge against the British gave them some leverage to get what they wanted, especially if they could exploit French fears of an Anglo-American reconciliation. They also understood that the favorable geography of an American union – an extensive territory with abundant natural and human resources in a part of the world with great strategic importance – made them a very attractive potential ally. The French also perceived the enormous potential power and importance of the United States. They were loath to antagonize the Americans owing to, as Chris Tudda observes, "their abundant natural resources, naturally increasing population, their capacity for agricultural production, and domestic manufactures seemingly limitless, and their willingness to use these resources to achieve their own ends."[30]

Indeed, some feared that the immense potential strength of the United States would make the French reluctant to assist them in achieving independence; such fears inhibited Spain from agreeing to a formal alliance with the Americans. But to override such concerns Franklin and the other American negotiators depended on France's unquenchable hatred of the British. They knew that they could count on the intensity of Anglo-French hostility to place them in a position of strength vis-à-vis the two mightiest powers in the world at that time. Equally important, Congress flirted with British offers of reconciliation while holding fast to the goal of independence. Even the possibility that the Americans might reconcile with Great Britain scared the French government and gave the Americans critical leverage in the delicate talks.

Events on the ground soon forced France's hand. The astounding victory at the Battle of Saratoga in October 1777, where 5,000 British regulars surrendered to a patriot army under Nathanael Greene, made it clear that it was now or never. By February 1778, two agreements had been made: a Treaty of Amity and Commerce establishing trade relations between the two states; and a military alliance, to take effect in the event of formal hostilities breaking out between France and Great Britain. The Treaty of Amity and Commerce was immensely favorable to U.S. interests, containing nearly all the neutral rights clauses called for in the Model Treaty, and as such represented a spectacular diplomatic victory.

The Treaty of Alliance, though essential to America's hopes for victory, entangled the United States in European rivalries. The ink had barely dried on the treaty when France undertook to widen the conflict in an effort to limit the dimensions of the American victory, especially in the west. Notwithstanding the republican sentiments of the philosophes, the French motives in making the alliance were entirely self-interested. They hoped to break up the British North American Empire and make the fledgling United States dependent on France. Although France agreed not to reclaim any its lost territories in North America, each of the two nations pledged not to make a separate peace with the British. This became a major problem for the United States in early 1779, when, after hostilities between France and Great Britain had commenced, the French negotiated the Treaty of Aranjuez (1779) with Spain. In that pact, Spain entered the struggle in exchange for France's commitment not to make peace until freeing Gibraltar from Great Britain and restoring it to Spain, its previous owner. In effect, U.S. independence had been chained to the Rock of Gibraltar.

THE TREATY OF PARIS, 1783

By 1779 Spanish efforts to mediate the conflict had broken down and another global war had begun, the second in less than thirty years to be caused by a North American controversy. The United States found itself in the middle of a conflict involving all the major European powers, essentially a sequel to the struggle that ended in 1763, a struggle that, as we have seen, also started in North America. Austria, Prussia, Russia, and Spain all anticipated advantages from the changed geopolitical situation that would emerge at the war's end, however it might turn out. The United States was bound by treaty to its former enemy France, which sought to limit the extent of any victory it might achieve even as it supplied large quantities of essential troops, materiel, and ships to the Patriot cause. The new union found itself deeply enmeshed in the larger geopolitical struggle. Americans generally perceived themselves as better than they generally perceived Europeans, whom they saw as politically corrupted by monarchical governments and morally dissipated by luxury. Americans were committed, in theory at least, to a new way of conducting foreign affairs, without recourse to war and secret treaties. Yet the importance of North America as perhaps the most crucial site of imperial rivalries in the world at that time rendered absurd its often-repeated desire to remain unentangled in European affairs.

In the midst of this perilous situation, in 1779 Congress sent John Adams to France to serve as a lead negotiator, in concert with Vergennes, in any prospective peace talks with the British. Adams's brusque manner and uncompromising belief that America owed nothing to France for its indispensable assistance grated on the French, who soon pleaded with Congress for Adams to be replaced with someone of a more diplomatic temperament. His instructions required that before any talks could begin, Great Britain must agree to treat with the United States as a sovereign, free, and independent state. Adams was to seek an extensive western boundary extending to the Mississippi River, among other desirable goals. It was not a diplomatic stance made from a position of weakness, notwithstanding the tenuous the state of the war effort at that time.

During the war, American diplomats also sought alliances or at least formal recognition of their cause from other European states in addition to France. It proved a fruitless endeavor. The Europeans, either fearing British retaliation, in the case of Prussia, or fearing the future potential might of a victorious United States, as in the case of Spain, shunned the American emissaries. American diplomat Francis Dana (ably assisted by his thirteen-year-old secretary, John Quincy Adams) spent two years in Moscow at the court of Catherine the Great in a futile effort to garner recognition by and admission to the czarina's League of Armed Neutrality. This was an ultimately unsuccessful effort by neutral states to defend a liberal definition of neutral rights in time of war, along the lines of the Model Treaty. That the Americans sought to join a league of neutral states despite being a major belligerent in an ongoing conflict offers insight into the intensity of their self-perception as a neutral trading nation.

The crucial victory at Yorktown in October 1781 – made possible not only by the French army and navy on the scene but also by the French military presence in the Caribbean, which drew off British forces that might otherwise have provided reinforcements for Lord Cornwallis's army – broke the diplomatic stalemate. In the aftermath of the capture of another British army, public and governmental opinion turned decisively against the war. Victory, even if obtainable, now seemed too costly to justify continuing the struggle. King George III, still not reconciled to submitting to the insolent colonists, nonetheless replaced Lord North and his war policy in January 1782 with Lord Rockingham, who was committed to bringing the war to a peaceful resolution even while lacking a definite plan to do so. Fortuitously for the Americans, Rockingham soon died, to be replaced as prime minister in July by Lord Shelburne, a former supporter of the war, who now, inspired by the economic theories of Adam Smith, sought both to recognize American independence and to split the United States off from its French allies by offering a generous peace. Shelburne, much like Franklin thirty years

earlier, saw an expansive and populous United States as a huge potential market for British goods so long as the bad feelings engendered by
the war could be put aside. His accession to power in such a timely
fashion was an astounding bit of good luck for the Americans.

Meanwhile, Franklin had begun private talks with British emissary
Richard Oswald, an old friend of his sent by Rockingham to thaw the
Anglo-American diplomatic deep-freeze. It soon became clear that a
treaty could be made quite favorable to U.S. interests, provided Franklin
was willing to disregard Congress's instructions of June 1782, which
had given Vergennes full power to make a comprehensive settlement on
any terms he chose so long as they guaranteed American independence.
American diplomats at this crucial time proved far more adept than one
might have thought given their relative inexperience. Philosophically
opposed to the concepts of Machiavelli as a guide to conduct, in practice
the team of Franklin, Jay, and Adams applied these principles expertly.
They did not allow a false sentimentality or unyielding devotion to principle to interfere with getting what they wanted for the United States.
As was the case in the negotiation of the French alliance, the key to the
U.S. diplomatic success in ending the war was remaining steadfast in
favor of independence, even though they had mortgaged that independence via the negotiation of the Treaty of Alliance with France. They
had pledged not to make a separate peace with Britain, as a loyal and
grateful ally. Yet the American negotiators (perhaps Franklin somewhat
less so) understood that French motives were entirely self-interested
and therefore could not fully be trusted to act in a manner befitting an
ally. For if the French wanted the colonies split off from Great Britain,
they also desired that they remain geographically hemmed in and politically reliant upon France. Although Franklin has received most of the
credit for the revolutionary diplomatic successes, it was John Jay who
saw through Vergennes's duplicity. It was Jay's urgings that were chiefly
responsible for the decision to, in effect, abandon the ally whose aid
had made victory possible.

Meanwhile, the U.S alliance with France alarmed the British, who
feared that if the relationship matured and strengthened it might
alter the balance of power, and not only in North America. Under the
new ministry of Lord Shelburne, feelers of conciliation were put out.
Shelburne began to advocate a generous peace with the Americans in
the hopes of wooing them back from the French orbit. Disregarding

Congress's instructions and over Franklin's objections, John Jay initiated secret peace talks with the British. The victory at Yorktown established the conditions for a decisive endgame.

Franklin's terms for a settlement fell into two categories. "Necessary" conditions included (1) unconditional acknowledgment of American independence, (2) evacuation of British troops and forts along the Canadian frontier, and (3) boundaries according to Congress's instructions of 1779, with the western limit along the Mississippi River. Conditions deemed "desirable" included (1) indemnities for destruction of Patriot property, including the liberation of slaves, (2) an Anglo-American treaty of commerce, and (3) the cession of British Canada to the United States. Given the relative weakness of the United States, Franklin's demands, especially the desire for Canada, seem unrealistic to say the least. However, the desire of the Shelburne ministry both to end the war and to entice the Americans away from too great a reliance upon France opened the door to an astounding outcome. Under the terms of the Treaty of Paris, the United States gained recognition of its independence, a western boundary along the Mississippi River from the Canadian border to the thirty-first parallel, and the right of Americans to fish the waters of the Grand Banks, the most productive fishery in the world at that time. In return, the United States (for the time being) gave up the demand for Canada, agreed not to interfere in the collection of debts owed to its British subjects, and pledged to compensate Loyalists for property seized during the war. It was an astounding achievement for a revolutionary movement whose very survival seemed doubtful as late as 1778. In the 1920s the eminent historian Samuel Flagg Bemis characterized the 1783 Treaty of Paris as "the greatest victory in the annals of American diplomacy," an assessment that still holds true.[31] Vergennes and the French were privately appalled by the way the Americans had played them, but circumstances were such as to force them into tight-lipped acquiescence with its terms. After all, they could not publicly be too disappointed at the success of their American allies.

The newly born United States had accomplished a political, diplomatic, and, above all, military miracle in declaring its independence

---

[31] Samuel Flagg Bemis, *The Diplomacy of the American Revolution* (Bloomington, Ind., 1935), 256.

from the most powerful nation in the world, bringing in the second most powerful on its side to support its cause, and then tacking back in the direction of their enemy to extract an immensely favorable peace treaty. They had accurately judged the interests of the world's two most powerful states and played them off one another flawlessly. Franklin, Jay, and the rest of the novice American diplomatic corps had pulled off a foreign policy high-wire act perhaps the equal of any in world history.

NATIVE AMERICANS AND THE WAR OF INDEPENDENCE

The War of Independence had dire consequences for Native Americans of the trans-Appalachian frontier. The revolt against Britain did not start the hostilities with Native Americans in the west. Violent conflicts between white settlers and Indians had been going on continually since at least 1755. However, it did greatly fan the flames of the struggle, making it difficult for Indians to remain neutral, as was the initial impulse of most of the tribes. Instead, pressure from multiple sources forced Indians to choose sides, and given the historic tension between Native American land claims and the rapacity of the settlers, it is not surprising that most tribes ultimately opposed the rebels. Since at least 1763, the British government had attempted, not always successfully, to regulate the tide and conduct of the settlers. Indeed the effort to control western immigration was one of the major causes of the breakup. Seeking to gain the loyalty of the settlers, in 1775 the Continental Congress began supplying them with soldiers and supplies for use against the British and their Indian allies.

For Native Americans, the rhetoric of liberty and self-government embraced by the Americans often served to justify the seizure of Indian lands. The steady stream of settlers who had been heading west became a torrent in the 1770s when an estimated 100,000 migrated into Kentucky, no longer inhibited by British restraints and determined to acquire as much land as possible.

The revolutionary faction led by Washington well understood that Indians could play a decisive role in the war with Great Britain and sought to guarantee their neutrality if not garner their active support. Nonetheless, attacks on British frontier outposts inevitably threatened the interests of their Indian allies, and therefore it is not surprising that by 1777 the United States was at war with most of the Indian tribes west of the mountains. As early as 1776, the Continental Congress had authorized a three-pronged, 5,000-man assault on the Cherokees of western North Carolina, who, at British instigation, had launched attacks on Patriot settlements in the early days of the war. In 1778, Colonel George Rogers Clark led 200 Virginia rangers on a campaign to attack Illinois, clear evidence that the revolution was about expansion as well as independence.

But the most important campaign of the war occurred in upstate New York in late 1779, after coordinated British-Loyalist-Iroquois attacks on Patriot settlements threatened to cut the united colonies in half. In an effort to smash the military might of the Six Nations (especially that of the Seneca) forever, Washington took a lead role in coordinating a three-pronged assault (the so-called Sullivan-Clinton campaign) on Seneca lands. Although the Seneca war parties retreated in the face of the American force of almost 5,000 troops, the unopposed Patriot force destroyed dozens of Indian towns and thousands of acres of crops in a systematic effort to starve the tribes into submission. The Continental army demonstrated an early and particularly brutal example of what John Grenier terms "the first way of war," a manner of American warmaking that for the most part did not distinguish between warrior and noncombatant, young and old, or male and female, and that sought to destroy the enemy's ability both to resist and to subsist. The ferocity of the 1779 American military campaign against the Seneca ironically legitimated a nickname given to George Washington more than a quarter-century earlier: Caunotaucarius, roughly translated as "destroyer of villages." The term had first been applied to Washington's great-grandfather John nearly a century earlier for his relentless assaults upon the Iroquois. Sensing a warrior lineage in the young officer whom he served as a guide, Seneca half-king Tanaghrisson had bestowed the title upon Washington as a sort of inheritance during their exploits in the Ohio Country in the 1750s.[32] Now, as architect of the devastating assault on the Iroquois led by Major General John Sullivan, Washington earned his terrible sobriquet. Retreating to Canada to avoid annihilation, the tribes of the Six Nations in 1780 joined with a British/Loyalist

---

[32] Fred Anderson, ed., *George Washington Remembers: Reflections on the French and Indian War* (Lanham, Md., 2004), 31.

force to invade the Mohawk Valley, laying waste to much of it, including the villages of the Oneidas, a member of the Six Nations aligned with the United States.[33]

By 1779, most of the Indian tribes from the Great Lakes to the Gulf of Mexico had united in opposition to the United States. Since at least the 1740s, intertribal unity had been the key factor in countering the expansion of the Anglo-Americans. Prior to 1775, it was the Indians who had used the advantages of unity to blunt the advance of the Anglo-Americans. This period of unity peaked during the revolution and after: Gregory Dowd writes, "From the final years of the Revolution through the critical engagements of 1794, the Indians of the trans-Appalachian borderlands trained their guns with more consistency, more unity, and more consequence than did any other Indians in the history of the United States."[34] Yet this courageous attempt by Native Americans to unify in the name of maintaining their independence now confronted an even more imposing unity, the new United States of America, inspired by a visionary prophet and led by a charismatic war chief. This new, more powerful North American Union would spell the Indians' doom in only a few years' time.

---

[33] On the Sullivan campaign of 1779, see John Grenier, *The First Way of War: American War Making on the Frontier, 1607–1814* (New York, 2005); Glenn F. Williams, *Year of the Hangman: George Washington's Campaign Against the Iroquois* (Yardley, Pa., 2005); Barbara Mann, *George Washington's War on Native America* (Westport, Conn., 2005).

[34] Gregory E. Dowd, *A Spirited Resistance: The North American Indian Struggle for Unity, 1745–1815* (Baltimore, 1992), 60.

A PERILOUS UNION

Every step by which they have advanced to the character of an independent nation seems to have been distinguished by some token of providential agency.... The preservation of the sacred fire of liberty and the destiny of the republican model of government are justly considered, perhaps, as *deeply*, as *finally*, staked on the experiment intrusted [sic] to the hands of the American people.

George Washington, First Inaugural Address, April 30, 1789

It appears to me that the union of the states depends under Providence upon his life.

Abigail Adams, referring to George Washington, 1790,
quoted in Richard Norton Smith, *Patriarch: George
Washington and the New American Nation*, xvii

THE DESTINY OF A PEOPLE

The achievement of independence and the acquisition of a claim to half of the North American continent by the infant United States appeared little short of miraculous to many observers of the time. Somehow a ragtag military led by an ad hoc collection of amateur politicians and diplomats had outwitted and outlasted the two most powerful nations on earth. Victory in the War of Independence gave a mighty boost to the presumption that the hand of God could be found at work in American history. Although the end of the eighteenth century is rightly remembered for the popularity of deism – a religious philosophy that envisioned God as a "great watchmaker" who, having created the universe, no longer directly intervened in human affairs – it by no means completely or even mostly replaced older conceptions of an activist God with a providential plan for humankind. Increasingly, this view situated the newly independent United States as a "redeemer nation" destined to be at the center of world history.

During the years prior to the revolution, religious and scholarly opinion often argued for a special role for the emerging American state. The 1771 poem "America," by Yale graduate Timothy Dwight, mapped a trajectory of national greatness, originating in Columbus's arrival in the New World and evolving into a blessed freedom destined to expand a Christian imperium to the far corners of the world – "the last and brightest empire of time." Similarly, Philip Freneau's Princeton commencement poem "The Rising Glory of America" (1771) predicted that a "new Jerusalem sent down from heav'n" would emerge in North America. In their work, both Dwight and Freneau presumed to see the hand of God in the inevitable westward movement of civilization and the destiny of the British North American colonies as the future center of world civilization.

Victory over Great Britain brought forth a wave of proto-nationalist literature, much of it emerging from the nation's few institutions of higher learning. To key members of the educated elite, the near-miraculous defeat of the strongest nation on earth seemed a visible manifestation of God's favor for the United States. Among the most widely disseminated productions of this sort was "The United States Elevated to Glory and Honour" (1783) by Ezra Stiles, president of Yale. Originally delivered as a sermon, Stiles's exegesis of politics and history saw the United States as "God's American Israel" whose destiny was to redeem humanity. Echoing Franklin, Stiles pointed to the "accelerated multiplication" of the American people as "a reason to expect that this will become a great people." He predicted that at some future time the collective wisdom and learning of Americans "may reblaze back from America to Europe, Asia, and Africa, and illumine the world with TRUTH and LIBERTY."[1] Joel Barlow's epic poem "Columbiad" (1809) is only the best known of a lifetime of work by a writer who devoted himself to heralding the future greatness of America. Jedidiah Morse's *American Geography* (1789) combined the first attempt at a comprehensive mapping of the new nation with an eschatological map that firmly located the Americans as a chosen people with a mission to redeem the world in

[1] Conrad Cherry, ed., *God's New Israel: Religious Interpretations of American Destiny*, revised and updated ed. (Chapel Hill, 1998; first published 1971), 84, 90.

their image. David Ramsay's *The History of the American Revolution* (1789) portrayed the political developments of the struggle both as in the tradition of classical republicanism and as a sign of providential favor. All of these authors framed American history both as a critical chapter in world history and as evidence of a divine plan.

Although literary elites did much to create a sense of the nation's special role in history, Americans of all backgrounds sensed the burgeoning cultural and economic upheaval going on around them. The "radicalism of the American Revolution" (as Gordon Wood has termed it) was not to be found in the political transformation caused by the struggle but rather in the wholehearted embrace of capitalism that emerged in its wake. Its role as the first liberal, capitalist modern state made the United States a source of fear and fascination to people everywhere. The revolution and the ideas that underlay it not only altered the relationship between the Mother Country and the colonies but also fundamentally changed the individual's relationship to himself and to society, giving rise to the frank embrace of ambition and self-interest that Alexis de Tocqueville would later term "individualism." All of these changes were subject to export to the rest of the world, either by example or by active propagation.

A new age seemed to be at hand, and the revolutionary generation created the Great Seal of the United States to reflect this sense. One side of the seal features an eagle, a symbol of the empire, gripping an olive branch of peace in one talon and thirteen arrows in the other, something the Romans termed a *fasces,* a symbol of strength through unity. In the eagle's beak is held a herald with the Latin motto *e pluribus unum,* "out of many, one." The reverse side features a pyramid symbolizing the edifice of the Union, topped by the all-seeing eye of God and the Latin motto *Annuit Coeptis,* "He has looked after us." Underneath the pyramid, the motto *Novus Ordo Seclorum,* "a new world order of the ages," suggests the grandiose pretensions of the founders of the new nation. Collectively, the symbolism of the Great Seal perfectly captures the origins, aspirations, and presumed Godly foundations of the new republican empire.

FOREIGN THREATS

In spite of the outpouring of triumphalist literature in the years after 1783, the survival and success of the United States were by no means assured. The immediate postwar period found the United States facing imposing challenges, both domestic and foreign, which threatened to shatter the unity essential to the nation's future. The most serious of these foreign challenges was Great Britain's refusal to abide by the terms of the Treaty of Paris. Lord Shelburne's astounding generosity at the negotiating table now spawned a backlash by those in the British government determined to punish the rebellious colonists. The complex document ending the war offered numerous opportunities to claim a breach. Arguing (with some merit) that U.S. state courts were not equitably settling the claims of British creditors and Loyalists, the new ministry of William Pitt the Younger took several steps back from the treaty. First, the British refused to evacuate seven forts along the Canadian border, cheering Britain's Indian allies in the area and leaving the entire northern frontier effectively beyond American control. Second, the British declined to pay compensation for the approximately three thousand black slaves who had fled with the British army at the end of the war, most of them having been liberated in the West Indies. Third and perhaps most importantly, the British refused to negotiate a commercial treaty guaranteeing equality of treatment for U.S. merchants. Instead, Parliament enacted discriminatory regulations against American shipping, requiring that British vessels carry all commerce to the lucrative British West Indies. In spite of the discriminatory treatment, Pitt's government considered American retaliation unlikely given that under the Articles of Confederation each state made its own commercial policy, thereby making concerted action difficult if not impossible. Less fearful now than formerly of a Franco-American alignment, the British sought not to conciliate the United States but to subordinate it into a quasi-colonial role.

Uncertainty loomed large in the Southwest, where control of the Mississippi River, and ultimately the loyalty of the people living within its reach, threatened national unity. Spain contested the western boundary granted the United States by the Treaty of Paris, affirming control of the eastern bank of the river and denying Americans the freedom to navigate on its waters. Sovereignty over the entire lower Mississippi watershed remained contested throughout the decade. American settlers in the region, the so-called men of the western waters, personified the acquisitive capitalist ethos of the new nation, so much so that their loyalty to their own economic interest outweighed their loyalty to the

United States. This made the Confederation Congress reluctant to do anything that might further diminish their allegiance and push them toward Spain. The national government, though fundamentally allied with the expansionist tendency that had in part prompted its creation, nonetheless sought an orderly process of imperial expansion that would limit conflict by keeping settlers from encroaching on Native American lands protected by treaty. In many ways it was the same challenge faced by the British government in the years after 1763, and it created similar sorts of resentments by frontiersmen eager to acquire new lands without regard to treaty obligations.

As had been the case in Ohio and would be true elsewhere in the future, land speculators drove expansion into the southwestern frontier. The search for the next great opportunity to make an easy fortune proved irresistible. As Arthur Preston Whitaker put it, "The importance of the land speculator in the history of western expansion in the United States ... can hardly be exaggerated."[2] Seeking to exploit the secessionist tendencies of American settlers, Spain adopted a policy that encouraged them to settle in the colony of Louisiana and allowed use of the Mississippi River, for a fee, beginning in 1788. Madrid extended a grant of religious toleration to the mostly Protestant settlers and made them subjects of the Spanish king. In spite of these concessions, the frontiersmen retained a near-mystical sense of loyalty, not so much to a government or to a leader, but to the idea of Anglo liberal capitalism. So long as the federal government did not do anything to damage their interests (such as concede navigation rights to the Mississippi for twenty-five years, as John Jay provisionally did in the unratified Jay-Gardoqui Treaty of 1785), the secessionist threat remained minimal. Spain had reconquered the Floridas during the war and retained nominal control of the Mississippi, including access to New Orleans. This meant an inevitable confrontation at some future time with the United States. Yet in the 1780s the fractious, lawless, go-for-broke acquisitiveness of the settlers posed the greatest threat to stability on the Mississippi frontier. It proved far more threatening to Spain than did the actions of the federal government. Whatever limits the Confederation Congress sought to place on the expansionist tendency in the name of justice and stability were contemptuously disregarded. Whitaker writes, "Grimly

[2] Arthur Preston Whitaker, *The Spanish-American Frontier, 1783–1795* (Lincoln, Neb., 1927), 47.

[the settlers] drove the Indians out before them, and exploited natural resources, slaves, and public offices, trampling down with pitiless determination every obstacle to prosperity."[3]

The challenges posed by Great Britain and Spain, though serious, ultimately proved less threatening to the United States than the ongoing resistance of Native American tribes along the western frontier. In spite of numerous campaigns waged against them during the War of Independence, Senecas, Shawnees, Miamis, Cherokees, Creeks, and others remained unvanquished, and they emerged more unified than ever in the war's aftermath. Their betrayal in the Treaty of Paris of 1783 stung a bit less when the British opted not to evacuate the forts (and the critical link to arms and other supplies that they represented) as had been agreed. Shawnee raids in Kentucky and Ohio in 1784 had prevented George Washington from visiting his claims along the Great Kanawha River in the course of his continued quest for an all-river route west. In spite of the Treaty of Paris, Indian resistance never really stopped at war's end, and by 1786 it had reemerged with renewed fury. Continuing Indian resistance demonstrated what a tenuous grasp the victorious rebels had on the western frontier. The Ohio Country stood unconquered. The Americans had gained the British imperial claim to the west by treaty; it remained unclear whether they could subjugate the natives who still claimed it as their own. Richard Butler, in charge of Indian affairs in the Northern Department, summarized the situation in a 1787 letter to Secretary of War Henry Knox: He warned that Native Americans had formed "a general confederacy among themselves from North to South in order to become formidable, and as far as they are capable of being bound to each other, I believe they are."[4] The Union now confronted another union comprised of Native Americans, one that seemed capable of stemming the expansionist tide, particularly if it could continue to receive British support.

THE CRITICAL PERIOD

The United States emerged from the revolution with both independence and an empire. The thirteen states, unified at least for the time being,

---

[3] Whitaker, *Spanish-American Frontier*, 32.

[4] Gregory Evans Dowd, *A Spirited Resistance: The North American Struggle for Indian Unity, 1745–1815* (Baltimore, 1992), 99.

collectively had acquired a claim to a western empire nearly as large as that of the original thirteen colonies. Geographically, the United States already stood as the fourth-largest country in the world. Yet its unity was sorely tested almost from the moment the ink dried on the Treaty of Paris. Friends and foes alike of the new union harbored expectations of its imminent demise. The newly independent entity seemed too big, to contain too large a diversity of interests, and its people collectively too resistant to the strong central authority needed to hold it together, for the Union to survive intact. Perhaps it would split into two or three separate confederacies. The very nature of its national compact, formed under the duress of war, seemed ill equipped to hold the states together for very long.

The states were bound as one by a document known as the "Articles of Confederation and Perpetual Union." Notwithstanding its pretensions to perpetuity, the nature of the plan was revealed in its opening paragraph, which described the United States as a "firm league of friendship," thereby highlighting the continuing ambivalence of the individual states toward a strong union. British tyranny made necessary the unity the states had resisted from the time of the Albany Plan, but they remained wary of sacrificing their freedom of action to a powerful central authority. The impotence of the Confederation Congress reflected that wariness, having been strictly confined to an enumerated list of powers that did not include the power to levy taxes. Such revenues as it could raise were by "requests" that the states by no means always granted. The Articles of Confederation proved little more than a mutual defense pact among the states and, lacking enforcement power, subject to being ignored as circumstances dictated. Comprised of a one-house Congress and requiring unanimity in order to approve legislation, the Confederation government reflected the desire of the states for a weak union with limited central authority. Most citizens still saw their primary political loyalty to their states; they aimed to take back powers ceded to the Confederation government as an exigency of war. The legacy of British tyranny meant that most citizens remained wary of conceding any power to a new central authority even as they eagerly contemplated continued westward expansion. David Armitage's observation about Great Britain – "How to achieve empire while sustaining liberty became a defining concern of British imperial ideology from the late 16th century onwards" – with equal force could also be applied to the new United States.[5]

In one crucial area, however, the Confederation Congress had been given substantial responsibility: control of the western lands. In order to head off future conflicts between individual states over western land claims, the articles entrusted control of those territories to the Congress. Controversy over this very question had held up final ratification of the articles until 1781. Historians judge the Northwest Ordinance of 1787 (successor legislation to the Land Acts of 1784 and 1785) as the most significant achievement of the Confederation Congress. It provided a blueprint for imperial expansion into land stretching from the Ohio River to the Great Lakes, a territory larger than the original thirteen states. Based on the anticolonial principle that new states would enter the Union as coequals, it allowed settlers to form their own governments and established a path to statehood, including the surveying of the land into township grids, each six miles square. Fred Anderson, perhaps the most astute scholar of the legislation, writes, "[T]he Northwest Ordinance established an empire capable of indefinite expansion because it was conceived as a league of self-governing republics, immune to the possibility of despotic rule from the center because (unlike the British empire) it was ultimately a voluntary association.... Thus the rhetoric of freedom supported and justified the reality of federal power on which the order of the imperial periphery depended."[6]

Thus the Confederation Congress had the responsibility for administering the western imperial domain but lacked the authority effectively to do so. This was one aspect of its generalized lack of the powers needed to conduct an effective foreign policy. In addition to lacking the power to tax, the Confederation Congress could not raise armies and navies and did not have the power to make a uniform commercial policy, and thus each state was allowed to make its own, often in competition with other states. The absence of a chief executive and the requirement of unanimity for passing legislation meant that even

---

[5] David Armitage, *The Ideological Origins of the British Empire* (Cambridge, 2000), 125.
[6] Fred Anderson and Andrew Cayton, *Dominion of War: Empire and Liberty in North America, 1500–2000* (New York, 2005), 191.

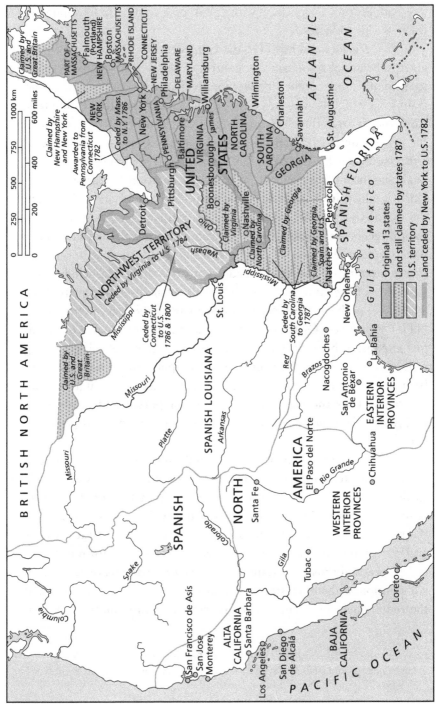

Map 2. The American Empire, 1787.

BRITISH NORTH AMERICA

UNITED STATES

Claimed by U.S. and Great Britain

PART OF MASSACHUSETTS
Falmouth (Portland)
NEW HAMPSHIRE
Boston
MASSACHUSETTS
RHODE ISLAND
CONNECTICUT
NEW JERSEY
Philadelphia
DELAWARE
MARYLAND
Williamsburg
Wilmington
Charleston
Savannah
St. Augustine

ATLANTIC OCEAN

Claimed by New Hampshire and New York
Awarded to Pennsylvania from Connecticut 1782
NEW YORK
Ceded by Mass. to N.Y. 1786
New York
PENNSYLVANIA
Baltimore
VIRGINIA
James
NORTH CAROLINA
SOUTH CAROLINA
GEORGIA

Pittsburgh
Detroit
Ohio
Boonesborough
Claimed by Virginia
Nashville
Claimed by North Carolina
Claimed by Georgia
Claimed by Georgia, Spain and U.S.
Natchez
Pensacola
Claimed by Georgia and U.S.
SPANISH FLORIDA

NORTHWEST TERRITORY
Ceded by Virginia to U.S. 1784
Wabash

Ceded by Connecticut to U.S. 1786 & 1800
St. Louis
Mississippi
Ceded by South Carolina to Georgia 1787
New Orleans
Gulf of Mexico

Claimed by U.S. and Great Britain
Missouri
Columbia

SPANISH LOUISIANA
Arkansas
Red
Brazos
Nacogdoches
La Bahia

Platte
Missouri

San Antonio de Béxar
EASTERN INTERIOR PROVINCES

SPANISH
NORTH AMERICA
Santa Fe
El Paso del Norte
Rio Grande
Chihuahua
WESTERN INTERIOR PROVINCES

Colorado
Snake
Gila
Tubac

ALTA CALIFORNIA
San Francisco de Asis
San Jose
Monterey
Santa Barbara
Los Angeles
San Diego de Alcalá

BAJA CALIFORNIA
Loreto

PACIFIC OCEAN

0   250   500   750   1000 km
0   200   400   600 miles

Original 13 states
Land still claimed by states 1787
U.S. territory
Land ceded by New York to U.S. 1782

if it had the requisite powers, the government could not chart a decisive course. Observers, both at home and abroad, interpreted the disintegrative tendencies that emerged after the War of Independence as foreshadowing inevitable collapse. Britain eagerly anticipated reuniting with some or all of the colonies; Washington, Adams, and other members of the revolutionary elite interpreted the outbursts of democratic fervor on a local level as evidence of a rising licentiousness in the populace, a loss of the republican virtue that had sustained the revolution, and a herald of dissolution.

Elite anxiety reached a fever pitch in the aftermath of Shays's Rebellion (1786), a grassroots tax protest in western Massachusetts. Facing difficulties paying down the war debt, the state imposed taxes that fell disproportionately on farmers, who lacked the hard currency needed to pay the tax. In the tradition of the Stamp Act Rebellion, mobs of farmers (many of whom were war veterans, including the man for whom the uprising is named) shut down court foreclosure proceedings, intimidated tax collectors, and called for the abolition of debts. State militia refused orders to act against the protestors, many of whom were their friends and family members. A rising fear of anarchy compelled Massachusetts authorities to raise a new military force paid for by private funds to restore order in the western part of the state.

Elite opinion, rightly or wrongly, viewed Shays's Rebellion with horror. It seemed to symbolize the incipient anarchy and disunion that loomed before them. In response to this perceived crisis, a core group of committed strong unionists, including James Madison and Edmund Randolph of Virginia, James Wilson and Gouverneur Morris of Pennsylvania, and Alexander Hamilton of New York, began to push for a plan that would head off the anarchic, disintegrative tendency by creating a strong union with a government possessed of the requisite "energy" to hold the union together and to represent it effectively abroad. Hamilton provides some insight into the mindset of the nationalist faction in a letter to Washington expressing his concerns that the Confederation Congress might stymie plans for a constitutional convention: "I fear we may let slip the golden opportunity of rescuing the American empire from disunion, anarchy, and misery."[7]

---

[7] Harold C. Syrett et al., eds., *The Papers of Alexander Hamilton* (27 volumes, New York, 1961–87), 4:224–225.

The fifty-four assembled delegates who met in Philadelphia in May 1787, though recently described by one historian as "plain, honest men," are better remembered as a remarkable assemblage of characters who in effect constituted, with a few notable exceptions, the vanguard of the revolutionary movement.[8] Although Washington and Franklin played more symbolic than substantive roles in the deliberations, their presence gave the convention a legitimacy it otherwise would have lacked. Almost all of the delegates were wealthy. A large majority of the delegates had served in either the war or in the Congress, or both. It is small wonder that they pledged a code of silence about the proceedings, for, instead of merely revising the Articles of Confederation as they had been instructed to do by the Confederation Congress, the delegates abolished the existing plan and drew up a scheme that fundamentally altered the nature of the Union.

Bound together by a common conviction that the Union had to be strengthened in order to survive, the framers faced divisions on a number of issues, none more important than the role of slavery under the new regime. Almost half of the delegates owned slaves; the abolition of slavery in most of the northern states fueled concerns of Southerners that the new, strengthened union not infringe on the property rights of slaveholders. In the years before the cotton boom of the nineteenth century, many white Southerners anticipated the demise of slavery in the relatively near future, but this did not mean that they desired to have the institutions of a new national government play a role in that transition. Creating a Constitution required compromises with slavery, including the infamous three-fifths clause; it could not have been ratified or even drafted without them. The framers wistfully calculated that time and changing circumstances would make the slave controversy diminish.

Widespread opposition existed to centralizing schemes that to many threatened to re-create the tyranny of George III. Had the public known about the centralizing schemes of the Philadelphia convention, popular opposition in the form of angry mobs likely would have stopped it from continuing its work. Recognizing this possibility, the framers boarded up the windows of Constitution Hall and refused to heed what they

---

[8] Richard Beeman, *Plain, Honest Men: The Making of the American Constitution* (New York, 2009).

saw as an uninformed public opinion. Rather than submit their plan for a constitution to the state legislatures for consideration, the framers lobbied successfully for the creation of individual state ratifying conventions, which offered the best chance for their unpopular proposal to be implemented.

The extent of the constitutional reform took even some of its supporters aback; Gordon Wood describes its opponents as "profoundly shocked at the revolutionary nature of the plan."[9] The issue of state sovereignty had to be finessed throughout. Although nominally still a loose confederation of states, the structure envisioned in the new Constitution represented a revolution in terms of the unionist compact. Its opening line – "We the People" – proclaimed the existence of an American people greater than the sum of the citizens of the individual states, a distinct nationality whose loyalty to the United States trumped all local ties, and in whom true sovereignty ultimately resided. In reality, a unified American nation remained mostly a fiction. It seems certain that a majority, perhaps a sizable majority, of the citizenry opposed the new Constitution. In spite of this resistance, ratification of the new compact required the assent of only nine of the thirteen states, on the assumption that states that refused to ratify it would be forced to join the new union or be cast adrift to go it alone. This proved the case with holdouts North Carolina and Rhode Island, both of which eventually consented to the document more out of necessity than choice.

The process of giving popular consent to the Constitution contained a critical asymmetry. The states entered the Union one at a time, via individual ratifying conventions. But under the terms of the new compact it would not be so simple to leave the Union. States that had of their own choice entered the Union could leave only by a three-fourths vote of the national Congress, in effect making each state's choice hostage to a supermajority of representatives from other states. Patrick Henry, one of the leading anti-Constitutionalists, drew the inescapable conclusion concerning this part of the plan: "[I]f sir, amendments are left to the twentieth or tenth part of the people of America, your liberty is gone forever."[10] Although not explicitly "perpetual" as the Articles

---

[9] Gordon S. Wood, *Creation of the American Republic* (Chapel Hill, 1969), 519.

[10] Ralph Ketcham, ed., *The Anti-Federalist Papers* (New York, 2003; first published, 1986), 205.

of Confederation falsely promised to be, the new compact had a structure that made it difficult to amend and almost impossible to withdraw from legally. This reflected the determination of the framers to create a permanent union that need not fear efforts to divide and conquer the states. This deprived future generations of the individual states any real choice as to their ongoing role in the Union. Consent, once given, could not easily be withdrawn. The framers sought to cement the bonds of union on a national level while reining in what they perceived to be the licentiousness and democratic extremism of the people. It was a bold political move, an effort simultaneously to use the states to restrain the actions of the people and to invoke a still largely fictive American people to constrain actions of the states.

The use of the term "framers" when referring to the men who created the compact suggests the structural nature of the entity created by the Constitution. The plan erected a legal, economic, and political structure that would substantially define the existence of the people within the frame while defining them as separate from those outside it. The continued autonomy of the states would be limited by the establishment of a national boundary around them and a national system of law over them, along with the increasingly vigorous enforcement apparatus that lay behind it. In this respect, it is an underappreciated fact that the states themselves became an early and essential conquest of the American Empire, bound together in de facto perpetuity under a strong central authority in defiance of majority sentiment.

Opponents of the new Constitution rightfully observed that the Union had been radically changed. One commentator writing under the pseudonym the Federal Farmer (likely Melancton Smith of New York) published a blast in 1787–8, putting the matter directly: "The plan of government now proposed is evidently calculated totally to change, in time, our condition as a people. Instead of being thirteen republics, under a federal head, it is clearly designed to make us one consolidated government." Opponents saw the Constitution as a judicial Trojan horse inevitably leading to a powerful central government, high taxes, military conscription, and schemes of imperial conquest. Robert Yates of New York, writing under the pseudonym Brutus, correctly perceived the implications of the legal regime being contemplated: "[T]he constitution and laws of every state are nullified and void, so far as they are or shall be inconsistent with this constitution, or the laws made in pursuance of it, or with treaties made under the authority of the United States."[11]

THE FEDERALIST

The pro-Constitution nationalist faction, though a minority numerically, had several advantages in the ratification fight. The support of nearly all the nation's newspapers served as one of the most important of these advantages. If the anti-Constitutionalist majority refused to change its position, a chorus of opposing views in the national press could at least drown it out. Of the dozens of commentaries published during the ratification debate, none had the intellectual firepower nor the long-term influence of *The Federalist,* a series of eighty-five short articles that appeared first in New York newspapers and then in two-volume bound form during the period November 1787 to June 1788. Authored primarily by Alexander Hamilton and James Madison, *The Federalist* also featured five selections on the foreign relations aspects of the Constitution by John Jay, who served as secretary of foreign affairs for the Confederation Congress. According to common practice of the time, the three authors wrote under a historical pseudonym, choosing the moniker Publius, one of the founders of the Roman Republic. Although it is remembered as the most important work of political science ever written by Americans, one should note *The Federalist*'s original function as a political tract designed to persuade. As such, it reveals a certain intellectual slipperiness that belies its iconic status.

Such slipperiness is found in the very title of the text. The Constitution, as has been emphasized, represented a dramatic shift from a loose confederation to a permanent union with a strong national government. Indeed, the defense of it by Hamilton, Madison, and Jay would more accurately be titled *The Nationalist.* But supporters of the Constitution had the audacity to appropriate the name "Federalist" (and the popular connotations that came with it) as their own, leaving their opponents in the position of being anti-Federalists, essentially the opposite of what they actually stood for. It was a brilliant verbal jujitsu that obscured awareness of the strong union they sought to create.

[11] Ketcham, ed., *Anti-Federalist Papers,* 260, 272.

Hamilton, the driving intellectual force behind *The Federalist,* emphasizes what is at stake in the very first paragraph of paper #1: "[N]othing less than the existence of the UNION [sic], the safety and welfare of the parts of which it is composed, the fate of an empire in many respects the most interesting in the world." The dominant theme of *The Federalist* is the necessity of a strong and perpetual union that would serve the purposes Franklin originally envisioned: making the United States secure, expansive, and prosperous. Madison notes this in #41: "Security against foreign danger ... is an avowed and essential object of the American Union." But Hamilton had perhaps the most expansive conception of the possibilities of union: "Under a vigorous national government, the natural strength and resources of the country ... would baffle all the combinations of European jealousy to restrain our growth.... It belongs to us to vindicate the honor of the human race.... Union will enable us to do it.... Let Americans disdain to be the instruments of European greatness! Let the thirteen states, bound together in a strict and indissoluble Union, concur in erecting one great American system superior to the control of all transatlantic force or influence and able to dictate the terms of the connection between the old and new world!"[12]

The Federalist, like much of the American revolutionary ideology, drew on preexisting notions, especially those of the Enlightenment. But in one critical respect – the notion that in order to remain viable, republics must remain small – it made a radical departure from existing assumptions. Contradicting the conventional wisdom of the time as suggested by Montesquieu, Madison argues that an extended republic, as part of a "well-constructed Union," offered an ideal remedy to the danger of faction, which had spelled the end of earlier republics, insofar as it could incorporate such a diversity of interests and outlooks as to ensure they could never comprise a majority. The various factions, permanently divided and geographically separate, could then never threaten to challenge that "chosen body of citizens whose wisdom may best discern the true interest of their county and whose patriotism and love of justice will be least likely to sacrifice it to temporary or partial considerations."[13] And even though historians have long commented on

[12] Clinton Rossiter, ed., *The Federalist Papers* (New York, 1961), 33, 256, 87, 91.
[13] Rossiter, ed., *Federalist Papers,* 82.

Madison's recommendation in #10 to "extend the sphere" of the Union in the name of limiting factionalism, it also must be noted that implicit in the concept of "the permanent and aggregate interests" of the Union that Madison suggests do exist is the assumption that the Union is greater than the mere sum of the particularistic interests of the states. This constituted yet another subtle undermining of state sovereignty.

Madison continued this line of thought in #14 by emphasizing that although democracies necessarily need to be small, republics are limited only by the ability of their representatives to get to congressional sessions in a timely manner, thus dramatically expanding the territory a republic might cover. Even states at the farthest remove from the center stood to benefit from being in the Union if only for the security it offered in case of attack. "It may be inconvenient for Georgia ... to send their representatives to the seat of government; but they would find it more so to struggle alone against an invading enemy." Indeed, Georgia's early and eager ratification of the Constitution resulted from its need for assistance in quelling Indian attacks. In #38, Madison offers another reason for expanding the republic: It was now certain "that the western territory is a mint of vast wealth to the United States" that could be used to pay down the national debt and fund the national treasury in the future.[14]

The Federalist emphasizes that the positive advantages of union are made greater by the catastrophe of disunion. Hamilton frames the choice as a stark dichotomy: Americans faced "the alternative of an adoption of the new Constitution or a dismemberment of the Union." Hamilton fails to note the possibility of the continuation of the Confederation, assuming, rightly or wrongly, its inevitable demise. John Jay warns in #2 that "whenever the dissolution of the Union arrives, America will have reason to exclaim, in the words of the poet: 'Farewell! A Long Farewell To All My Greatness.'" Madison echoes this theme in #41: "Every man who loves peace, every man who loves his country, every man who loves liberty ought to have it ever before his eyes that he may cherish in his heart a due attachment to the Union of America and be able to set a due value on the means of preserving it." Indeed, the overarching theme of *The Federalist* is the central importance of the Union to each state's survival and success: "We have seen the necessity of the

---

[14] Rossiter, ed., *Federalist Papers*, 103, 239.

Union as our bulwark against foreign danger, as the conservator of peace amongst ourselves, as the guardian of our commerce and other common interests."[15]

The authors of *The Federalist* understood that a truly durable Union needed to be bound together by something more than mere rational consent. On this point Madison anticipates Lincoln when in #14 he warns his fellow citizens to beware of divisive, disunionist sentiments: "No, countrymen, shut your ears to such unhallowed language. Shut your hearts against the poison it conveys; the kindred blood which flows in the veins of American citizens, the mingled blood which they have shed in defense of their sacred rights, consecrate their Union."[16]

The authors of *The Federalist* took pains to assure skeptics that the new Constitution posed no threat to their liberties. Hamilton speculated that it was more likely that the states would intrude on the powers of the national government rather than the other way around, that there existed greater potential danger in the "anarchy in the parts" rather than in the "tyranny in the head." Hamilton denied that the states need ever fear the military might of the proposed government: "The resources of the Union would not be equal to the maintenance of an army considerable enough to confine the larger states within the limits of their duty; nor would the means ever be furnished of forming such an army in the first instance." Yet he argued vehemently for the creation of "an energetic government," for anything less could "certainly never preserve the Union of so large an empire."[17]

The Federalist, though rooted mainly in the secular realms of history and politics, is not entirely lacking in redeemer nation ideology. Characterizing the unanimity of the Constitutional Convention behind the final draft as an "astonishment," Madison concludes, "It is impossible for a man of pious reflection not to perceive in it [the making of the Constitution] a finger of that Almighty hand which has been frequently and signally extended to our relief in the critical stages of the revolution."[18] A "miracle in Philadelphia" had occurred. But would the people's representatives ratify it?

---

[15] Rossiter, ed., *Federalist Papers*, 37, 41, 259, 99.
[16] Rossiter, ed., *Federalist Papers*, 104.
[17] Rossiter, ed., *Federalist Papers*, 115, 157.
[18] Rossiter, ed., *Federalist Papers*, 230–1.

Given the democratic pretensions of America nationality it is important to remember that, had the Constitution been put to a referendum of the people, it almost certainly would have been defeated. All acknowledged the right to popular government as a bedrock principle of the American Revolution. Hamilton himself argues in #22, "The fabric of American Empire ought to rest on the solid basis of THE CONSENT OF THE PEOPLE [sic]. The streams of national power ought to flow immediately from that pure, original fountain of all legitimate authority."[19] Yet recognition of this basic principle did not mean that the Founders of the republic presumed to make themselves hostage to what they considered to be an untutored and ill-informed public opinion. Madison postulated in #51 that "[a]ll government rests on opinion," and from that time forward, the key to success in American politics would be to mold public opinion so as to gain the consent desired by elites. Elites need not fear democracy so long as they could control the terms of the debate.

Ratification by nine states led to the Constitution's formal adoption in 1788, and the inauguration of George Washington as the first president of the United States in April 1789. Only one other person had even a shadow of a claim to the office: Benjamin Franklin. In rapidly failing health, the aged prophet nonetheless had lived long enough to see his mid-century vision of a durable North American union come to fruition, albeit as an independent entity. But he was not content to depart the scene without making one more contribution. In February 1790 he presented a petition to Congress calling for the abolition of slavery in the United States. Although a slave owner for much of his life, beginning in the 1780s he began to question the morality of human bondage. Now he sought to bring the issue before the new Congress. Southerners responded to Franklin's last plan for human progress with predictable hostility. Congress rejected the petition, claiming it had no authority to interfere with the internal matters of the states.

HAMILTON CENTRALIZES POWER

In his inaugural address Washington joined the chorus of those thanking God for His assistance to the American people: "Every step, by which

---

[19] Rossiter, ed., *Federalist Papers*, 152.

they have advanced to the character of an independent nation, seems to have been distinguished by some token of providential agency."[20] The popular fear of a centralized tyrannical authority was somewhat muted by Washington's role as president. Yet the new government of 1789 remained a mystery in terms of the extent of its powers and the impact it would have on American life. As it happened, the original plan proved quite flexible under a doctrine of implied powers countenanced by the president and energetically pushed by Hamilton, his most relied upon assistant.

No one did more to define the new nationalist compact than Hamilton. He continued his role as an indefatigable advocate of a strong union as the first secretary of the treasury, where his unparalleled understanding of money and finance made him the only logical choice for the job. From Treasury, Hamilton made his influence felt far and wide in the new government, even in foreign affairs, where he often outflanked and outthought Jefferson, designated as the first secretary of state. With Washington's blessing, Hamilton intellectually and philosophically dominated the first decade of the new national government unlike anyone to follow. He later explained his role this way: "I conceived myself to be under an obligation to lend my aid towards putting the machine in some regular motion."[21]

One of Hamilton's first contributions at Treasury proved one of his most enduring: the recommendations contained in his "Report on Public Credit," presented to Congress in January 1790. It was a master financial plan for the new government, a complex scheme in which all the parts combined to make a coherent whole. Assumption of the Revolutionary War debts of the states formed the core of the plan. Hamilton proposed that the national government pay them off, along with the war debts incurred by the Confederation Congress, at their original value. Expectations that this debt would not be repaid had led bondholders to sell them at a fraction of their face value. Hamilton recognized that for the new national government to assume the entire national debt and begin to make good on the obligation would do more than anything else to legitimate it in the eyes of the financial community,

[20] James D. Richardson, ed., *Messages and Papers of the Presidents* (Washington, D.C., 1903), 1:33.
[21] Ron Chernow, *Alexander Hamilton* (New York, 2004), 287.

especially the European banking community. Hamilton understood that an appropriately sized and serviced national debt would energize the entire American economy by allowing the bonds to serve as collateral for private transactions. A creditworthy government would be a stable government. To facilitate handling of the debt, he proposed a national bank formed from both public and private funds that would ease the borrowing of money for public purposes such as the raising of an army. He devised an excise tax on distilled spirits to provide a dedicated stream of revenue to pay the debt. In sum, Hamilton laid the foundations of a fiscal-military state modeled very much along the lines of that of Great Britain.[22] Nothing could have been better calculated to solidify the new government and prepare it to act with vigor on the world stage.

THE FRENCH REVOLUTION

Even as the first administration and first congress sought to install the apparatus they had created, the foreign policy challenges facing the nation proliferated and intensified. The first summer of the new regime saw the fall of the Bastille in July 1789, heralding the onset of the French Revolution. It is one of history's great ironies that the European government whose support made possible American independence, itself fell victim to revolutionary violence in no small measure owing to the debts incurred during the American war.

Initial enthusiasm for the French revolutionary cause cooled when it became clear that the revolutionaries aimed not only to overthrow the king but also to transform the basic structures of society down to the remaking of the calendar and that, if necessary, violence on a vast scale would be utilized to implement these changes. The sacred flame of liberty burned ferociously in revolutionary France, feeding on the combustible elements of centuries of class privilege and oppression to turn into a raging firestorm consuming all in its path. It is not surprising that many Americans distinguished their revolt against a foreign power in the War of Independence from the internecine bloodletting of a true revolution (although Native Americans and the American Loyalist community

---

[22] On the creation of the British fiscal-military state, see John Brewer, *The Sinews of Power: War, Money, and the English State, 1688–1783* (New York, 1989).

might dispute this point). Even the arch-Francophile Jefferson lost some of his enthusiasm for the struggle when, literally, the heads began to roll in revolutionary France.

The execution of the royal couple in 1793 and the continent-wide war that soon followed complicated the U.S. response to the upheaval. The historic loathing that marked the Anglo-French rivalry worsened with the introduction of a revolutionary and ideological dimension to the struggle. Great Britain now saw itself fighting not only to preserve its own national interest but also to defend the monarchical status quo against a state that sought to overthrow God as well as the king.

In the short run, the Washington administration faced two key questions: First, how should the United States respond to the French Revolution? Second, did the treaties of commerce and alliance of 1778 remain in force? Although both Secretary of State Jefferson and Treasury Secretary Hamilton agreed that the United States should remain neutral, they differed on the nature of that neutrality. Jefferson proposed a biased neutrality tilted toward France, both out of ideological sympathy for the revolutionaries and out of gratitude for France's past support. Hamilton just as vehemently argued for an evenhanded neutrality based neither on sympathy nor gratitude but rather on a hardheaded assessment of U.S. national interest, which, in his (and Washington's) mind, required the maintenance of peace until such time as the new government could be stabilized and a strong military (especially a navy) could be built.

After much deliberation, in April 1793 Washington issued a Proclamation of Neutrality, notwithstanding the fact that he had no explicit authority as president to do so. The first neutrality proclamation in the modern world, the statement became a critical precedent for presidential handling of future foreign crises. Once again Hamilton's views had triumphed in the mind of the president. But neutrality did not mean uninvolvement in the struggle. Americans did not let concerns about the French revolutionary experiment prevent them from attempting to profit from the European war. However, they did not anticipate the refusal of the European states to allow them to trade unhindered in vital supplies with their mortal enemies. The British, especially, vigorously opposed American commercial vessels' trading with their enemies. Between 1793 and 1796, hundreds of American ships were taken as prizes on the high seas and their cargoes seized. In spite of these outrages, the enormous profits of the wartime trade led shipowners to react to the seizures as merely a cost of doing business, increasing their insurance coverage and raising their prices to absorb the added costs.

The forcible abduction of sailors from American merchant vessels (a practice known as "impressment") proved more troubling than the ship seizures. Better pay and working conditions on American ships made them a magnet for deserters from the harsh existence and meager pay of the British navy. This created an ongoing serious shortage in the Royal navy, compelling British captains to remove any deserters or suspected deserters that might be aboard an American vessel. Citizenship being at times hard to confirm in the eighteenth-century world meant that in certain cases American citizens found themselves impressed into the British navy.

The British attacks on American shipping and the impressment of American sailors outraged all Americans, but especially the faction associated with Jefferson and Madison, who harbored an almost Oedipal rage against their former compatriots. For the Virginians, the British transgressions had a personal, even psychological, impact. They began to call for commercial and, possibly, military retaliation. They could not stand to see U.S. independence compromised by what they saw as Britain's malicious and malignant actions. They reverted to the revolutionary-era discourse of equating themselves to slaves and raised the fear of recolonization by the oppressive British lion. The fact that Britain had made no agreement with the United States stipulating that "free ships made free goods" – or that it might not be reasonable to expect Britain to acquiesce in American maritime principles and allow its enemies to be supplied while it was fighting for the survival of its way of life – did not faze the critics. Instead they were obsessed with punishing Britain for its perceived transgressions of natural law and national honor.

James Madison had been pushing for commercial discrimination against British imports since 1791 as part of an effort to reduce U.S. commercial dependence on that nation. The ship seizures broadened support for action. Congress responded to the provocations by clamping a sixty-day embargo on all American shipping in April 1794, aiming primarily at exports to Britain. This action threatened to undermine the Anglo-American trade nexus vital to national prosperity: During this period of the 1790s, England supplied approximately 90 percent of

U.S. imports and absorbed 50 percent of its exports. Faced with a congressional challenge to executive control of foreign affairs, Washington, with the Senate's approval, dispatched John Jay to London to negotiate an end to Anglo-American differences, hoping to head off congressional efforts at commercial discrimination. The controversy over the agreement he returned with proved to be one of the first great foreign policy debates under the new Constitution and established a critical precedent for resolving future disputes between Congress and the executive branch.

THE OHIO WAR

Facing challenges to their economic interests on the high seas, Americans also confronted an ongoing war with the Indians on the western frontier, especially in the Ohio Country. Nearly forty years of warfare had failed to vanquish the tribes of that region; indeed, by 1790 resistance by Native Americans continued seemingly as strong as ever in spite of the decimation of their numbers by war, disease, and upheaval. The Ohio War, little known in U.S. history, took approximately five-sixths of the federal budget between 1790 and 1795. Initial efforts to deploy the power of the national government met with failure. In October 1790, Brigadier General Josiah Harmar and 1,400 regular troops and militia suffered a disastrous defeat near present-day Fort Wayne, Indiana. This fiasco was soon followed by an even bigger defeat. In November 1791 an army of Miami, Shawnee, and Delaware warriors led by Little Turtle annihilated a poorly trained and poorly led force commanded by Arthur St Clair. Approximately 940 of St. Clair's 1,400 soldiers were killed or wounded, the worst defeat ever suffered by the United States at the hands of the Indians and rivaling that of the Braddock disaster of nearly forty years earlier.

Washington and Secretary of War Henry Knox recognized that the difficulties on the western frontier were largely the fault of white settlers who would not be constrained by treaties negotiated with the Indians. Nonetheless, the two men took strong measures to affirm U.S. sovereignty in Ohio. In the aftermath of St. Clair's defeat, Knox reconstituted the army as the Legion of the United States, comprised of 5,000 regular troops and led by Revolutionary War hero "Mad" Anthony Wayne. In August 1794 a portion of this disciplined and determined force engaged approximately 1,000 Indian warriors in what became known as the Battle of Fallen Timbers, so called because the conflict took place in the tangled remnants of thousands of fallen trees likely downed by a tornado. Although the battle ended in a draw militarily, the retreat of the Indian force left the Americans in control of the region. Wayne's army then proceeded to destroy every Indian village and every Indian crop field in the vicinity, exposing the tribes to starvation when their British allies, fearing American retaliation, refused to aid them. Indian resistance in Ohio finally came to an end in August 1795 with the signing of the Treaty of Greenville, in which the Native Americans of the region surrendered their claims to most of the Ohio Country once and for all. More than that, the treaty sought to impress upon the Indians that the United States was now the imperial power on whom their continued existence depended and to whom they should offer their cooperation and submission. The historian Fred Anderson writes, "Voluntary submission to the authority of the federal government was what Washington sought above all on the frontier, and it was crucial that it came as much from whites as from Indians. When Wayne cut roads through the forest, built and manned forts, defeated hostile warriors and bid defiance to the British, he made the most convincing possible demonstration of the power of the United States government."[23]

THE WHISKEY REBELLION: FEDERAL AUTHORITY AFFIRMED

Hamilton's plans to stabilize the financial condition of the country required revenue, more revenue than could be raised via the traditional and accepted method of import tariffs. To address this shortfall Hamilton conceived of a tax on distilled spirits, a burden that fell disproportionately on farmers in the areas west of the mountains. Excise charges – traditionally the most hated of taxes – were payable only in hard currency, and western farmers found it difficult to see what benefit was derived from their payments. Hamilton's insistence, in the name of full compliance, that federal policy require distillers to keep meticulous records of their production or face penalties aggravated local sentiments. Careful record keeping proved quite burdensome to

[23] Anderson and Cayton, *Dominion of War*, 195.

small producers, more so than for larger operations accustomed to regular accounting procedures. By 1793, the reviled tax had inspired uprisings all along the western frontier. Later known as the Whiskey Rebellion, essentially a sequel to Shays's Rebellion of a few years earlier, it proved the largest internal uprising in the United States before the Civil War. Producers refused to pay the excise; tax collectors fell victim to mob violence when not being routinely harassed. The uprising directly challenged the authority of the new government. The revolt symbolized an existential threat to the new central authority: A government incapable of exercising authority over its own citizens could hardly expect respect on the world stage. British officials in North America saw the revolt as a manifestation of the inherently centrifugal tendencies of the not-so-united states and eagerly anticipated its collapse.[24]

Both Washington and Hamilton recognized the need for the incipient uprising to be decisively put down in the name of asserting the authority of the central government. The president also had personal reasons for securing the western country: For forty years he had accumulated property claims totaling more than sixty thousand acres west of the Appalachians. He had no desire to see either the Union dismembered or his land claims nullified by a secessionist tendency.[25] In August 1794, Washington declared western Pennsylvania to be in revolt and federalized militia from New Jersey, eastern Pennsylvania, Maryland, and Virginia. Washington personally oversaw the reconstitution of the officer corps. In September 1794, a force of nearly 13,000 troops with Washington at its head rendezvoused at Fort Cumberland, the same place where he and Braddock had started their ill-fated expedition forty years earlier. From there the army marched toward western Pennsylvania to crush the rebels. The ragtag collection of locals disbanded in the face of an overwhelming federal force marching west, thereby avoiding a violent confrontation. Several leaders of the rebellion suffered arrest and the charge of treason, but soon even they were released without severe penalty. Harsh measures proved unnecessary; the massive show of force decisively affirmed the authority of the national government. Washington's personal investment in western lands also benefited from

---

[24] Thomas Slaughter, *The Whiskey Rebellion: Frontier Epilogue to the American Revolution* (New York, 1986), 171.
[25] Slaughter, *Whiskey Rebellion*, 82.

the government's strong action, increasing approximately 50 percent in value after the defeat of the rebellion. And while the massive display of force did not necessarily assure the loyalties of Americans west of the mountains, it did, as Thomas Slaughter notes, "demonstrate the federal government's commitment to a perpetual Union and its ability to enforce that commitment hundreds of miles distant from the center of its power."[26]

THREE TREATIES: GREENVILLE, PINCKNEY, AND JAY

Between late 1794 and early 1795, the perilous condition of the new union greatly improved. Wayne's defeat of the Miami Confederacy in August 1794 had paved the way for the Treaty of Greenville in 1795, finally securing the Ohio Country for the United States. The crushing of the whiskey rebels in November 1794 had served notice far beyond western Pennsylvania that the new sovereignty established by the Constitution had teeth and was not to be taken lightly. That same month, Jay concluded the treaty that bears his name in London, sending it home for a hoped-for ratification by two-thirds of the Senate.

Armed with Hamilton's peace-at-any-cost instructions, Jay, an Anglophile, had minimal difficulty reaching an agreement with British officials. While the treaty was not wholly unfavorable to the United States, the British refused to budge on the maritime questions at the heart of the controversy. The pact allowed renewed access for Americans to the British West Indies but only in vessels of seventy tons or smaller, a distinct disadvantage. Rather than face the criticism of what many would see as capitulation, Washington withheld the treaty from the public; the Senate debated and ratified it in June 1795 by 20–10, a bare two-thirds majority – and only then by removing the limitations on American commercial access to the British West Indies. Before the president could sign the ratified treaty a leaked copy found its way into press, igniting a firestorm of controversy that scholars point to as the first significant partisan debate of the emerging two-party system. As had been feared, members of the emerging Jeffersonian faction viewed it as craven submission to Great Britain and a betrayal of France. The Democratic-Republican societies that sprang up at this time in

---

[26] Slaughter, *Whiskey Rebellion*, 226.

opposition to the treaty represent the origins of the first oppositional party in U.S. history.

While it is true that the Jay Treaty did not achieve any British concessions to the American definition of neutral rights, the British did agree finally to evacuate the western forts, thereby depriving the Indians of a critical source of supplies. They now would have to confront the growing might of the United States on their own. The treaty also extended U.S. shipping limited access to the rich markets of the British East Indies and allowed U.S. commercial vessels to enter British ports on a most-favored-nation basis. Most importantly, it preserved peace at a time when the Union had neither the economic nor the military means to engage in another conflict with Britain. From the perspective of American nationalism, it must be judged a success. Yet the nascent Jeffersonians waged an all-out effort to defeat it in the name of preserving the nation's honor. Public denunciations of the treaty, Jay, and, most shockingly, Washington, sprang up in almost every major American city.

Washington's signature on the treaty in August 1795 should have marked the end of the battle. But members of the Jeffersonian clique, having whipped themselves into a fever pitch about the dire consequences that allegedly would follow, attempted to stop the treaty by refusing to vote funds for its implementation. In an effort to discredit the treaty, they also demanded that the executive branch turn over all documents and correspondence relating to its negotiation. This move represented a bold attempt by the House to gain some measure of control of the foreign policy process. As with the debate over the Constitution, a solid majority of citizens seemed to oppose the treaty. Washington responded cagily, waiting six months for passions to cool before requesting implementation funds and flatly refusing to share any documents relating to its negotiation as an intrusion on executive privilege. Hamilton, by now a private citizen, produced another blizzard of articles (under the pseudonym Camillus) defending the treaty as essential to the national interest and wearing down opponents by both the cogency and the quantity of his arguments. On April 30, 1796, the House voted 51–48 to fund the treaty. Yet passions remained inflamed. Representative Frederick Muhlenberg of Pennsylvania was stabbed and beaten by his brother-in-law for changing his vote in favor of funding the treaty, a disturbing indication of the intensity of political divisions in the country at that time.[27]

Critics who blasted the Jay Treaty as a sell-out of the nation's commercial rights and its honor did not grasp the agreement's importance to the security of the Union. Essentially a follow-up to the treaty ending the War of Independence, the Jay Treaty served notice that the chance for a second Anglo-American war had been, for the time being, greatly reduced. This fact made Spain much more willing to deal with the Americans on the southwestern border dispute. Fears of an Anglo-American assault on Spanish Louisiana or the Floridas prompted Spanish prime minister Manuel de Godoy to capitulate to every demand of American negotiator Thomas Pinckney. In Pinckney's Treaty (1795), the United States secured navigation rights to the Mississippi River, the right to deposit goods at New Orleans preparatory to transshipment overseas, a southern boundary at the thirty-first parallel as originally called for in the 1783 agreement with Great Britain, the withdrawal of Spanish troops from territories now owned by the United States, and a Spanish pledge (which ultimately proved hollow) to prevent Indian attacks on American settlements.

The Senate unanimously ratified Pinckney's Treaty, reflecting the widespread popular acclaim it received. The vociferous critics of the Jay Treaty for the most part either did not understand or did not want to acknowledge the critical role that maintaining peace with Britain had played in securing the southwestern boundary from Spain. Indeed, between August 1794 and August 1796, England and Spain withdrew from the western territories and successful military campaigns had substantially reduced the Indian threat. In only two years, the United States, possessed of a new, invigorated foreign policy apparatus, had greatly increased its security.

WASHINGTON'S FAREWELL

After nearly half of century of public service, George Washington eagerly looked toward retirement after his second term as president.

---

[27] On the Jay Treaty ratification fight, see Todd Estes, *The Jay Treaty Debate, Public Opinion, and the Evolution of Early American Political Culture* (Amherst, Mass., 2006).

Especially during the last two years in office, he had suffered harsh public criticisms of a sort he had never before experienced, and it stung. These attacks, however, did not diminish his astounding achievements as both a soldier and a citizen. From that uncertain beginning in western Pennsylvania in the early 1750s, he had literally presided over the conception, creation, and institutionalization of what was presumed to be a permanent union of Britain's now independent North American colonies. The United States had assumed a sovereign role amid the world's nations and had expanded prodigiously during its short existence, making real Washington's vision of a great western Empire. He was the one indispensable man to the entire process, rightly known as the "father of his country."

Before leaving office, Washington decided to bequeath to his fellow citizens a political testament representing in brief what he in his accumulated experience and wisdom felt should be the future path of the Union. Never formally delivered as a speech, the Farewell Address became one of the most widely reproduced public documents in American history, quickly assuming the role of a type of national holy writ. While historians have noted the prominent role of Hamilton in writing and revising the text, it is wrong to think that the ideas are Hamilton's, for the themes of the Farewell Address reflect the concerns of Washington's entire career. First among them was the critical importance of union, "a main pillar in the edifice of your real independence, the support of your tranquility at home, your peace abroad, of your safety, of your prosperity, of that very liberty which you so highly prize." In the name of preserving the Union, Washington warned against the rise of factions, of either a geographic or a partisan nature, which even then threatened stability. Along the same lines the retiring president, in a thinly veiled reference to the Jeffersonian Republicans, cautioned against "permanent, inveterate antipathies against particular nations and passionate attachments for others" as prone to making America "a slave to its animosity or to its affection, either of which is sufficient to lead it astray from its duty and its interest."[28]

Washington's acute sense of the favorable geography enjoyed by the United States informed much of his Farewell Address. Not surprisingly, he urged Americans to honor any agreements already made, but

[28] Richardson, ed., *Messages and Papers of the Presidents,* 1:215, 1:221.

once they were fulfilled he strongly counseled them to "steer clear of permanent alliances with any part of the foreign world." Instead, he recommended a policy of maximum commercial engagement with foreign states and minimum political engagement. This he termed "the great rule of conduct" for American foreign relations, designed to involve Americans in foreign commerce without entangling it in foreign controversies. While historians in the twentieth century have deemed, anachronistically, that the Farewell Address counsels an isolationist foreign policy, in fact Washington advises his fellow citizens to make use of the favorable geography of their "detached and distant situation" in the Western Hemisphere to consolidate and stabilize the Union. "If we remain one people, under an efficient government, the period is not far off when we may defy material injury from external annoyance; ... when we may choose peace or war, as our interest, guided by justice, shall counsel."[29] Washington hoped, according to Burton Kaufman, "to assure that the rising empire of the New World would not fall victim to the struggles of the Old."[30]

It was left to Parson Mason Weems, transplanted Anglican priest and Washington's most popular biographer, to eulogize the first president's awesome legacy. Weems lauded Washington's role in establishing "a mighty Empire for the reception of a happiness unknown on Earth, since the days of blissful Eden.... An Empire that shall afford a welcome retreat to all the uncorrupted sons of freedom, an Empire that shall open a vast theatre for the display of the grand transactions of providential wisdom."[31]

[29] Richardson, ed., *Messages and Papers of the Presidents*, 222.
[30] Burton Kaufman, ed., *Washington Farewell Address: The View from the 20th Century* (Chicago, 1969), 181.
[31] Richard Van Alstyne, *Genesis of American Nationalism* (Waltham, Mass., 1970), 139–40.

3

EXPANSION, EMBARGO, AND WAR

Louisiana ... became an unexpected experiment in empire ... it challenged Americans' view of themselves as well as others, and it began to give the word empire another and not altogether comfortable connotation for America ... an America that included a bloc of captive peoples of a foreign culture that had not chosen to be Americans.

D.W. Meinig, *The Shaping of America: Continental America, 1800–1867*, 23

The creation of an empire for liberty was pushed forward by the activities of thousands of land-hungry western settlers.

Eric Hinderaker, *Elusive Empires, Constructing Colonialism in the Ohio Valley, 1673–1800*, 186

THE QUASI-WAR WITH FRANCE

The Jay Treaty greatly reduced Anglo-American frictions along the Canadian border and on the high seas. With peace assured with Great Britain, trade with that nation prospered in a manner not seen since before the War of Independence, a prosperity made even greater by a rapid rise in the price of American agricultural exports as a result of the demands of the continent at war. The rapidly expanding overseas trade set off a boom in shipbuilding and in the industries related to it: lumber, naval stores, carpentry, and the like. Paine's dream of the United States as the chief supplier of a Europe at war seemed to be coming true. While some Jeffersonians continued to snipe at the agreement as an insult to national honor, France wound up as the real loser from the Jay Treaty. America's one formal ally felt betrayed that the United States had made concessions on neutral rights to the British that were far more generous than had been established in the Treaty of Amity and Commerce of 1778. Franco-American commerce now operated at a disadvantage compared to U.S. trade with Britain, a huge slap in the face for a nation whose aid had made American independence possible.

The French, far more experienced than the Americans in the ways of diplomacy, knew better than to feel sincerely aggrieved. Americans made concessions to Britain at the negotiating table because their national security required it and the balance of forces compelled it. Any chance that the United States might have refrained from making the best deal it could with Britain out of a misplaced sense of gratitude to revolutionary France ended with Hamilton's ascendance in the cabinet. Raison d'état of the sort counseled by Hamilton allowed no room for sentiment. Nonetheless, the French chose to respond to news of the Jay Treaty with the vengeance of a jilted lover. In July 1796 they announced they would no longer honor the premise of "free ships/ free goods" articulated in the Treaty of 1778; by June 1797 the French navy had seized more than three hundred American vessels trading with the West Indies. A new international crisis loomed for the Americans with their former ally, led now by a revolutionary junta known as the Directory. The Directory's insistence that the United States acquiesce in its demands to modify the commercial terms of the alliance as a precondition to receiving the new American minister, Charles Cotesworth Pinckney, prompted new president John Adams to escalate the war of words in a special message to Congress. He declared to Congress that France's high-handed treatment of the American minister "is to treat us neither as allies nor as friends, nor as a sovereign state.... Such attempts ought to be repelled with a decision which shall convince France and the world that we are not a degraded people, humiliated under a colonial spirit of fear and sense of inferiority, fitted to be the miserable instruments of foreign influence."[1] Having defused tensions with the world's most powerful state, the United States now escalated them with its second most powerful state.

Seeking a peaceful solution to the crisis, Adams dispatched a bipartisan team of envoys to Paris to attempt both to negotiate an end to the immediate dispute over commercial policy as well as to reestablish diplomatic ties with the French revolutionary regime. But before he would

---

[1] James D. Richardson, ed., *Messages and Papers of the Presidents* (Washington, D.C., 1903), 1:235.

talk to the Americans, French foreign minister Talleyrand repeatedly sought to extract bribes for him and a U.S. loan to the French government. Talleyrand apparently thought this was the least the Americans could do, both for him and for France. After months of fruitless diplomatic efforts, in March 1798 Adams asked Congress to begin preparations for war, turning over to that body documents relating to the failed diplomatic mission, including written requests for bribes by French negotiators identified only as X, Y, and Z.

The so-called X, Y, Z Affair caused a sensation in the public mind and gave a mighty boost to the fortunes of the Adams administration. War fever raged, as Americans rallied to the sentiment that pledged "millions for defence, but not one cent for tribute." At the behest of the administration, Congress prepared for war: It nullified the French treaties, launched an ambitious expansion of the navy (including the construction of six new frigates), and increased the size of the regular army. Adams even urged a reluctant Washington out of retirement to take command of the reconstituted national army. As a precondition to accepting leadership of the new force, Washington requested that Hamilton be made inspector general, in effect making him the day-to-day head of the army. Hamilton used his new post to advance schemes for an Anglo-American conquest of Spain's American colonies in the event of a war with France.

The war scare of 1798 had ominous domestic consequences in the form of the Alien and Sedition Acts. Seeking to curb an influx of Irish – who, it was feared, might tend to side with the Republicans in any future political conflicts – the Federalist Congress used its power over naturalization to enact two Alien Acts limiting new immigrants to the United States and asserting the right to deport resident aliens of nations with whom the country was at war. The Sedition Act made written political dissent a crime, punishable by a fine of $2,000 or two years in jail. Hamilton justified this outrageous abridgement of First Amendment rights as necessary in the name of "unanimity" in wartime. Prosecutions under this onerous law soon began, with devastating consequences for press freedom.

Resisting calls from members of his own party for a formal declaration of war against France, President Adams instead engaged in a unilateral executive action known as the Quasi-War against the French navy. Lasting more than two years, the Quasi-War showed off the reconstituted navy's newfound strength in a series of brilliant victories over French naval vessels in the West Indies. The superb display of sea-going might by the new nation had the intended effect. America's firm response to French diplomatic provocations soon forced Talleyrand to let it be known that he would receive a new American envoy without preconditions or bribes in the name of avoiding all-out war. Yet, having threatened war to gain concessions from France, Adams now defied members of his own party in order to send William Vans Murray to Paris to seek a settlement. This so outraged the pro-war members of the Federalist party that they deserted him politically. In a notable act of political courage, Adams sacrificed his standing in his own party and cut short his political career by standing firm on his determination to limit the conflict with France to the high seas only.

France, now led by Napoleon, vindicated Adams's limited war policy by quickly agreeing to settle the dispute. The Treaty of Mortefontaine, also known as the Convention of 1800, abrogated the Franco-American Treaties of 1778 as the United States desired, although at a cost: The United States agreed to assume the claims of American merchants whose goods had been illegally seized by the French since 1793, totaling approximately $20,000,000. It was a considerable expense but, given the cost of a full-scale war, qualified as a bargain. Adams had hewed to Washington's policy of avoiding a major war with the two dominant powers but at the cost of his own reelection. He went to his grave believing it had been one of his greatest accomplishments.

The 1790s proved a crucial decade in American history. Domestically, the fiction of a harmonious one-party state intended by the framers of the Constitution broke down amid intense partisan acrimony, much of it related to differences over foreign affairs. The political strife precipitated the rise of the Jeffersonian Republicans and the emergence of the first party system. Resistance to the heavy-handed Alien and Sedition Acts resulted in resolutions issued by the legislatures of Virginia and Kentucky in 1798 reserving the right of the states to nullification or interposition of federal legislation deemed oppressive, carrying with them the distinct whiff of disunion. At the same time, the enormous centralization of power rendered theoretically possible by the Constitution and made real by the policies of Hamilton led to remarkable achievements in American foreign relations. In a little over a decade under the new Constitution, the United States had won a major victory over the

Indians in the Ohio War, put down a serious internal rebellion in the trans-Appalachian west, secured navigation rights on the Mississippi River from Spain, stabilized both the Canadian border and trade relations with Great Britain, and escaped from an entangling alliance with France after besting that nation in a protracted, undeclared naval showdown. In spite of the toxic domestic political environment, visionary political leadership and adroit diplomacy combined with decisive applications of force to make the period 1789–1801 a time of great success for the United States in foreign affairs.

THE REVOLUTION OF 1800

The Convention of 1800 with France and the temporary cessation of hostilities in Europe combined to create a period of calm in the days before the accession in March 1801 of Thomas Jefferson to the presidency. The Federalist party, divided internally and widely loathed for its heavy-handed rule, set the stage for the first transfer of power to another party in American history in what historians sometimes term "the revolution of 1800." As the undisputed head of a party in control of both houses of Congress (but not the judiciary, thanks to John Adams's last-minute appointments to the federal bench), Jefferson had wide latitude to craft the policies of his choice. The bitter political antagonisms of the late 1790s had resulted in a new regime's coming to power that promised to take back the American Revolution from the moneychangers and "Anglomen," who, it was thought, had corrupted the dream. With the excesses of the French Revolution fresh in the public mind, no one was quite sure how far the new administration might go in its purification ritual.

As it turned out they need not have worried. In his inaugural address (which was, like Washington's Farewell Address, widely printed and reprinted), Jefferson signaled that the changes he would make would not be drastic and sought to bury the bitter feelings of the recent past in the warm glow of consensus: "Every difference of opinion is not a difference of principle.... We are all Republicans, we are all Federalists. If there be any among us who wish to dissolve this Union or to change its republican form, let them stand undisturbed as monuments of the safety of which error of opinion may be tolerated where reason is left free to combat it."[2] Appeals to bipartisanship are enduringly popular U.S. history, but such appeals overlook the fact that partisan differences are often rooted in differing principles, particularly regarding the size and function of the national government. The new president's appeal to unity rang a bit disingenuously given Jefferson's significant role in drafting the Virginia Resolutions of 1798, which contained an implicitly secessionist aspect. Most observers, however, relieved at the smooth transfer of power, chose to overlook these seeming contradictions and instead hope for better times ahead.

Playing to the resentments of his Jeffersonian Republican base, the new president inaugurated both his administration and the new capital in Washington, D.C., by vowing to shrink the size and function of a central authority that many felt had become too big and too powerful. Jefferson proposed a minimalist government with large cuts to the army and navy, and he promised to reduce the bloated federal bureaucracy with its 130 or so employees. Most popular of all, Jefferson pledged to end all internal taxes (including the hated excise on distilled spirits) while at the same time eliminating the national debt in short order. In foreign affairs, Jefferson committed to a policy of "peace, commerce and honest friendship with all, entangling alliances with none." The overarching vision was that of a "wise and frugal government, which shall restrain men from injuring one another, shall leave them otherwise free."[3]

Given this staunch small-government stance, it is ironic that Jefferson is remembered as the most expansionist of all the Founders, more so than even Franklin or Washington. Jefferson wrote to James Monroe in 1801 of his belief that "[h]owever our present interests may restrain us within our limits, it is impossible not to look forward to distant times, when our rapid multiplication will expand it beyond these limits, & cover the whole northern if not the southern continent, with people speaking the same language, governed in similar forms, and by similar laws."[4] Though he never traveled west of the Blue Ridge Mountains of Virginia, Jefferson from his earliest days had a consuming vision of

[2] Richardson, ed., *Messages and Papers of the President*, 1:322.
[3] Richardson, ed., *Messages and Papers of the President*, 1:323.
[4] Richard Van Alstyne, *The Rising American Empire* (New York, 1974; first published, 1960), 87.

the possibilities of continental expansion. He zealously advocated for American navigation rights on the Mississippi River, early on recognizing that maintaining unhindered access to the Gulf of Mexico was critical to securing the loyalty of the trans-Appalachian west. But his continentalist vision extended far beyond the Mississippi, the Lewis and Clark Expedition being only the most famous of several exploratory missions to the west sponsored by the Jefferson administration. The ostensible scientific purpose of the Lewis and Clark endeavor was joined to another, more practical, concern. Jefferson's instructions to the two explorers called for them to explore the streams and rivers from the Missouri River west for the purpose of discovering which waterway might "offer the most direct & practicable water communication across this continent for the purposes of commerce."[5]

Jefferson's interest in the west encompassed more than the commercial opportunities it represented. In a theoretical sense, territorial expansion also functioned as crucial to the continued success of the republican experiment. Jefferson's version of agrarian Republicanism required an expanding dominion so that the trends that might threaten its future – such as the development of a large urban proletariat – could be averted. As formulated by Drew McCoy, expansion through space could ward off the inevitable deterioration over time of a hemmed-in population with declining opportunities.[6] Like Washington and Franklin before him, Jefferson's republican vision for America included an indispensable role for expansionism. His continentalist vision of an "Empire of Liberty" incorporated Franklin's racially exclusive outlook found in "Observations Concerning the Increase of Mankind" along with Madison's theorizing of an extended republic capable of indefinite expansion. Yet to these earlier visions Jefferson added a new dimension: the special role of freehold farmers as a sort of chosen people of God, calling no one master and redeeming humanity by their example of unfettered liberty even as they tilled the soil. If Americans could stay close to the soil and to God, their virtue would be sustained and their nation's uniqueness assured. But to be realized, that vision required large amounts of new territory, thus making expansion not a choice but

5 D. W. Meinig, *The Shaping of America: A Geographical Perspective on 500 Years of History*, 4 vols. (New Haven, 1986), 2:65.
6 Drew McCoy, *The Elusive Republic: Political Economy in Jeffersonian America* (Chapel Hill, 1980).

a necessity. Ironic, too, is that even though Jefferson idealized yeoman farmers as producing little more than a subsistence living for themselves and their local communities, the reality is that even at that early date the enormous productivity of American farmers meant they had to seek international markets for their crops in order to be prosperous and thus were subject to its fluctuations. Most glaringly, Jefferson's vision of a nation of white freehold farmers expanding westward ignored the presence of a rising slave population in the southern states whose critical role in the nation's labor force meant that they, too, would at some point need to be moved into the western territories.

Jefferson's expansionist vision was not merely continentalist. He foresaw expansion to the West Coast as only one step toward the realization of a "passage to India," the establishment of an American commercial presence in Asia and the Pacific. Ultimately his expansionist vision encompassed virtually the entire world, which he did not see as becoming part of the United States but rather becoming like the United States – that is, republican politically and capitalist economically. Only in a world guided by the principles of liberal capitalism could the safety of republican government be assured. It is in this respect that Jefferson entertained what could be said to be the most expansive, the most far-reaching of the foundational visions of the founders of the American Empire.

THE LOUISIANA PURCHASE

It was against this ideological backdrop that the momentary calm on the international scene that had ushered in the Jefferson presidency gave way in the summer of 1801 to fears that Spain, in control of the Louisiana territory since it had been ceded to the Spanish crown by the French at the end of the Seven Years War, planned to "retrocede" the province back to Napoleonic France. Alarming reports suggested that a huge French expeditionary force under the command of Napoleon's brother-in-law, General Victor Leclerc, was headed to Saint Domingue in a final effort to defeat the rebels under the command of Toussaint L'Ouverture, a former slave whose brilliant leadership had sustained the Haitian independence movement since its inception in 1791. Taken together, the reports presented a thorny challenge. Jefferson, initially sympathetic to the idea of crushing a black revolution occurring in

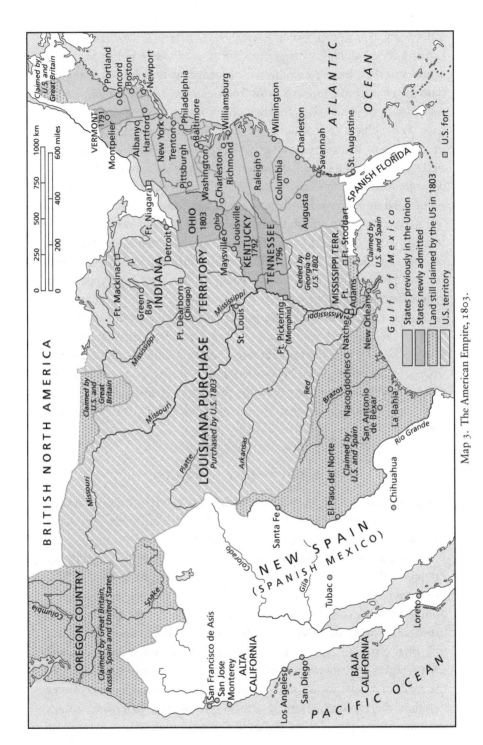

Map 3. The American Empire, 1803.

Labels within the map:

BRITISH NORTH AMERICA

Claimed by U.S. and Great Britain

VERMONT 1791

Portland
Concord
Boston
Newport
Philadelphia
Montpelier
Albany
Hartford
New York
Trenton
Baltimore
Williamsburg
Pittsburgh
Washington
Richmond
Charleston
Raleigh
Wilmington
Columbia
Charleston
Savannah
St. Augustine

ATLANTIC OCEAN

OHIO 1803

KENTUCKY 1792

TENNESSEE 1796

Augusta

Ft. Niagara
Detroit
Ft. Mackinac

INDIANA

Green Bay

Ft. Dearborn (Chicago)

TERRITORY

Maysville
Ohio
Louisville
St. Louis

Mississippi

SPANISH FLORIDA

Ft. Stoddart

Ceded by Georgia to U.S. 1802

MISSISSIPPI TERR.

Ft. Adams

Claimed by U.S. and Spain

Ft. Pickering (Memphis)

Missouri

LOUISIANA PURCHASE
Purchased by U.S. 1803

Claimed by U.S. and Great Britain

Missouri

Platte

Arkansas

Red

Brazos

Natchez
New Orleans

Gulf of Mexico

Nacogdoches
San Antonio de Bexar
La Bahia

Rio Grande

Claimed by U.S. and Spain

El Paso del Norte

Chihuahua

Santa Fe

NEW SPAIN
(SPANISH MEXICO)

Colorado

Gila

Tubac

OREGON COUNTRY

Claimed by Great Britain, Russia, Spain and United States

Columbia

Snake

San Francisco de Asis
San Jose
Monterey

ALTA CALIFORNIA

Los Angeles
San Diego

BAJA CALIFORNIA

Loreto

PACIFIC OCEAN

Scale:
0   250   500   750   1000 km
0   200   400   600 miles

Legend:
States previously in the Union
States newly admitted
Land still claimed by the US in 1803
U.S. territory
□ U.S. fort

close proximity to the United States, soon came to fear a large French expeditionary force in the Western Hemisphere even more. The administration speculated that Leclerc's ultimate mission was to secure New Orleans and hence control of the Mississippi after the defeat of the Haitian revolutionaries. Like a recurring nightmare, the specter of western expansion being blocked once again haunted the sleep of Americans, even more so than the equally recurring dream of a slave uprising. Once again, America's imperial ambitions entangled it in the maelstrom of European imperial intrigues even as it continued to see itself as apart and uninvolved in world affairs.

Jefferson, temporarily elbowing Secretary of State Madison to the side, took personal control of American diplomacy in this time of crisis. In a letter designed to become public knowledge, Jefferson in April 1802 wrote to the American minister in Paris, Robert Livingston, warning that the day France took possession of New Orleans, Americans would have to "marry themselves to the British fleet and nation." It was a continuation of the "Mississippi question" of the 1780s, a threat both to commerce and to the Union itself. Jefferson's inveterate Anglophobia did not prevent him from at least contemplating an alliance with Great Britain in the face of a massive expansion of French power in North America. Napoleon at first appeared unconcerned with this threat and sought to augment France's reinvigorated New World Empire by acquiring the Floridas from Spain, too. The crisis came to a head with the closing of the port of New Orleans to American shipping by the Spanish Intendant of the city in October 1802, in direct violation of Pinckney's Treaty. Occurring before the formal transfer of the colony to France, many Americans assumed (probably incorrectly) that Napoleon was behind the suspension of the right of deposit. For at least the third time since the adoption of the Constitution, war fever swept the nation. Congress made plans to raise an army of 80,000 militia, and settlers in Kentucky, Tennessee, and elsewhere began to make their own preparations for defense.

Hoping to avoid a war, in early 1803 Jefferson dispatched fellow Virginian James Monroe to Paris. Monroe was charged with assisting Livingston in the negotiations and empowered to purchase New Orleans and West Florida for $10 million. This was nearly as much as the Revolutionary War debt Jefferson had seen as such a threat and vowed to reduce. Nevertheless, the demands of the moment took precedence over the principles of the past. The chance for successful talks seemed remote. Why should Napoleon forgo his dream of a reborn New World Empire for France in order to placate the Americans?

Circumstances came to both Jefferson's and America's rescue in the form of the courageous resistance of the Haitian revolutionaries and the deadliness of the mosquito. By early 1803, Leclerc's 30,000-strong army was in tatters and its general dead, a victim of the fever that had consumed many of his troops. With their demise died Napoleon's dream of a reconstituted French New World Empire centered in New Orleans. In the wake of defeat in Sainte Domingue and contemplating a renewed struggle with the allies in Europe, Napoleon acted decisively. He instructed Talleyrand to sell all of the vaguely defined Louisiana territory to the Americans for $11 million, plus the assumption of $4 million in claims by Americans (mostly merchants) against the French government. Monroe arrived in Paris to find a radically different negotiation. Yet he and Livingston did not hesitate to disregard their instructions and to agree to Tallyrand's astounding offer of a huge, indeterminate expanse of North America peopled by approximately 50,000 French Creoles and 150,000 Indians. Both men knew that, given Jefferson's long interest in the west, if they had not been given instructions to buy all of Louisiana it was only because the president had not considered it a possibility in this particular negotiation.

The immensity of the Louisiana Territory challenged the imagination of Americans at a time when its population scarcely exceeded five million people. It must be recalled that Jefferson's proclamation of America as "a chosen country, with room enough for our descendants to the thousandth and thousandth generation" occurred in his inaugural address, before the acquisition of Louisiana territory. Nonetheless, Monroe and Livingston instinctively sensed that Americans would embrace, with few exceptions, this approximate doubling of the nation's imperial domain if only to ensure that no other nation controlled it. The ill-defined boundaries contained in the deal did not give the two men any hesitation, for they knew that their very ambiguity would be the basis for future expansionist bids, in all likelihood against a weak Spain.

Some Federalists at the time and some historians since have portrayed the Louisiana Purchase as a stroke of diplomatic luck that owed little to Jefferson's presidential leadership. True, the Haitian resistance better explains Napoleon's willingness to deal than does Jefferson's statecraft. Jefferson, however, had placed the United States in a position to benefit from the unexpected turn of events, most notably by the perceived tilt toward Great Britain. Napoleon, following in the footsteps of Vergennes, acted to affirm "forever the power of the United States" by creating a rival to Great Britain that he thought "sooner or later [would] lay low her pride." Once again, the United States gained an advantage as a result of the Anglo-French rivalry. From the start, American diplomacy consistently sought to exploit Anglo-French antagonism; in that sense, the Louisiana Purchase was no more the result of luck than was the Treaty of Paris. As the two dominant European powers contended, the United States took advantage of their distraction to realize its own imperial ambitions.

However large the territory of Louisiana actually turned out to be, its acquisition presented two major constitutional challenges: first, could a president acquire new lands by treaty? Second, was it constitutional or just to incorporate non-Indian peoples into the Union without their consent? On the first point Jefferson himself had serious doubts, scuttling a hurried attempt to amend the Constitution granting him permission to purchase territories only when he feared that further delays might lead Napoleon to change his mind about the entire deal. The second objection loomed even larger. The framers of the Constitution did not authorize the colonization of a Euro-American population by presidential treaty-making power, an outright act of imperial domination. Jefferson made matters worse by depriving Louisianans, for a time, of the right to self-government, instead making himself the de facto emperor of the "Empire of Liberty" in 1805. Notwithstanding these and other objections, most notably that the massive extension of territory would eventually lead to the collapse of the Union, the Republican-dominated Senate ratified the purchase 24–7 in October 1803.

FREEING THE SEAS: THE WAR ON BARBARY PIRACY

Jefferson's conception of a minimalist federal government domestically stood in sharp contrast to his maximalist conception of the power of the state, and of the executive in particular, to wield power abroad. The Louisiana Purchase signified a major expansion of both territory and executive power. On the high seas, Jefferson's war on Barbary piracy represented a similar expansion of both the imperial reach of the United States and the power of the executive to make war.

Whatever the commercial advantages of independence as envisioned by Paine and others, the loss of the protection of the Union Jack proved a distinct disadvantage to the nation's commercial fleet, which quickly fell prey to piratical attacks by the North African states of Morocco, Tripoli, Tunis, and Algiers. Known by Americans as the Barbary Coast, for several centuries these states had terrorized shipping in the Mediterranean, compelling Europeans to pay protection monies or face seizure. Wealthy states with strong navies, such as Great Britain, found it advantageous to make the payments rather than crush the lightly armed pirates so as to leave the ships of their less-well-off commercial competitors facing capture of their vessels and enslavement of their crews. In the short run, capitulation to extortion seemed expedient. In 1786, over Jefferson's objections, the United States agreed to make payments totaling $1 million to Morocco in return for a guarantee of safe passage for American-flagged vessels. In the late 1790s, similar payments made to Algiers totaled $1 million. The protection these payments afforded seemed to justify the national humiliation they entailed.

As president, Jefferson faced a number of foreign policy challenges. The first was the resumption of the attacks by Tripolitan corsairs on American shipping, supposedly the result of late tribute payments to the pasha. Without asking Congress for permission, Jefferson dispatched a squadron of navy frigates to chastise Tripoli for its actions and, more generally, bring a measure of American-style freedom to the Mediterranean. Jefferson deeply resented both the fact and the idea of the United States continuing to pay tribute to the Barbary states. Although he had garnered political support by vowing to reduce the size of the Federalist navy, Jefferson did not hesitate to use some of those same ships in his attempt to make the Mediterranean safe for American commerce. Underfunded and conducted far from home, Jefferson's Barbary War (1801–5) did not fully succeed in ending Mediterranean piracy. Although substantially more expensive in lives and money than continuing to pay tribute would have been, the campaign did enhance the security of American commercial vessels by putting the North African states on notice that piracy would be challenged. The undeclared campaign produced some stunning victories and memorable national heroes. Lieutenant Stephen Decatur turned out to be the most famous of these heroes. His 1804 stealth mission into the harbor of Tripoli to burn the USS *Philadelphia*, which had been taken captive along with its crew after running aground, captured the imagination of more than merely Americans. Lord Nelson, celebrated British admiral and hero of the Battle of Trafalgar, described Decatur's exploits as the "most spectacular story of the age." Almost as remarkable, in January 1805, a squad of seven marines and 400 mercenaries under the command of William Eaton marched five hundred miles across the Libyan desert "to the shores of Tripoli" to capture the port of Derna, part of a first effort at regime change by the United States. The capture of Derna, combined with the intense shelling of Tripoli by American naval vessels offshore, eventually did force the pasha to cut a deal freeing the hostages in exchange for $60,000 and agreeing to forgo tribute payments from the Americans. Yet it was not the last campaign against the North Africans. Algiers resumed attacks on American shipping in 1807 and continued them until defeated by U.S. naval forces in the Second Barbary War in 1815. Although mostly forgotten today, the Barbary Wars remains significant as an early step in a long-term American campaign to free the seas and a vivid early example of the emerging U.S. capacity to project power far from home.

FREEING THE SEAS: AFFIRMING NEUTRAL RIGHTS

The naval assault on the North African states in the name of freedom of the seas, while significant, is historically overshadowed by the lengthy, determined campaign to expand neutral rights, which ultimately resulted in the War of 1812. Once again, Americans found themselves entangled in European controversies as a result of their unquenchable thirst for big profits. Conflict had first arisen in 1793 as a direct result of the beginning of the wars of the French Revolution. At that time it had first become clear that the United States stood to profit hugely from a general European war, and equally clearly, the belligerents were not about to stand idly by while vessels with American flags trafficked with their enemy. Particularly valuable was the so-called carrying trade, the highly profitable movement of the goods of belligerent states in American vessels, effectively making them "free." The controversy surrounding this issue had been behind Jay's Treaty and the Quasi-War. The renewal of hostilities in Europe in May 1803 set the stage for a new round of conflict on the high seas that the United States, by far the world's leading neutral carrier at that time, could not hope to avoid.

As was the case in the 1790s, the British denied American notions of international law as it concerned neutral rights in wartime. London was determined to maintain a system that supported its role as the world's preeminent naval power. In particular, the British did not want neutral vessels being employed to carry goods between France and Spain and their respective colonial ports in the West Indies, a trade normally closed to neutrals in peacetime. Indeed, this prohibition of opening a colonial trade in war that was normally closed in peace was known as the Rule of the War of 1756. The *Polly* case of 1800 exposed a large loophole in this policy. In that decision, the British Admiralty court ruled that neutral vessels might legally carry enemy goods to enemy ports if they first stopped at a home port and unloaded their cargoes and paid import duties, effectively changing their aspect from "unfree" to "free." The goods could then legally be reexported. American shippers eagerly exploited this technicality. The wartime reexport trade quickly proved enormously lucrative, amounting to $53 million in 1805. While the British Admiralty court had assumed that changing the nature of the goods would be so burdensome as to drain the reexport trade of its profitability, the broad requirements for a so-called broken voyage invited fraud or evasion, which occurred on a massive scale. American shippers often did not even unload the "enemy" goods in question, and port officials often reimbursed shippers for import duties if the items were reexported in a timely fashion, a practice known as "drawbacks." Faced with this unexpected consequence of the *Polly* decision, in May 1805 the Admiralty court reversed itself, ruling in the *Essex* case that the American ship in question had not paid bona fide duties on its cargo. British Admiralty law now effectively outlawed trade between a belligerent colonial port and a neutral port. British warships assumed patrol stations outside American ports, effectively placing much of the East Coast under a blockade.

The impressment of sailors from American merchant vessels proved the most controversial British action. American shippers were not innocent victims of this practice. The dire need for able-bodied sailors prompted some American ship captains to "entice" British sailors they encountered in foreign ports. By the thousands, jack-tars deserted the

Royal navy and sought refuge on American merchant ships, resulting in a serious, ongoing drain for the Royal navy and a determination by ship captains to replenish their crews by any means necessary. Between 1803 and 1812, the Royal navy impressed approximately 10,000 crewmembers from American vessels – an imposing number but by no means surprising when placed next to Secretary of the Treasury Albert Gallatin's 1807 calculation that half of the 18,000 sailors serving in the American commercial fleet were of English nationality.

James Monroe, fresh from his purchase of Louisiana in Paris, now went to London, where he took charge of negotiating a successor agreement to the Jay Treaty, set to expire in 1806. He had already spent two fruitless years trying to get the British to bend on the issues of blockade, impressment, and the carrying trade when Congress sent William Pinkney to assist him. Britain negotiated with the Jay Treaty as a starting point and sought in essence to renew it. They stuck to this position, feeling no need to compromise given the current balance of forces. The agreement the two sides reached – the so-called Monroe-Pinkney Treaty – offered little to assuage American concerns over impressment, blockades, and the carrying trade. It, like the Jay Treaty, did promise a period of lessening Anglo-American tensions. But this was not nearly enough for the Jefferson administration. After consulting a committee of elders on the merits of the draft treaty, Jefferson declined even to submit it to the Senate for ratification. With the treaty's demise went what would turn out to be the best hope for settling Anglo-American differences without resort to war.

THE *CHESAPEAKE* AFFAIR

Disappointment over the allegedly deficient Monroe-Pinkney Treaty led to a period of drift and uncertainty, giving circumstances a chance to take control. On June 22, 1807, the British warship *HMS Leopard*, patrolling the lower Chesapeake Bay, overtook and broadsided an American frigate of the same name, which was en route to the Mediterranean to take part in the Barbary War. Its crew unseasoned and its guns virtually unfired, after a brief exchange Commodore James Barron quickly surrendered the *Chesapeake* to the British, who searched it and seized four alleged deserters. The impressment of American sailors from merchant vessels outraged the public; their seizure from an American warship was both an affront to national honor and a seeming act of war. A second Anglo-American war appeared to be imminent.

Britain's sudden conciliatory tone in the aftermath of the *Chesapeake* affair demonstrated the extent to which Anglo-American relations in the years since the Treaty of Paris had been a game of diplomatic chicken. The two countries' mutual interest in sustaining good trade relations was balanced by the fear each had for the other. To the Jeffersonian majority, the British malevolently had sought to reenslave the United States in quasi-colonial subordination as punishment for the revolutionary victory. Britain's struggle to stop Napoleon – whom Jefferson feared greatly – from dominating all of Europe, played an increasingly small role in American calculations. As Burton Spivak put it, the Jeffersonians "transformed England's desire to defeat Napoleon and to defend its commercial empire into a cruel obsession with America's death."[7] For their part, the British governing classes perceived the Americans as a rapidly rising competitor with a propensity to break the rules. The Anglo-American crisis was sustained by a dynamic in which Britain was determined to exercise the prerogatives of its power and the United States was equally determined not to accept those dictates. Neither party really wanted another war, but both demonstrated a willingness to threaten it to further their policy goals.

So the saber rattling that followed the *Chesapeake* affair was to be expected, and this kind of thing had worked in the past to help Americans get what they wanted. In this case, however, a lack of sabers to rattle, the result of the Republican fiscal austerity campaign, made the threats less effective. The dry-docking (another Jeffersonian innovation) of half of the planned navy frigates, the reduction in the army's size from 5,000 to 3,000 troops, and an Army officer corps notorious for nepotism and incompetence took much of the bite out of Americans' collective snarl. The administration's secret efforts during the summer of 1807 to mobilize 100,000 militia for a planned assault on Canada ran into intense resistance from the states, some of which expressed reluctance to cede control of their forces to the federal government. Treasury Secretary Gallatin, suddenly having to shift from a program of fiscal austerity to massive projected borrowing, found that the federal government had to compete for capital with insurance companies that

---

[7] Burton Spivak, *Jefferson's English Crisis* (Charlottesville, 1979), 96.

had large claims to be paid related to ship and cargo seizures. Gallatin even schemed for a while to reduce government borrowing costs by artificially inflating the market value of government paper.[8]

While the Jefferson administration cast about for an effective response to the *Chesapeake* affair, both Britain and France continued to look for ways to stop the Americans from carrying the goods of their enemy. Locked in a battle to the death, the world's two largest powers would now resort to any means necessary for victory. In May 1806, Britain had declared a de facto paper blockade of all the ports of Europe between Brest and the Elbe River. This made American vessels anywhere near the continent subject to search and seizure. In November, Napoleon countered by declaring a similar blockade of the British Isles, the so-called Berlin Decrees. Britain, upping the ante, issued special orders-in-council in 1807 requiring that all vessels heading to French-controlled ports anywhere in the world first submit to British inspection and pay a special tax. Once again, Napoleon countered in December 1807 with the Milan Decrees, proclaiming that any American vessel that showed signs of submitting to Britain's policy of fees and inspections would be treated as a British ship. The hazards to neutral shipping greatly increased, as both antagonists sought ways to starve the opponent into submission. Although the restrictions of both nations placed onerous burdens on American interests, those of the British provoked the most American complaints owing to the numbers and aggressiveness of the Royal navy in confiscating cargoes and impressing seamen. The British seized roughly 60 percent of the estimated 1,500 American merchant ships seized between 1803 and 1812.

THE EMBARGO

Jefferson and the Republicans now had to confront a European system seemingly unified in stymieing American commerce. With the military option temporarily off the table, Congress, after secret deliberations and at the administration's urging, passed on December 22, 1807, the first of five Embargo Acts of successively increasing severity. The lawmakers aimed to cut off all American trade with the world as a means of economically coercing Britain and France into respecting neutral rights.

[8] Spivak, *Jefferson's English Crisis*, 84.

The Jeffersonians hoped that Anglo-French efforts to starve the other into submission could be trumped by an American campaign aimed at forcing both sides into changing their policies toward neutral shipping. Harking back to the non-importation campaigns of the 1760s and 1770s, Jefferson saw the embargo as a means of bringing back the self-sacrifice and patriotism that epitomized "the Spirit of '76." What Jefferson termed "peaceable coercion" would use the means of withholding America's economic bounty to the end of bending the world to its national will. When the public proved less than unanimous in its support of the embargo and looked for ways to evade it, Jefferson tightened the screws. The foreign policy power of the national government was turned inward, as the Republicans finally increased the size of the army and the navy, not to fight a foreign war but to enforce the domestic side of a foreign policy. The president seemed to acknowledge no limit in his drive to enforce the law, which, to a disturbing degree, became just another way to impose his own will on the American people and on the world. Jefferson wrote to Gallatin, "Congress must legalize all *means* that may be necessary to obtain its *end*."[9] By mid-1808, the army was being used to enforce tyranny disguised as law. Republican fears about the danger to liberty of a standing army had apparently come true.

It seems clear that the framers of the commerce clause giving the national government the right to regulate commerce did not imply the right to cut it off completely, but Jefferson and the Republicans did not shrink from another massive expansion of the implied powers of the national government. The embargo created widespread economic hardship and dislocation; ships rotted, and businesses went bankrupt when they could not pay debts incurred prior to the embargo; exports fell from $108 million in 1807 to $22 million in 1808. Jefferson rationalized the suffering as an opportunity to purify American society of what he saw as an excessive zeal for commerce – ironic, given the commercial motives behind the embargo. A nightmarish experiment, the embargo rendered absurd Jefferson's promise of a government that would not impose its arbitrary will on the people.

In the end, the embargo never had the slightest chance of success. Americans could not maintain the needed pressure for the length of

---

[9] Robert Tucker and David Hendrickson, *Empire of Liberty: The Statecraft of Thomas Jefferson* (New York, 1990), 224.

time required to create real hardships as a result of the embargo. This, combined with Britain's determination to maintain its control of the high seas and Napoleon's capacity to find alternative sources of food supplies, meant that the real victims of the embargo were the American people, who had to contend with an increasingly aggressive, increasingly invasive national government. One historian writes of the president, "His energy was prodigious, his direction detailed, his resolution implacable, and his spirit remorseless.... To avoid foreign war, Jefferson made domestic war."[10]

Jefferson's continued campaign to coerce Britain and France economically in the face of widespread evasions of the embargo by Americans culminated in January 1809 in the Fifth Embargo Act. It gave draconian powers of enforcement to the government, empowering the military to arrest individuals and to seize property without a warrant, effectively nullifying the Fourth Amendment. Goods even suspected as being intended for export could summarily be seized. The Fifth Embargo Act still stands as one of the most repressive pieces of legislation ever passed by Congress.

The outrageous disregard for constitutional liberties embodied in the Fifth Embargo Act concerned even diehard supporters of the president's campaign of peaceable coercion. Relentless enforcement had resulted in widespread violations of the rights of American citizens and a devastated economy, with nothing to show for it in terms of altering the behavior of either Britain or France. Once the likely failure of his policy became evident Jefferson seems to have lost interest both in it and in the presidency. He began to look forward to retiring to his estate at Monticello, where he could focus his attention on his books and on his experiments and be done with the messy world of politics. Shortly before leaving office he wrote to Du Pont de Nemours of his eagerness to return "to my family, my books, and my farms ... Never did a prisoner, released from his chains, feel such relief as I shall on shaking off the shackles of power."[11] When Jefferson's administration ended in March 1809, Congress allowed his embargo to expire with it.

[10] Leonard W. Levy, *Jefferson and Civil Liberties: The Darker Side* (Chicago, 1989; first published, 1963), 104–5.
[11] Levy, *Jefferson and Civil Liberties*, 141.

INDIAN TROUBLE ON THE IMPERIAL FRONTIER

While Anglo-American relations remained in crisis, things heated up on the western imperial frontier. In 1806, Tenskwatawa, an Indian medicine man known as the Shawnee Prophet, experienced a powerful vision in which all the remaining Indian tribes east of the Mississippi River united in one last-gasp effort to roll back the advance of the American Empire onto their lands. Tenskwatawa was joined by a charismatic war chief named Tecumseh, also a Shawnee, whose inspired leadership helped foster what soon became a formidable pan-Indian resistance. This was only the most recent of a number of Indian unity movements extending back to Pontiac's, all of them motivated by a desire to evict the American invaders and return to traditional ways of living.

Few Americans of the time, especially westerners, acknowledged these motives. Most attributed the Indian uprising to scheming British agents in Canada who incited the tribes with anti-American rhetoric and who armed them with guns and ammunition to attack frontier settlements as a means of further undermining the sovereignty of the United States. Once again Indian resistance threatened to block westward expansion. Westerners began to demand the conquest of Canada and the eviction of the British from North America so as to deprive the Indians of a sanctuary and to cut them off from the military supplies that westerners wrongly alleged were being supplied to Indians by British agents.

MR. MADISON'S WAR

Jefferson handed off the dreadful mess of his failed embargo to his faithful protégé, James Madison, who was easily elected in this era of one-party rule in spite of the political upheavals of the previous two years. Madison's skill as a constitutional scholar did not necessarily prepare him to be a political leader, and during his tenure as secretary of state Jefferson frequently eclipsed him. Still, the foreign policy cul-de-sac created by Jefferson's failed embargo left Madison with few moves to make short of declaring war. Neither Madison nor the country was quite ready for that. As a face-saving measure, Congress passed the Non-Intercourse Act three days before Madison assumed office. This measure reopened foreign trade with all nations except for

Great Britain and France (and places controlled by them) but offered the possibility of reopening trade with one or both of the belligerents if they agreed to respect neutral rights. When British minister David Erskine pledged that London would repeal its orders-in-council so long as non-intercourse against France continued, Madison, without waiting for formal ratification of the agreement, reopened trade with Britain in June 1809. More than six hundred American ships soon departed for the British Isles filled with two years' worth of formerly embargoed goods. To Madison's great embarrassment, British foreign secretary Canning repudiated Erskine's diplomacy, keeping the orders-in-council in place and welcoming the American goods en route. Whatever pressure had been accumulated on Britain by the embargo was now lost.

Macon's Bill Number 2 replaced the Non-Intercourse Act in 1810. This anomalously named legislation reopened all foreign trade but pledged to renew non-intercourse against one of the belligerents if the other suspended its attacks on American shipping. Perhaps seeing how Britain had profited from Madison's gullibility, Napoleon now promised repeal of the Continental System if the Americans retaliated against the British. Naïvely taking the French dictator at his word, the president dutifully closed trade with Britain and reopened it with France, only to find that Napoleon did not mean what he had said. Madison's prestige as a leader sank even further. The debacles over the successor legislation to the embargo set the tone for Madison's entire administration; after this humiliating debut he never really regained mastery of the political stage.

During the critical period of 1810–12, when effective communication and accurate information might have prevented a war, neither Britain nor the United States had effective representation in the other's capital. A series of British diplomats, each more condescending and contentious than the last, followed David Erskine's ignominious departure in the wake of his failed treaty bid. The legacy of bad feelings and estrangement existing between two nations that had so much in common prevented effective diplomatic communication. On the American side, after Minister William Pinkney left London in a huff in February 1811, no ministerial-level diplomat replaced him. The U.S. government lacked good intelligence as to the state of the British economy and society in the midst of total war. This failure to stay well informed as to the state of the British state and nation resulted in the Madison administration's failure to anticipate the June 18, 1812, repeal of the offending orders-in-council. For a year and a half, a severe economic downturn, caused in part by the embargo policy, had caused bread riots by the poor and great remonstrance by manufacturers, who pleaded with Parliament to find a way to reopen access to the American market. These pressures, combined with a growing fear that the Americans might declare war if only for lack of a better strategy, prompted the British government to change course.

The British concession happened too late. The game of diplomatic chicken had gone too far. Two days after the repeal of the onerous orders-in-council, Congress at Madison's urging voted to declare war. In the days before instantaneous communication, a concession that almost certainly would have delayed if not halted the march to war went by the boards. Goaded by the rhetoric of the hypernationalists of the Twelfth Congress (known as the War Hawks) and at a loss to know what to do next, on June 1 Madison formally requested the beginning of hostilities. His war message (the first in U.S. history) offered a laundry list of reasons for war, starting with impressment. In expressing his outrage at the practice ("this crying enormity") Madison did not reference Gallatin's finding that the impressment–enticement balance sheet greatly favored the American side, and that a just settlement of the question would actually hurt American bottom lines. The second major grievance concerned harassments that handicapped American commerce, including the "pretended blockade" of European ports. Madison denied that the effort to deprive Napoleon of supplies motivated these policies but rather that they served as a means to defend "the monopoly that she covets for her own commerce and navigation."[12]

Next, Madison moved to the western imperial frontier, decrying "the warfare just renewed by the savages ... a warfare which is known to spare neither age nor sex and to be distinguished by features peculiarly shocking to humanity" and linking that warfare to the tribes' "constant intercourse with British traders and garrisons." In a rhetorical ploy extending at least as far back as the Declaration of Independence, Madison pleaded long American forbearance in the face of British provocations. The case was clear: "We behold, in fine, on the side of Great Britain a state of war against the United States, and on the side of the

---

[12] Richardson, ed., *Messages and Papers of the Presidents*, 2:502.

United States a state of peace toward Great Britain." War was the only course appropriate for "a virtuous, a free, and a powerful nation."[13]

Congress debated Madison's request for two weeks, split both along sectional and along partisan lines. Shipping and commercial interests, the ones most directly affected by the British maritime policies, for the most part opposed war. The windfall profits of wartime trade outweighed the costs of the possibility of British seizure of ships and goods, the expense of which was factored in to prices. Westerners, on the other hand, were nearly unanimous in favor, as the uncertainties of the wartime trade limited agricultural exports. Politically, Madison had strong (though not universal) support from the Republicans but faced a Federalist party nearly unanimous in opposition. Intensely divided, and still woefully unprepared for war, Congress voted 79–49 in the House and 19–13 in the Senate for war. All thirty-nine Federalists in Congress voted nay. For a second time in less than thirty years, the United States went to war with the world's greatest power.

[13] Richardson, ed., *Messages and Papers of the Presidents*, 2:504; 2:504; 2:505.

4

CLAIMING THE
HEMISPHERE

The Universal feeling of Europe in witnessing the gigantic growth of our population and power is that we shall, if united, become a very dangerous member of the society of nations.

> John Quincy Adams, January 17, 1817, quoted in Robert
> Kagan, *Dangerous Nation: America's Place in the World from
> its Earliest Days to the Dawn of the 20th Century*, 130

A feature of our modernity is projecting on other cultures impulses we believe we do not possess and deeds for which we claim no capacity. By remaining displaced observers of our most important acts, we define ourselves as a nation.

> Carolyn Marvin, *Blood Sacrifice and the Nation: Totem
> Rituals and the American Flag*, 3

THE CIVIL WAR OF 1812

President Madison's message to Congress offered no immediate *casus belli* to justify a declaration of war. In the end the president chose war because he seemed to have run out of strategies for maintaining the peace. No one seemed to have a sure sense of what to try next. At one point an exasperated Congress nearly voted for war against both Great Britain and France. The declaration of war surprised most American citizens; the drumbeat for conflict had been nearly constant since 1805, and yet no war had been forthcoming. Now, seemingly without immediate provocation, Congress commenced hostilities by a vote split along partisan lines. J. C. A. Stagg writes that Congress's "response to war was determined, with few exceptions, more by partisan and political considerations than by any individual or sectional attitudes toward the issues which had produced the crisis."[1] Certainly one political advantage gained by Madison was to put an end to New York Federalist Dewitt Clinton's campaign for the presidency in 1812.

Even after so many years of delay the decision to go to war had a rushed quality about it. The repeal of the orders-in-council might not have been such a surprise had the Madison administration had better intelligence. As it was, after the departure of Minister William Pinkney in 1811, the United States had only minimal understanding of political climate in Britain. Obsessed with what they perceived to be the malevolence of Great Britain toward the United States, Republicans in general had made up their minds for war long before the actual vote. Historians have never agreed about the root cause of the war. Beginning in the 1920s, some claimed the chief motive to be an expansionist desire for Canada and Florida. More recently, historians have reemphasized the maritime issues, especially impressment as the primary cause. In this view, the indisputable ambition to conquer Canada has been seen as "defensive expansionism," done in the name of depriving Great Britain of a source of raw materials. But a consensus as to the war's causes remains elusive. The war occurred not because of race, nor was it about religion, and it occurred in spite of potentially thriving economic relations between the two states. This leaves the subjective concept of "honor" invoked by Madison as a cause of the war, hardly enough it seems to justify or explain full-scale hostilities unless one understands honor in this case to be a duel between the dominant power of the era and a rising challenger having the audacity to refuse subordination to the reigning hegemon. Great Britain remained determined to limit the growth of what it perceived to be a future rival, and the United States was just as determined to assert its position, at whatever the cost. The contest took place on the land, on the seas, and in the realm of ideology, where Republicans treated the contest as a test of national resolve and national identity.

The congressional split over going to war mirrored that in the society. If anything, the public was even less unified for a fight than were the politicians. So great were the internal divisions over the conflict that

---

[1] J. C. A. Stagg, *Mr. Madison's War: Politics, Diplomacy, and Warfare in the Early American Republic, 1783–1830* (Princeton, 1983), 111.

Alan Taylor has renamed it "the Civil War of 1812." The new struggle rekindled the Patriot-Loyalist clashes of the War of Independence, this time with many members of the Federalist party tarred as Loyalists in disguise. A June 1813 letter to the Philadelphia *Aurora* by "An American Farmer" captured this sentiment: "As much as the people of the two nations resemble each other in face, it is notoriously evident that there are some in America whose souls are perfectly British ... It is not where a man was born or who he looks like, but what he thinks, which ought at this day to constitute the difference between an American and a British subject."[2] Taylor sees four intertwined dimensions to the Civil War of 1812: first, a struggle between Loyalists and Americans for control of the new province of Upper Canada; second, the efforts of Irish immigrants to the United States, many of them recent, to continue their ongoing struggle against British colonialism, this time in Canada under the American flag; third, the involvement of Native American tribes on both sides of the conflict, pursuing their individual agendas, often against other Indians; and fourth, an intense domestic partisanship that spilled over into outright treason as some members of the Federalist party served as spies and smugglers for the British.

Once war had begun, the passionate political rivalry between Republican and Federalists turned violent. Federalists who openly opposed the war were subject to mob violence, the worst example of which occurred in Baltimore shortly after the war began. There, controversy ensued over the actions of Alexander Hanson, youthful publisher of the *Federal Republican* and an outspoken critic of the war. After a series of assaults on Hanson and his newspaper, in late July a mob stormed the paper's office and the two dozen or so people harbored there. After a tense night holding off the mob, Hanson and his followers – all members of the Federalist party – agreed to surrender themselves to the protective custody of the local police. The following evening, a mob broke into the jail where they were being held, dragging nine of the captives into the street to be brutalized and left in a bloody pile. Over the next several hours, rioters beat and stabbed Hanson and his associates while the authorities did nothing to stop it. Some of the victims reputedly suffered hot candle wax poured into their eyes to see if they were still alive. The mob assaulted

---

[2] Quoted in Alan Taylor, *The Civil War of 1812* (New York, 2010), 8.

retired general James Lingan, a veteran of the War of Independence, and stabbed him to death as he pleaded for his life. Local police and state militia largely stood aside as these atrocities unfolded. A subsequent report by the Maryland House of Delegates described the shocking incident as "[a] scene of horror and murder ... which for its barbarity has no parallel in the history of the American people, and no equal but in the massacres of Paris."[3]

THE CLOSE CALL OF 1814

Knowledge of how the War of 1812 turned out has obscured the recklessness with which it was commenced and prosecuted. A three-pronged invasion of Canada in 1812 failed miserably, as many of the state militias that had been federalized for the war refused to cross the border to fight. Jefferson had confidently predicted that conquering sparsely populated and lightly defended Canada would be "a mere matter of marching," but he had not anticipated that his vaunted militia might not be willing to make the march across a foreign border in the name of imperial conquest. Moreover, Jefferson and others seriously underestimated the intense loyalty of Canadians to the Crown; many of them were the descendants of Loyalist exiles of the War of Independence.

The U.S. navy performed magnificently in spite of the deep cuts to naval construction and readiness done in the name of Republican economy. While the superior size of the British fleet required the Americans to focus on harassing British commerce rather than pursue large-scale naval showdowns, in numerous individual engagements with British warships over much of the Atlantic, American frigates staffed by able crews more than held their own against the number one navy in the world. Also noteworthy was the epic voyage (1812–14) of battle and plunder by Commodore David Porter at the helm of the USS *Essex*. Porter, in the first U.S. naval action in the Pacific Ocean, sailed the *Essex* far up the west coast of South America, doing an estimated $2.5 million in damages to the British whalers in the area before being captured. Major naval victories on Lake Erie in 1813 and Lake Champlain in 1814 proved decisive in the final outcome. Although the war ended

---

[3] Donald Hickey, *The War of 1812: A Forgotten Conflict* (Baltimore, 1989), 65.

in a draw, the United States had conclusively demonstrated its ability to defend the coastal waters of the nation and to project naval power to the far reaches of the globe.

Perhaps as much as anything, the war revealed the tensions between Republican small-government ideology and the realities of Jeffersonian foreign policy. Political dissent was crushed in the name of unity in time of war. The intense fear of a standing army as a threat to liberty and the corresponding heavy reliance on state militias to prosecute the war proved disastrous. Republican antitax ideology meant that Congress refused to raise internal taxes during the war. The failure in 1811 to renew the charter of the First Bank of the United States, as called for by Republican ideology, added to the difficulties and cost of financing the war and resulted in a bankrupt government beholden to the nation's wealthy elite in order to regain solvency. The Jeffersonians attempted to pursue the foreign policy of a fiscal-military state while dismantling the fiscal-military apparatus put in place by the hated Federalists. Predictably, this approach failed, and in 1813–14 the nation found itself wedged between internal chaos and foreign conquest.

This wrongheaded policy culminated in the close call of 1814. Napoleon's initial defeat gave Britain the chance to concentrate its accumulated rage and resentment on its erstwhile colonists and compatriots, who had been a thorn in their imperial side at the very moment they had sought to quell the Napoleonic threat. Now temporarily at peace on the continent, the British planned a three-pronged assault for late summer on the United States in an attempt to divide if not destroy the Union. At the minimum, the offensive aimed to block further U.S. expansionism. At first it seemed this strategy might pay off. The invasion up the Chesapeake met with ineffective resistance, and news of the capture of Washington, D.C., and the burning of the White House on August 14 rocked the peace talks occurring in the city of Ghent. After news of the fall of the capital arrived in early September, American negotiators John Quincy Adams, Henry Clay, and James A. Bayard were presented with onerous peace terms that included territorial concessions allowing for British navigation of the Mississippi, a U.S. demilitarization of the Great Lakes, a quarter-million-square-mile Indian buffer zone between Canada and the United States, and recognition of the treaty rights of Britain's Native American allies. At Clay's behest, the Americans bluntly refused the British demands and threatened to break off the talks. This bold move prompted the British to moderate their terms to the *uti possidetis*, or state of possession, at the war's end. This still would have left substantial portions of Maine as well as control of Fort Niagara in British hands.

The burning of the White House and the capture of Washington, D.C., in August 1814 held more symbolic than strategic importance. It was done largely in retaliation for the sacking of York, the capital of Upper Canada, by American troops the previous year. Madison, like Jefferson when he was wartime governor of Virginia, suffered the ignominy of having to flee into the night to evade capture by the advancing British forces. Baltimore, a major port, the nation's third-largest city, and a hotbed of Anglophobia, was of far greater importance to British plans. As British forces advanced by land and by sea on that city after the fall of Washington, no one could say where the enemy offensive might end. On September 14 a British naval task force arrived at the mouth of the Patapsco River beneath Fort McHenry, a modest earthen-walled fort dominated by an enormous 30-foot × 42-foot American flag flying above, the faithful handiwork of Mary Pickersgill, a local seamstress. During the night, the British frigates pounded the fort with approximately eighteen hundred bombs and rockets. When the sun rose and the smoke cleared, the flag, the fort, and the Maryland militia defending it, all were still standing, and the British invasion fleet, its firepower spent, retreated down Chesapeake Bay. Jefferson's militia had come through after all, but as defenders, not conquerors. Although famous as the inspiration for Francis Scott Key's "Star Spangled Banner," the Battle of Baltimore is underrated in its strategic importance. Together with Lt. Thomas McDonough's naval victory on Lake Champlain three days earlier, the victory in Baltimore stopped the British invasion in its tracks. News of the defeats ended British hopes for territorial concessions from the Americans. Fiscal necessity now prompted a peace treaty based on the status quo ante, with the maritime issues that had been the putative cause of the war unaddressed. The determined and courageous military resistance of the citizenry amid severe internal political dissension averted what could have been a punitive treaty creating endless future headaches for the United States.

THE PEACE OF CHRISTMAS EVE, 1814

Two weeks after the signing in London of the peace treaty ending the war on Christmas Eve, 1814, the decisive victory of Andrew Jackson's unlikely assortment of Tennessee volunteers, state militia, Native Americans, and French Creoles over a British force attacking New Orleans put an exclamation point on the heroic defense of the home-land. Although its timing rendered the Battle of New Orleans irrelevant to the treaty ending the war, it nonetheless prompted euphoria among Americans. They had gone toe-to-toe with the mightiest power in the world and had emerged, if not wholly victorious, at least unvanquished. American sovereignty and independence had been established once and for all. The struggle confirmed to a new generation of Americans their role as worthy successors to their revolutionary forebears. The war seemed to some to have a purifying effect on the public mind, a regenerative struggle to counteract the perceived degeneration of a commercial society. No one emerged from it with more luster than Andrew Jackson of Tennessee. In many ways he seemed to epitomize the successors to the revolutionary generation: born on the frontier, experienced in war against both Native Americans and the British, heavily involved in speculation in western lands, personally ambitious, and faithful to a code of honor that judged violence as an appropriate response to even the smallest personal affront. In many respects, both good and bad, Jackson personified the emerging energies of post-1815 America. John Quincy Adams had unknowingly heralded the rise of Jackson and his ilk when he had characterized the war as an opportunity to recover "the great and glorious qualities in the human character which as they can unfold themselves only in time of difficulty and danger seem to make war from time to time a necessary evil among men.... God grant that in suffering the unavoidable calamities we may recover in all their vigor the energies of war!"[4]

As had been the case in the War of Independence, the Native American tribes who counted on British support to resist the American expansionist advance proved the real losers of the War of 1812. Beginning in 1811 at the Battle of the Thames, in which Tecumseh's "spirited resistance"

---

[4] Steven Watts, *The Republic Reborn: War and the Making of Liberal America, 1790–1820* (Baltimore, 1987), 206.

met its end with his death and his followers scattered, American forces sought bloody retribution against those tribes allegedly instigated by the British to harass American settlements. The Creek War of 1813–14 resulted in another gigantic land grab, but only after the death of thousands of Creeks from war, famine, and dislocation. Jackson's decisive victory at the Battle of Horseshoe Bend in 1814 led to the imposition of the Treaty of Fort Jackson, which transferred 23 million acres to the United States, most of which had belonged to Creek factions allied with the Americans. Although Article Nine of the Treaty of Ghent pledged to restore to Indians any land lost in the conflict, in the aftermath of the conflict London showed no inclination to hold the Americans to that stipulation. The year 1815, then, marked the final defeat of the Indian resistance in the United States east of the Mississippi River, after nearly three-quarters of a century of war. What had been the primary obstacle to expansion had been defeated; those Indians who survived would soon be removed. In this regard, the War of 1812 stands as an important victory for the American Empire.

POSTWAR CHALLENGES, FOREIGN AND DOMESTIC

The return of peace and the end of the high seas controversies caused by the Napoleonic Wars did much to change the national mood after 1815. In spite of the near-defeat, near-bankruptcy, and near–civil war caused by the recent conflict, an ebullient optimism emerged in its wake. A new burst of westward expansionism, rising economic prosperity, and the distinct cooling of ideological passions explain this new national consensus. The Federalist party, tainted by secession as a result of the Hartford Convention and treason owing to its members' widespread sympathy and support for the British, almost disappeared after the war. Its principles, however, survived to a considerable degree in a reimagined Jeffersonian Republican party whose leaders now embraced a new national bank, a limited program of federally financed internal improvements, and a moderate protective tariff in the name of encouraging domestic manufactures and restoring national stability. This created the space for the brief reemergence of a one-party state of the sort originally envisioned by the framers of the Constitution.

Movement toward true reconciliation with Great Britain proved to be the most significant ideological shift by the Republicans. Their intense, almost Oedipal hostility to all things British ebbed, replaced by a desire for commerce and cooperation reminiscent of the Federalists in the 1790s. Having affirmed the autonomy of a new generation of Americans in a Second War of Independence, the Jeffersonian Republicans now looked to construct a relationship with Great Britain based on mutual interest and respect, although residual hostility to John Bull persisted for decades.

Although the United States emerged from the War of 1812 in far better shape than might have dared been hoped, the postwar world presented major challenges in foreign affairs. The war and the years running up to it effectively had shelved other preexisting issues that now had to be addressed, starting with the resolution of outstanding issues regarding trade and boundaries with Great Britain that the peace treaty ending the war had left unaddressed. European observers perceived that the two nations had achieved only a brief armistice and that renewed conflict was only a matter of time. Equally threatening, a long-standing dispute with Spain over ownership of East and West Florida and the specifics of the western boundary offered no easy solution. Spain had contested the legality of France's sale of Louisiana from the start and now hoped to define its uncertain limits so narrowly as to effectively stop expansion to the southwest. The ancient fear of being encircled by European powers that so worried Franklin and others in the 1750s remained a serious concern in the first decades of the nineteenth century.

The issue of formal sovereign control of the "borderlands" along the southern frontier was made immeasurably worse by the role those borderlands played as a refuge for Indians and blacks fleeing the wrath of the Americans. While West Florida, in effect, had been annexed by the Madison administration after being revolutionized by a pro-American faction in 1810, East Florida (that area east of the Apalachicola River) remained beyond U.S. control and ineffectively governed by Spain, creating a political refuge that allowed for Indians and runaway slaves (at times joining together in single communities) to resist capture. White Southerners along the Georgia-Florida border found this intolerable. The so-called Negro Fort on the lower Apalachicola River, on the site of an abandoned British garrison, symbolized a particularly ominous manifestation of the racial autonomy of the region. Several hundred runaway slaves and Indians occupied this site until in 1816 cannon fire from an American naval patrol sent to take down the fort destroyed it. The enormous blast from a direct hit on its gunpowder cache obliterated the Negro Fort, killing an estimated 250 of its inhabitants. Yet this spectacular event by no means pacified the Florida frontier. Remnants of the Creek tribes defeated by Jackson had fled across the border into the province, where they now joined with other Indian tribes and runaway slaves to become the Seminoles, not so much a distinct Indian tribe as an amalgam of races and cultures bound together by their common resistance to American expansionism. White Georgians deemed the existence of this black-Indian refuge as intolerable and demanded that the national government act to suppress it.

While the presence of European powers in North America threatened to block U.S. expansionism to the west and south, the rest of the hemisphere faced political uncertainty owing to the collapse of European colonialism in Spanish America. Specifically, the revolt against Spanish authority in the Americas that began in 1808 now included most of its colonies, although by 1817 none had achieved complete victory. It is fair to say that citizens of the United States overwhelmingly supported in principle the idea of South American independence, seeing it as a natural consequence of their example. In practice, the revolutions presented, from the U.S. perspective, a host of potential problems: Would the insurgents be capable of creating true republican liberty? Would a new, homegrown tyranny merely replace Spanish despotism? A far more troubling prospect was related to fears that the European powers would deploy an expeditionary force in an attempt to restore Spain's New World Empire. That seemed a distinct possibility in the years after 1815.

Any thought of an expedition to restore Spanish colonial authority rested on British policy and specifically British naval power. Britain had championed the restorationist push on the Continent, and European governments assumed they would back a similar policy in the Americas. Emerging free-trade liberalism increasingly aligned British interests with a free Latin America open to British commerce. The easing of colonial trade restrictions during the Napoleonic Wars had given the British a taste of lucrative markets such as Cuba, and they now had no desire to assist in the reestablishment of Spanish mercantile barriers. British policy moved aggressively to assert commercial influence in Latin America, at least in part to head off the Americans, many of whom themselves coveted the economic opportunities represented by a South America freed of Spanish colonial restrictions.

Henry Clay of Kentucky led those pushing to give the United States a head start on access to the emerging markets of South America. As speaker of the House in 1817, Clay led the campaign attempting to force the Monroe administration to take the lead in recognizing the rebellious states. Clay combined passionate appeals on behalf of liberty with a hardheaded assessment of what the United States stood to gain by backing their cause, chiefly the role as its primary trade partner. He envisioned the states of the trans-Appalachian west as standing to benefit from a lucrative commercial connection to the South American republics via New Orleans, thereby freeing the west from its neocolonial economic dependence on the states of the Atlantic Seaboard. Politically, Clay sought to exploit Madison's precedent of weak presidential leadership to affirm the right of the House to make foreign policy and to position himself for a future run for the presidency. Monroe, at Adams's urging, staunchly resisted precipitous action, even mere diplomatic recognition, on behalf of the Latin American revolutions as both premature and as needlessly complicating the ongoing talks with Spain and Great Britain. Both of those states, albeit for somewhat different reasons, signaled that American aid to the patriot movements would have adverse consequences on their relations with the United States. Resisting congressional attempts to seize control of foreign policy from the executive branch proved one of the biggest domestic political challenges facing Monroe.

The most pressing foreign policy difficulty faced by the incoming Monroe administration and its new secretary of state, John Quincy Adams, concerned the outstanding issues with Spain. The Spanish government initially claimed that Napoleon, under the terms of the retrocession to France in 1800, had no right to transfer Louisiana to the United States. This impractical and ultimately unenforceable position gave way in 1815 to grudging recognition of the legality of the sale and efforts to define the vague boundaries of Louisiana as narrowly as possible. On the U.S. side, the ambiguity of the boundary had been from the start seen as advantageous in that it created the conditions for an essentially open-ended claim on western North America. American assertions that Louisiana included West Florida, dubious at best, served as justification for its absorption in the aftermath of the West Florida

Revolution of 1810. The Napoleonic Wars interrupted talks to resolve the matter; restoration of the Spanish royal family in the aftermath of the fall of Napoleon did not lead immediately to the resumption of negotiations, as Madrid judged that it had more to gain from a policy of delay. Finally, in late 1817 the two sides resumed direct talks, but the Spanish remained minimally inclined to compromise. Of all the major European powers, Spain had long been the most suspicious of the rising American Empire. Emblematic of this sentiment, in the aftermath of the War of Independence the Spanish minister to France had observed, "This federal republic is born a pygmy," but "the day will come when it will be a giant, even a colossus."[5] Spain now hoped to erect a bulwark to prevent the United States from encroaching on the remaining Spanish colonies in the New World.

Control of the Floridas had been an American obsession for years. Its geography led some to see it as a pistol pointed at New Orleans, and more generally as an invasion route for attacking the entire southern United States. In 1806, Jefferson pushed though Congress the Two Million Act allocating monies (never utilized) to bribe Napoleon into pressuring Spain to cede the province to the United States. In 1811, after the failed Mathews mission to revolutionize East Florida had left Spanish sovereignty intact, Congress, citing the "security, tranquility, and commerce" of the United States, had resolved that the United States "cannot without serious inquietude see any part of the said territory pass into the hands of any foreign Power," reserving the right to occupy the Floridas as necessary to prevent this from occurring. This resolution became the grounds for the annexation of that part of West Florida between the Perdido and Pearl Rivers in 1812. Yet East Florida remained in Spanish hands in 1815, and there seemed no easy way to alter that situation.

Minister to the United States Don Luis de Onis did most of the negotiating for Spain. Although not formally recognized as a diplomatic representative until 1815, Onis had informally represented Spanish interests in the United States since 1809. His lengthy time in the United States made him decidedly suspicious of the motives of Americans. He wrote in his *Memoria,* "The Americans believe themselves superior to all the nations of Europe, and see their destiny to extend their dominion

---

[5] Donald Kagan, *Dangerous Nation* (New York, 2006), 4.

to the Isthmus of Panama, and in the future to all of the New World."[6] As per instructions from the Consejo de Estado in Madrid, Onis staunchly resisted any significant compromise on the western boundary. The Spanish judged that the restorationist tide sweeping Europe and contemplating intervention in the Latin American revolutions could be counted on to back Madrid in standing up to the Americans. For years the Spanish had attempted to designate the Mississippi River as the westernmost boundary of Louisiana. This, of course, would have invalidated most of the Louisiana Purchase, containing U.S. expansionism in the process. In late 1817, Onis began talks with Adams by placing the western boundary at the Mermento River (located only a few miles west of the Mississippi) and extending northward to the Missouri River. This would have deprived the United States of virtually all of the lands west of the Mississippi and south of the Missouri Rivers. Onis adamantly refused to transfer either of the Floridas, repeating the long-held claim that they formed no part of Louisiana. Adams countered with a proposal transferring all Spanish-controlled territories east of the Mississippi to the United States and fixing a western boundary along the Rio Colorado of Texas to its source and thence northward to the Rocky Mountains. In early 1818, the United States seemed caught between the rocks of Spanish intransigence and European reaction.

A brewing confrontation over the institution of slavery and its spread complicated the challenges the United States confronted internationally in the post-1815 world. Having failed to die a natural death as people north and south had hoped for in the 1790s, slavery now made a dynamic comeback thanks to the suddenly burgeoning demand for cotton. The resumption of peace in 1815 set off a land rush westward, especially to the rich lands opened up in Georgia and Alabama by the Treaty of Fort Jackson, which promised to be enormously profitable for cotton and the slave labor essential to its production. Yet a small but passionate opposition to the further spread of slavery came to life politically, building on the opposition to human bondage evident at the Constitutional Convention. The final incorporation of the immense Louisiana territory into the Union presented a number of challenges, none more serious than how to handle the explosive issue of slavery.

---

[6] William Earl Weeks, *John Quincy Adams and American Global Empire* (Lexington, Ky., 1992), 72.

Finessing this potential threat to the Union would be a major task for the incoming administration of James Monroe in 1817.

JAMES MONROE: THE ORIGINAL "HIDDEN HAND" PRESIDENT

James Monroe, it is fair to say, is the least renowned of the three Virginians elected to the presidency between 1800 and 1820. Although he neither coauthored the Declaration of Independence (as did Jefferson) nor received acclaim as one of the framers of the Constitution (as did Madison), Monroe's lengthy record of service as a diplomat and as a soldier of distinction in the War of Independence deserves respect. Monroe's time as president usually is remembered as less accomplished than either Jefferson's or Madison's, and his administration's achievements are usually overlooked, underappreciated, or chiefly credited to his able cabinet members, especially John Quincy Adams. A sparse paper trail has also contributed to Monroe's relative invisibility, as little of his personal correspondence survives and his formal addresses were not noted for their eloquence. In contrast, both Jefferson and Madison left enormous caches of written records for historians to peruse. Yet scholars are beginning to realize that Monroe – an eminently calm man who was given to speaking in platitudes and who preferred to see others take the credit for achievements that arguably were his – was in fact one of the most effective presidents in all American history. Monroe's capacity to manage a fractious cabinet of talented egos, a complex domestic political environment, and a host of challenges internationally while, in the tradition of Washington, seeming to be above the fray marks him as the original "hidden hand" president, a term usually reserved for his latter-day successor Dwight D. Eisenhower. Like Eisenhower, Monroe combined a placid exterior appearance with a dissembling style in order to mask his behind-the-scenes influence from the press and his political foes.

Monroe, in the tradition of Washington, sought to strengthen the Unionist consensus that he saw as crucial to national survival. It is not surprising that the phrase "Era of Good Feelings" first appeared in a Boston newspaper as Monroe conducted a grand tour of the northern and western states in 1817 in an attempt to banish the memory of the divisiveness of the recent war with Britain and cultivate loyalty to the national government. The first president to make a national tour since Washington, Monroe encountered large and enthusiastic crowds at every stop, people who welcomed his eighteenth-century manner of dress as a visible symbol of his ties to the revolutionary era. Throughout his administration, Monroe sought to balance the diversity of interests and outlooks that comprised the Union. He projected an air of unity, consensus, and calm amid some of the sharpest divisions yet to arise in American history.

Politically and philosophically, Monroe proved less doctrinaire than either Jefferson or Madison. Monroe did not have the intense loathing of England characteristic of the two earlier presidents, preferring to adhere to Washington's maxim of avoiding both passionate attachments and passionate hatreds in international affairs. His fundamentally pragmatic approach to politics led to his eager embrace of the turn toward a neo-Federalist policy of centralization at home and rapprochement with Great Britain abroad. Although in conflict with Republican ideology, these policies seemed most likely to enhance the prosperity and security of the Union. Consistent with these goals, Monroe favored federally supported internal improvements and the resurrection of the Bank of the United States, whose charter the Republican Congress had allowed to expire in 1811. He backed a dramatic expansion in the number of post offices, doubling the miles of post roads in the name of knitting the Union together more tightly. He also advocated a significant expansion of the navy and upgrades of coastal defenses in order to make the United States respected abroad and protected at home. Monroe, both more cosmopolitan and more broadly experienced than either Jefferson or Madison if less respected intellectually, charted a dramatic new course as president of the United States.

One of Monroe's primary goals as president was aimed at encouraging and expanding American foreign trade via the negotiation of commercial reciprocity treaties. Surplus production of raw materials and agricultural produce threatened to glut the national economy unless foreign markets could be found on good terms. A policy of reciprocity promised to level the tariff playing field with other states while the United States retained a comparative advantage in shipping costs. At the same time, Congress in 1816 enacted tariff protection for American manufactures in the name of strengthening the Union. The net result was a uniquely American form of neo-mercantilism designed to gain access to foreign markets while protecting key sectors of the economy from destructive competition. This was yet another startling departure from Republican orthodoxy.

The recovery of the economy and the success of the Monroe administration both hinged on improving relations with Great Britain. The postwar consensus on the advisability of a rapprochement with Great Britain combined with the fact that the two nations were each other's largest trading partner speeded the reconciliation. Negotiation of a commercial treaty in 1815 had been the first sign of this reconciliation, followed by the signing of the Rush-Bagot Treaty reducing naval forces on the Great Lakes in April 1817. Britain's postwar financial distresses and movement toward liberalizing its mercantile restrictions also contributed to reconciliation of the former foes. But the international community was slow to notice this change in Anglo-American relations. Indeed, the vitriolic tone that continued to characterize much press opinion on both sides of the Atlantic contributed to a sense that another war might break out at the slightest provocation.

Settling into the presidency, Monroe evolved a comprehensive strategy aimed at expanding the Union externally while solidifying it internally. In addition to the aforementioned efforts to expand foreign trade and further the rapprochement with Great Britain, Monroe's plan of action consisted of five distinct parts: first, a strategy of increasing pressure on Spanish possessions along the Gulf Coast in an effort to extract concessions at the negotiating table; second, the declaration of "an impartial neutrality" as concerned the Latin American revolutions so as not to further antagonize Spain; third, refraining from the acquisition of any more territories, such as Texas, that were favorable to the expansion of slavery; fourth, the colonization of free blacks in a new colony in Africa in the name of "diffusing" America's black population abroad; fifth, the removal of Native Americans from lands in the southeast that were demanded by frontiersmen for gold-seeking or cotton production. Some of these policies, such as Monroe's active support of the American Colonization Society, predated his time in office; others, such as the policies toward Spain and toward the South American revolutions, emerged from his consultations with cabinet members. Collectively they represented a bold if ultimately not wholly successful attempt to respond to a complex political reality.

PRESSURING SPAIN: THE FIRST SEMINOLE WAR

Confronted with a tangled skein of foreign and domestic difficulties, James Monroe assembled a talented cabinet of ambitious, capable people of diverse political backgrounds whose capacity for infighting anticipates Lincoln's "team of rivals."[7] Two of them – John Quincy Adams of Massachusetts at the Department of State, and John C. Calhoun of South Carolina at the War Department – proved to be among the most accomplished cabinet members in U.S. history. The distinguished resume of William Crawford of Georgia made him a capable choice for treasury secretary, but his relentless political maneuvering limited his effectiveness as a member of the administration. All three men harbored ambitions to succeed Monroe as president, jockeying to improve their positions even as they maintained a façade of unity.

In order to end Spanish intransigence at the negotiating table, Monroe, at Adams's urging, began to apply military pressure on Spanish possessions. It was a risky policy that if improperly done might blow up in the face of the administration. The first application of force occurred at Amelia Island, on the Georgia–East Florida border. There a ragtag band of Latin American revolutionaries, mercenaries, and smugglers had occupied the island undisturbed by Spanish royal authority, which lacked the resources to recapture it. In early December 1817 and without congressional approval, the administration ordered a small force of sailors and marines to evict the supposed freedom fighters, taking possession of the site in the name of suppressing smuggling and increasing security along the southern border. Minister Onis protested this action as an outrageous violation of Spanish sovereignty (as did some of the administration's political opponents), but Adams deemed it justified by Spain's manifest failure to exert effective control over what the administration deemed to be a lawless region.

A far more serious challenge to Spain's authority in East Florida occurred in late December 1817. Accelerated efforts to remove the scattered bands of Native Americans remaining in southern Georgia had led to rising tensions in the border region. Frontiersmen, mercenaries, and speculators agitated continually to drive out the last remaining Indians

---

[7] Doris Kearns Goodwin, *Team of Rivals: The Political Genius of Abraham Lincoln* (New York, 2005).

by any means available. In early November 1817, American forces commanded by General Edmund P. Gaines had attacked the village of Fowltown, just north of the border, where a band of Creek Indians resided who were allied with the United States during the war and who were not subject to removal according to the Treaty of Fort Jackson. Nonetheless, Gaines and his troops killed several members of the tribe, ran off the rest, and burned Fowltown to the ground. This provocation prompted a grisly retaliation. In late November, a Creek war party attacked an American naval supply vessel ascending the Apalachicola River in Spanish territory just south of the Georgia border, killing forty of its passengers. Georgians howled at this outrage, and Monroe and Secretary of War Calhoun responded decisively, dispatching orders to General Andrew Jackson in Tennessee to gather a force, proceed to East Florida, and "chastise" the perpetrators of the deed. Although authorized to cross into East Florida in pursuit of the enemy, Jackson was not explicitly directed in the official orders to conquer the province. That would be an act of war prosecuted without congressional authorization and potentially would involve the United States in a direct confrontation with Spain and its European allies, especially Great Britain. The full extent of Jackson's orders will never be known for sure; he later claimed that he had been given expanded authority from the administration to conquer East Florida via an unofficial (and therefore deniable) channel. Yet it must be asked, Why would Monroe and Calhoun summon Jackson, famous for his boldness, from Tennessee for this mission with the competent Gaines readily available?

Jackson's force of approximately 3,000 Tennessee volunteers, regular army troops, and Native American allies pillaged and burned Seminole villages, the inhabitants vanishing into the swamps in the face of Jackson's huge force. Under the pretext that his troops had been threatened with expulsion, Jackson seized Spanish garrisons at St. Mark's and Pensacola, setting up a revenue district there and deporting its few defenders to Havana. The Seminoles by and large did not resist the Americans' overwhelming force, but Jackson did capture and execute two key Creek chiefs: Hillis Hadjo (known as Francis the Prophet) and Himmilemico. More controversially, Jackson captured two British subjects: Royal Marine Robert Christy Ambrister and Scots trader and Seminole adviser Alexander Arbuthnot. In a bold display of frontier imperial justice, Jackson accused the two Britons of instigating the Seminoles to wage "savage war" on Americans and had them tried and executed. By late May the United States controlled both East and West Florida.

Jackson's relentless campaign of conquest shocked observers on both sides of the Atlantic. Few could believe that an American president would have the audacity to ignore the will of Congress, the requirements of the Constitution, and the potential wrath of the European powers. Spanish minister Onis demanded the immediate return of the Floridas and a formal apology. At this crucial moment in American history the choice appeared to be between national humiliation and another European war, with potentially disastrous consequences for the Union. President Monroe and his cabinet, motivated by geopolitical fears and political ambitions, contemplated abandoning Jackson to his critics. Only Adams fought to support Jackson, if not wholly to back his campaign and its outcome, then at least to offer a rousing patriotic defense of the general that might salvage the American negotiating position with Spain. In two official notes that were later "leaked" to the public – to Onis in July and to Minister to Madrid George Erving in November – Adams crafted a narrative of Spanish-British-Indian depravity that in the name of self-defense necessitated the invasion of the Floridas. Adams uncompromisingly defended Jackson's actions even as he offered to return the Floridas to Spain. Adams played the situation both ways: on the one hand, withdrawing from the Floridas to cool European anger over the situation and yet, on the other hand, refusing to acknowledge any wrongdoing on Jackson's part, refusing to apologize for the invasion, and threatening to take the Floridas again if the province remained a refuge for runaway slaves, recalcitrant Indians, and smugglers.

Far from characterizing Jackson as a threat to constitutional government as did some of his critics (most notably Henry Clay), Adams cast Jackson as a valiant hero defending American lives, territory, and honor. The secretary of state's super-patriotic narrative had the desired effect, both at home and abroad. Domestically, it made Jackson – already a national hero from his exploits during the War of 1812 – into the most popular individual in the country and positioned him as a future president. Congressional opponents saw themselves castigated as tools of Spanish diplomacy, notwithstanding the abundance of evidence that Jackson had indeed stretched the executive power to make war far

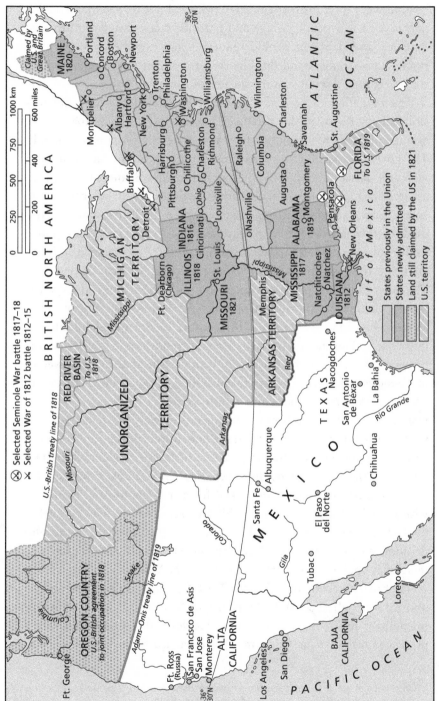

Map 4. The American Empire, 1821.

beyond what its framers intended. Critics did not realize that Adams's narrative of American courage and patriotism contrasted with foreign duplicity and depravity would render all facts to the contrary irrelevant. Adams understood that the rhetoric of American empire would trump rational discourse in the theater of American politics.

The unyielding defense of what seemed at first glance to be indefensible caught the Spanish off-balance. Initially, Onis had expected the events in Florida to strengthen his hand in resisting Adams's demands. The governments of Europe expressed outrage at the situation as a violation of accepted international practices. The Spanish government assumed that Jackson's brutal treatment of two British subjects would ensure London's support. Nevertheless, while the British public clamored for revenge, the British government understood it had no motive to disrupt the ongoing rapprochement with the Americans in order to vindicate the lost honor either of its two dead subjects or of Spain. The other European powers acquiesced in Britain's restrained response, lacking the means effectively to project armed force so far from their shores. Onis soon realized that the capture of Amelia Island and the invasion of Florida foreshadowed an uncompensated seizure of the province. With the approval of the government in Madrid, he moved to make the concessions necessary to conclude a treaty while he still could. At this critical point, the administration made a bold move. Adams's new offer of July 1818 contained a surprising new twist: Instead of a western boundary extending from the headwaters of the Rio Colorado and thence north to the Rockies, the Americans now proposed to draw the line at the Sabine River, thus excluding Texas. In exchange for this major concession, Adams now asked for a transcontinental boundary with a northern limit running roughly along the forty-second parallel to the Pacific. The acquisition of the Floridas assured, the Monroe administration unexpectedly introduced an entirely new dimension into the talks with Spain: a boundary extending to the West Coast.

The bid for a claim to the Pacific Coast did not originate with Monroe and Adams; Jefferson and Madison had first envisioned a transcontinental republic some years earlier.[8] However distant and abstract a presence on the Pacific Coast may have seemed to most Americans at

---

[8] On this point see J. C. A. Stagg, *Borderlines in Borderlands: James Madison and the Spanish American Frontier, 1776–1821* (New Haven, 2009).

the time, government policy, prompted by the urgings of prominent citizens such as John Jacob Astor, aggressively moved to establish an American foothold on the Northwest Coast. In July 1818, the USS *Ontario,* commanded by Commodore James Biddle, had arrived at Astoria with orders to reassert U.S. sovereignty over the region, as per the terms of the Treaty of Ghent. Astor, one of the richest men in the country at the time and a creditor to President Monroe, had personally lobbied for the recovery of the spot where he had hoped to establish a fur trading empire before being forced to transfer Astoria to the British-owned Northwest Fur Company. Biddle's largely symbolic act of repossession prepared the ground for a more formal assertion of a claim to the Northwest Coast via talks with Spain and Great Britain.

As all of this went on during the summer of 1818, the Monroe administration worked to further solidify relations with Great Britain. In July, Richard Rush and Albert Gallatin began talks with British officials in London designed to reach agreements on several outstanding issues between the two states: the status of the fisheries off the coast of Newfoundland; the demarcation of a northern boundary from the Lake of the Woods to the Rockies; control of the Oregon country along the Northwest Coast; compensation for slaves liberated by British forces during the War of 1812; and the end of the practice of impressment. The resulting Convention of 1818 resolved the first four of these issues, removing most of the remaining obstacles to amicable relations and smoothing the way to a massive expansion of Anglo-American trade. Thus it is not surprising that Jackson's execution of Ambrister and Arbuthnot did not seriously threaten bilateral ties, though it did provoke heated denunciations of the Americans by members of Parliament and the press.

A policy of steadily increasing military pressure combined with the progressive separation of Spain from British support led to an agreement in February 1819. The Adams-Onis Treaty ceded the Floridas to the United States in exchange for assumption of claims by U.S. citizens against Spain totaling approximately $5 million. The western boundary began at the Sabine River on the Gulf Coast, from the source of that river northward to the Red River, along its course to the hundredth meridian, thence due north to the Arkansas River to its source, extending due north to the forty-second parallel, and from there to the Pacific Ocean. Popular enthusiasm for this spectacular diplomatic victory meant that almost no one at the time took notice of the concession of Texas. Why did Adams, at Monroe's direction, prove willing to concede the claim to Texas? It cannot be blamed on Onís's resistance, for his instructions gave him the authority to draw the western boundary along the Rio Colorado if necessary. Rather, this momentous decision resulted from Monroe's concerns regarding the dangers of acquiring new territories amenable to slavery. The president foresaw the looming battle over slavery in the Missouri statehood debate and sought to avoid, as a threat to the Union, future such controversies. Monroe explained his thinking in letters to Jefferson and Jackson in May 1820. To Jefferson, Monroe expressed his concerns over the passions raised by the slavery issue: "[I]t is evident, that the further acquisition of territory, to the West and South, involves difficulties of an internal nature which menace the Union itself." He advised that no more territories to the west or south be acquired without the consent of "at least a majority of those who accomplished our Revolution." To Jackson, Monroe again expressed his concerns over "the repugnance with which the eastern portion of our Union" had viewed expansion to the west and south. He recommended that "we ought to be content with Florida for the present, and until the public opinion in that quarter shall be reconciled to any future change."[9] Monroe and Adams had committed a first-rate diplomatic sleight of hand, conceding an expansionist claim not owing to foreign opposition but because of internal political strife, and successfully disguising that fact to the public, at least for a while.

Although the Senate unanimously approved the Adams-Onís Treaty within days after it was presented for consideration, the refusal of elements in the Spanish government to accept its terms delayed final ratification. Members of the Consejo de Estado lamented that the deal contained no agreement by the United States to refrain from recognizing the rebellious Latin American colonies. More seriously, three land grants by Ferdinand VII effectively ceding most of East Florida to Spanish noblemen threatened to nullify the original agreement. Erving had alerted Adams to the existence of these grants the previous spring, but the secretary of state had overlooked the warning. Now they seemed likely to upset the entire deal. The six-month period for ratification

---

[9] Monroe's letters to Jefferson and Jackson can be found in Stanislaus M. Hamilton, ed., *Writings of James Monroe*, 7 vol. (New York, 1896), 6:119–23; 6:126–30.

came and went, leaving the treaty unratified by either side just as the first of two congressional debates on the admission of Missouri to the Union began.

Even as the Floridas gradually came under the power of the United States, the Seminoles and their African American allies retreated deeper into the swamps, defeating efforts to conquer them and continuing their resistance even in the face of a second war of extermination against them between 1838 and 1842. Although the Floridas nominally were acquired by treaty, perfecting the claim would require the spilling of blood.

"THE MISSOURI QUESTION": BREAKDOWN OF THE EXPANSIONIST CONSENSUS

Although the political brouhaha resulting in the Missouri Compromise has long been understood to be an important chapter in the history of the domestic conflict over slavery, its aspect as a foreign policy controversy has been underappreciated. The admission of Maine as a free state to balance Missouri's admission as a slave state reflected an internal political compromise, the demarcation of the 36-degree, 30-minute line as the dividing line between future slave territory and free territory. This arrangement demonstrates the extent to which the expansionist consensus (and thus the Unionist consensus) had already collapsed, with ominous implications for the future. From at least the time of the Constitutional Convention, differences over slavery had been growing, not lessening, although both sides tacitly agreed to refrain from speaking of these differences. Thus, when Representative James Tallmadge of New York, motivated apparently by nothing more than an intense repugnance for human bondage, arose on February 13, 1819, to introduce an amendment to the Missouri statehood bill effectively abolishing slavery in the new state, it set off a vitriolic debate that threatened immediately to end the Union. The congressional speeches in the weeks to follow as recorded in the Annals of Congress proved to be a rehearsal of almost every argument over slavery to appear for the next forty years. Did the national government have the power to regulate slavery in the territories? Did the Declaration of Independence inevitably point in the direction of black freedom? Was slavery an oppressive institution, or was it mostly benign and ameliorative of the presumed civilizational shortcomings of blacks? Tallmadge's defense of his amendment captures this intensity: "If dissolution of the Union must take place, let it be so! If civil war, which gentlemen so much threaten, must come, I can only say, let it come!"[10]

The rhetorical furnace of the Missouri Debates forged both the proslavery and the antislavery ideologies that defined American politics until the Civil War. The Era of Good Feelings evaporated as a rising moral and ideological objection to the institution of slavery collided with its increasing profitability in the cotton kingdom and the rising fears by white Southerners of slave revolts. Representative Thomas Cobb of Virginia reputedly accused Tallmadge of having "kindled a flame which all the waters of the ocean cannot put out, which seas of blood can only extinguish." But a startling number of Northern members of Congress began to frame it as, in the words of Arthur Livermore of New Hampshire, "a sin which sits heavy on the souls of every one of us," encouraging his fellow representatives "if not to diminish, at least to prevent" its growth. By doing so, Livermore continued, "we may retrieve the national character, and in some degree, our own."[11]

The future of the republican empire hung in the balance as congressional leaders and the Monroe administration looked for a compromise that could leave both sides feeling victorious and, more importantly, still firmly committed to the Union. Monroe opposed slavery for both practical and ideological reasons. He recognized it to be an outrageous contradiction of the Declaration of Independence and of America's pretensions as the world's preeminent champion of freedom. He also knew that its continued existence left the South in a perpetual state of anxiety regarding the prospect of slave uprisings: As governor of Virginia, Monroe himself had been targeted for kidnapping as part of Gabriel Prosser's Virginia Slave Rebellion of 1800, a plot foiled only by a chance torrential downpour that disrupted the conspirators' plans.

Typical of his hidden hand presidential style, Monroe's behind-the-scenes role in brokering the series of compromises that made up the Missouri Compromise has only recently been discerned, a result of his efforts to disguise his role in persuading the various factions to go

---

[10] Robert Pierce Forbes, *The Missouri Compromise and Its Aftermath: Slavery and the Meaning of America* (Chapel Hill, 2007), 43.
[11] Forbes, *The Missouri Compromise and Its Aftermath*, 40, 42.

along with them. Monroe attempted to maintain a Unionist consensus in the face of potentially irreconcilable political differences by meeting the needs as he saw it of all sections. In this case, Monroe hoped that the acquisition of Florida would mollify Southern concerns for their security as well as offer the promise of more slave-state representation in Congress. At the same time, Monroe began to implement the policy of removing the defeated Indian tribes of the Southeast from their ancestral homelands to the western territories, thereby opening huge new tracts to cotton cultivation. He also vigorously supported the colonization of freed blacks in some new colony in Africa in the hopes of diffusing future problems related to their increasing numbers in many southern states. Yet to assuage the concerns of Northerners about the growth of the institution of slavery, he conceded the claim to Texas and in 1822 negotiated an agreement with Great Britain for the suppression of the African slave trade. Suffering no illusions about the severity of the slave question, Monroe took comprehensive and reasonably effective steps to ease it even as he continued to push an expansionist agenda. Robert Pierce Forbes concludes that Monroe aimed "to secure a compromise that would permit the expansion of slavery in principle, while prohibiting it in practice from the rest of the Louisiana Territory excepting Arkansas.... Monroe quietly built a majority for compromise while simultaneously assuring skittish slaveholders that he would give no quarter. He then secured their acquiescence in precisely the result he had promised to prevent by convincing them that his capitulation had saved the nation from a Federalist-abolitionist takeover."[12]

In the aftermath of the Missouri Debates, all sides came to a tacit agreement not to speak again of the potentially volcanic topic of slavery. However, it proved an enormously polarizing event, crystallizing a critique of slavery even as it galvanized support for it by white Southerners. Those, such as John Quincy Adams, who fashioned themselves as staunch nationalists found their consciences pricked by the debate. As it unfolded he wrote in his diary that the debate was "a mere preamble – a title page to a great tragic volume." He went on to predict that "[i]f slavery be the destined sword in the hand of a destroying angel which is to sever the ties of this Union, the same sword will cut in sunder the bonds of slavery itself. A dissolution of the Union for the

---

[12] Forbes, *The Missouri Compromise and Its Aftermath*, 10.

cause of slavery would be followed by a servile war in the slave-holding states, combined with a war between the two severed portions of the Union. It seems to me that its result must be the extirpation of slavery from this whole continent; and calamitous and desolating as this ... must be, so glorious would be its final issue, that as God shall judge me, I dare not say that it is not to be desired."[13] Southerners responded equally strongly to the Missouri controversy, accusing Rufus King's incendiary Senate denunciation of slavery of being contrary to the laws of God and of instigating the foiled Denmark Vesey South Carolina slave uprising of 1820. One Virginian protested that antislavery rhetoric "would sound the tocsin of freedom to every Negro of the South and we may have to see the tragical events of Santo Domingo repeated in our own land."[14] If, as some scholars claim, the origin of the South as a distinct region dates from the Missouri controversy, this was in no small measure the result of a rapidly increasing threat of servile rebellion that united Southern whites in a republic of fear.

CREATION OF A HEMISPHERIC DOCTRINE

Final passage of the Missouri Compromise in February 1821 came only four days after final ratification of the Adams-Onis Treaty, and two weeks prior to Monroe's second inauguration. His first term had seen major achievements in foreign affairs, including important agreements with Great Britain and Spain, and the position of the United States was far less precarious than it had been in 1817. Yet major challenges remained concerning the continued prospect of European intervention in the Western Hemisphere on behalf of Spain as well as a looming collision with Russia along the Northwest Coast.

In September 1821, the tsar had issued a *ukase* asserting Russian control of the Northwest Coast as far south as 51 degrees and prohibiting Americans from its offshore waters in an area extending for one hundred nautical miles. Adams and Monroe immediately made plans to respond to this provocative attempt to expand Russian influence in the hemisphere. In 1822, the administration began to recognize the independence of the South American states even as the Holy Allies schemed

---

[13] John Quincy Adams, *Memoirs*, ed. Charles Francis Adams (Philadelphia, 1874–7), December 29, 1820, 5:210.
[14] Forbes, *The Missouri Compromise and Its Aftermath*, 145.

to preserve monarchy in the New World by considering transferring some of the rebellious colonies to France. This, combined with the Holy Alliance's interventions in the Italian and Iberian peninsulas, provoked British anxieties by threatening to tilt the balance of power in Europe as well as the New World. Anglo-American relations, steadily improving since 1815, now stood nearly perfectly aligned in opposition to the Holy Alliance's schemes for a New World intervention.

This set the stage for a series of conversations in August and September 1823 between British foreign secretary George Canning and American minister Richard Rush. Ultimately, Canning proposed to the Americans that the two nations make a joint declaration acknowledging the inevitable independence of the South American colonies from Spanish control, renouncing any intention to possess any portion of them, and opposing their transfer to any other European power. In effect, it was an offer of a de facto alliance with the world's largest power to guarantee the independence and autonomy of the new South American republics. It seemed an excellent opportunity to commit British seapower on the side of nonintervention; initially, Monroe responded favorably to the proposal, as did both Jefferson and Madison, whom he consulted on the matter. To Jefferson, the prospect of aligning the Royal navy with U.S. interests outweighed the requirement that the annexation of Cuba be postponed indefinitely. Madison was enthusiastic, suggesting that the United States join with Britain in making statements opposing the interventions of the Holy Alliance in Europe and supporting the Greek independence movement. Calhoun, too, supported the idea of an Anglo-American front to oppose foreign intervention in the hemisphere.

Once again Adams stood apart from the other members of the cabinet and opposed the seemingly irresistible offer of an Anglo-American alliance. As secretary of state, he clearly understood that the whole course of British policy since 1815 had shifted from supporting the restoration of monarchy to advocating open markets and liberal capitalism. In the Western Hemisphere, this meant opposing the restorationist schemes of the Holy Alliance and cultivating an independent Spanish America open to British commerce. London could be relied upon to oppose European intervention without any formal agreement with the United States, and therefore what possible advantage could there be in the United States renouncing future claims to former Spanish colonies, most notably Cuba? Always wary of agreeing to self-denying ordinances that might hinder future American expansionist plans, Adams now feared that the British were more eager to contain the expansionist tendencies of the United States than to prevent the intervention of the Holy Alliance. Adams, perhaps owing to the perspective offered from his many years abroad, understood that without British support the chances for a successful European invasion of the hemisphere were nil. Napoleon's disastrous campaign to reconquer Sainte Domingue had proven that the New World could be a graveyard for Old World armies. Adams did not count on British power to stop an invasion. Rather, he counted on the inability of the Holy Allies to mount an invasion without it. The Holy Alliance, lacking the capacity effectively to project power across the Atlantic Ocean and throughout the extensive landmass of the Americas, by itself posed no threat to the hemisphere: "They will no more restore Spanish dominion on the American continent than the Chimborazo will sink beneath the ocean," he said, referring to the famous Ecuadoran volcano.[15] Confident that he had discerned Britain's true aim of containing U.S. expansionism, Adams opposed calls for an alliance and instead pushed for an independent statement of American hemispheric policy. This included the firm admonition to resist making any statement about the Greek independence movement as an unnecessary interference in European affairs. Rather than position the United States as subordinate to British policy, Adams urged that the administration make hemispheric policy "an American cause" unrelated to European concerns. In essence, Adams urged a reprise of the strategy from the War of Independence, in which American diplomats assiduously cultivated European support and then abruptly changed course once that support was assured.

Monroe gave public voice to his emerging hemispheric foreign policy in his seventh annual message on December 2, 1823. In it, he detailed two distinct principles that would be the foundation of U.S. hemispheric policy to the present day. The first of these two principles, noncolonization, arose in response to the ongoing efforts of the tsar to assert his claims to the Northwest Coast. Alluding to the negotiations with Russia over the tsar's *ukase*, Monroe set it down as a matter of unyielding principle that "the American continents, by the free and independent

---

[15] George Dangerfield, *The Era of Good Feelings* (New York, 1952), 296.

condition which they have assumed and maintain, are henceforth not to be considered as subjects for future colonization by any European powers." It was a bold statement given the inability of the United States to enforce unilaterally the concept and the still-uncertain outcome of the South American independence struggles. Yet the whole course of American foreign policy since independence pointed in this direction, and circumstances now dictated that a stand be taken affirming it. More immediately, the implicit support of the British navy for this principle rested on its own changing economic interests and philosophies. Adams, especially, perceived this change and understood that it could be relied upon with far more certainty to control British policy in the future than any bilateral agreement. Hence, the United States could take its stand with confidence. Later in the address, Monroe articulated a second foundational pillar of American foreign relations: the principle of non-intervention. Acknowledging the sympathies many Americans felt for the Greek independence movement, Monroe emphasized that the United States would take no part in the struggle: "[I]n the wars of the European powers in matters relating to themselves we have never taken any part, nor does it comport with our policy to do so. It is only when our rights are invaded or seriously menaced that we resent injuries or make preparations for our defense." Observing that "[t]he political system of the allied powers is essentially different in this respect from America," the president warned, "We owe it ... to candor and to the amicable relations existing between the United States and those powers to declare that we should consider any attempt on their part to extend their system to any portion of this hemisphere as dangerous to our peace and safety.... It is impossible that the allied powers should extend their political system to any portion of either continent without endangering our peace and happiness; nor can anyone believe that our southern brethren, if left to themselves, would adopt it on their own accord."[16] It was a breathtaking assertion of hemispheric dominance, a message to the Europeans that the New World was now off limits to further imperial adventures, except of course those launched by the United States itself. Monroe had demarcated the entire hemisphere as an American security zone; European powers could enter at their own risk.

---

[16] James D. Richardson, ed., *Messages and Papers of the Presidents* (Washington, D.C., 1903), 2:206, 2:218, 2:219.

The audacity of the president's bold stand startled the courts of Europe. Surely, the Americans, so recently nearly destroyed by war, did not have either the power or the position to dictate hemispheric affairs. Yet the alignments of power and interests in both the Americas and in Europe had shifted dramatically since 1815, thereby making the president's stand plausible. In fact, unbeknownst to Monroe at the time he gave his address, the British had communicated their resolute opposition to any plans by the Holy Alliance to intervene in the revolting Spanish colonies. In the so-called Polignac Memorandum, Canning had finally removed all doubts as to Britain's unequivocal embrace of South American independence and the limits of its restorationist fervor. Lacking the expected support of the British navy, Spain gave up plans for a New World expedition to quash the independence movements and abandoned a scheme to transfer one or more of Spain's former colonies to France.

The net result of Monroe and Adams's statecraft was a post-1823 world in which a de facto Anglo-American condominium had been established in the Western Hemisphere. The centuries-long multilateral European imperial competition for dominance had effectively been reduced to two players: Great Britain and the United States. The two states could now engage in what Jay Sexton terms the "collaborative competition for ascendancy in Latin America," cooperating and competing as specific circumstances dictated.[17]

Confronted with this new Anglo-American solidarity, in April 1824 Tsar Alexander I capitulated to U.S. pressure over the Northwest Coast. Adams's warnings of the previous July that the United States would vigorously contest any new colonial establishments, combined with the president's public affirmation of that intention, resulted in the Convention of 1824. To the surprise of European diplomats, the tsar agreed to repeal his *ukase* of 1821 banning Americans from offshore waters, established a southern boundary of Russian Alaska at 54 degrees, 40 minutes north latitude, and allowed Americans to land and take furs along unoccupied regions of the Northwest Coast. The deal constituted another major victory for American statecraft.

---

[17] Jay Sexton, *The Monroe Doctrine: Empire and Nation in Nineteenth-Century America* (New York, 2011), 64.

James Monroe rapidly faded from the public mind upon leaving office in 1825. But under his leadership eight years of purposeful diplomacy had resulted in the promulgation of the benchmark principles of noncolonization and nonintervention, themselves best understood as the implicit goals of American foreign policymakers from the time of the War of Independence. Although Secretary of State John Quincy Adams had done much to establish the conditions necessary for the promulgation of doctrinal principles of American foreign relations, esteemed diplomatic historian and Adams biographer Samuel Flagg Bemis nonetheless affirms Monroe's primary role: "The 'most significant of all American state papers' appropriately bears the name Monroe Doctrine."[18] The authority with which Monroe could pronounce his principles flowed from the stark transformation of the U.S. geopolitical position between 1815 and 1825. Fears of encirclement at the hands of Spain and Great Britain had given way to Spain's cession of the Floridas and recognition of a transcontinental boundary between the United States and Hispanic America. Historic enmity with Great Britain had been replaced with burgeoning trade ties, resolution of the most pressing conflicts between the two states, further demarcation of the U.S.-Canadian border, and a joint occupancy agreement in the Pacific Northwest. The Anglo-American rapprochement blunted Russian pretensions to expansion southward from Alaska. Perhaps most importantly, South American independence from Spanish rule had been assured, and the danger of a European intervention to restore Spanish sovereignty had effectively been ended. In three-quarters of a century, Franklin's vision of a durable union of the North American colonies achieving hemispheric preeminence had been realized.

Beyond the formal articulation of the foundational principles of U.S. hemispheric policy, the Monroe administration's conduct of foreign affairs established crucial precedents for future presidents to refer to and stand upon when engaging in their own activist foreign policies. The First Seminole War and the controversy surrounding it demonstrated that framing foreign policy crises in ultranationalist terms could trump facts contrary to the official story and cast dissenters as unpatriotic, thereby emboldening future presidents to engage in foreign

---

[18] Samuel Flagg Bemis, *John Quincy Adams and American Foreign Policy* (New York, 1949), 408.

policy adventurism. In addition, the concession of the Texas claim in the Adams-Onis Treaty and the partial concession of the Oregon claim in the Free and Open Occupation Treaty of 1818 would later give rise to charges that the Monroe administration had sold out American interests at the negotiating table. Just as important, Monroe and Adams's conception of an American security perimeter encompassing the entire Western Hemisphere in the long run had a profound influence on future policy. Jay Sexton observes, "[P]remised upon a curious mixture of imperial ambitions and perception of internal vulnerability, the national security of the United States required more than just the safety of its borders – it required an entire hemispheric political system conducive to its political system and economic practices."[19]

Although not formally given the status as a doctrine, or axiomatic principle of American foreign policy, until the 1840s, Monroe's statement of hemispheric hegemony made an immediate impact. The newly independent states of South America were disappointed to discover that what seemed like an offer of multilateral cooperation in resisting foreign penetration was actually a statement of hemispheric unilateralism by the North American republic that saw itself as inherently superior to the states to the south. Political leaders in Washington would decide when and where to invoke the principles of noncolonization and nonintervention and assert them without the aid or consultation of the South American republics. Once again, favorable geographic circumstances created the conditions for a favorable outcome in the name of the burgeoning American Empire.

Yet even as American policy diminished European imperial influence in the hemisphere, a division over the nature of freedom split the Imperial Republic. From the 1820s until the Civil War the most serious obstacle to further American expansionism arose from within.

---

[19] Sexton, *The Monroe Doctrine: Empire and Nation in Nineteenth-Century America*, 60.

5

FREEDOM'S EMPIRE, AT HOME AND ABROAD

We are great and rapidly – he was about to say fearfully – growing. This, said he, is our pride and power – our weakness and our strength.... Let us then ... bind the Republic [sic] together with a perfect system of roads and canals. Let us conquer space."

> John C. Calhoun, February 1817, Annals of Congress,
> 14th cong., 2nd sess. 854

It is equally plain that the religious and political destiny of our nation is to be decided in the west.

> Rev. Lyman Beecher, "A Plea for the West," 1835

Land is the footstool of our power; land is the throne of our empire.

> Caleb Cushing, July 4, 1850

MANIFEST DESTINIES

The period 1815–61 looms especially large in U.S. history, a time of massive territorial and commercial expansion and dramatic technological change. This dynamic process of expansion, change, and outsized accomplishment gave rise to an outlook known as Manifest Destiny, the dominant ideology of that time. It is a term most often associated with the 1840s and most often attributed to the journalist and publisher John L. O'Sullivan.[1] But it is appropriate to employ it for the entire period from the end of the War of 1812 to at least the beginning of the Civil War; in other words, the existence of the ideology predates the most commonly used term to describe it. As is the

---

[1] Linda Hudson, *Mistress of Manifest Destiny: A Biography of Jane McManus Storm Cazneau* (Austin, 2001), makes a strong case that the journalist/speculator/agitator Jane McManus Storm Cazneau was actually the originator of the term.

case with any ideology, Manifest Destiny, though oriented around a few basic concepts, did not belong exclusively to any one group or have one precise meaning. Perhaps it is best understood as a web of justifications, rationalizations, and idealizations designed to legitimate the seizing of North America (or at least a large portion of it) from its Native American residents and European claimants.

In one sense, Manifest Destiny heralded the destiny of the United States to spread its limits throughout North America and perhaps the rest of the hemisphere. Rooted in Franklin's continentalist vision in the 1750s, this outlook subsequently was modified by Jefferson, John Quincy Adams, and others; these changes, combined with the palpable successes experienced by the young nation, resulted in the vision morphing into a messianic conception of the American people as the chosen agents of God's will. After 1815, having twice stood up militarily to the most powerful nation in the world, having expanded across North America, and having created a dynamic society built on a broadly (but by no means universally) shared freedom, many Americans began to feel that the country's long-anticipated destiny was being realized before them. Nothing else could explain the astounding and rapid success of the United States as anything other than a part of a godly plan – or Divine Providence, the term commonly used. Each victory in battle, each technological breakthrough, each foreign revolution in the name of liberty and republicanism spoke to the American people as another sign of their chosen role as agents in God's master plan. Manifest Destiny functioned as an enabling ideology, a potent mix of American patriotic nationalism, evangelical Christianity, and material self-interest.

In its most basic form, the ideology of Manifest Destiny rested on three assumptions: the special moral virtue of the American people; their mission to redeem the world in the name of their own distinct concept of freedom; and their presumed destiny under Divine Providence to accomplish that mission. The facts of any particular case could be adapted to fit within these foundational assumptions. John Quincy Adams had demonstrated the power of this nationalist/imperialist narrative in defending Andrew Jackson from his critics in 1818–19. By the 1820s, many Americans looked back to the revolution as part of a sacred past en route to a seemingly boundless future.

Even as the ideology of Manifest Destiny coalesced in the 1820s, it began to evolve into two distinct strands based on different readings of the nation's sacred past and future. One school of Manifest Destiny remained closely tied to the Declaration of Independence and its promise of universal freedom and equality. To its adherents, the Declaration stood as the Magna Charta of American nationality; the ultimate realization of its principles constituted the essence of the American mission. In theory, the Declaration of Independence applied to people of all backgrounds, whatever qualms or uncertainties may have existed regarding how this fundamental human equality might be accommodated in practice.

A second conception of Manifest Destiny emerged in the 1820s and gained strength thereafter. This conception rejected the universal application of the promises of the Declaration of Independence. Basing its belief on a traditional reading of the Bible, a new scientific consensus on the supposed truth of racial inequality, and a rapidly increasing economic and cultural interest in racial subordination, this view would energize the expansionist thrust to the southwest during this time. This second conception of Manifest Destiny connoted a romantic racial nationalism that hypothesized a putative Anglo-Saxon people as the prime movers of modern world history. Its conception of American destiny justified the enslavement of the African, the removal of the Indian, and the conquest of the Mexican. This version of the ideology of Manifest Destiny, unlike the ideology that informed the founding generation, had an explicitly racialist component. Only white people could enjoy the benefits of American freedom; nonwhite people were considered undeserving of equality. The conviction of racial superiority joined with assumptions regarding the superiority of Protestant Christianity, of the superiority of republican government, and of the superiority of free market capitalism to create a comprehensive worldview that informed the era, at least for one segment of the population.

These diverging notions of America's apparent destiny only loosely correlated along free state–slave state lines. Many white Southerners remained staunch believers in the universality of the Declaration of Independence and continued to wish to see slavery ended even if they could not envision the transition to true racial egalitarianism. Just as many, if not more, white Northerners themselves rejected the radical implications of the Declaration of Independence in the name of maintaining a white imperial republic that countenanced slavery. Ultimately, the ideological divide that developed after 1820 is best understood not along sectional or party or racial lines but as a philosophical difference splitting the country according to individual conscience.

This ideological split regarding the precise meaning of American destiny and American freedom dated at least to the framing of the Constitution. Yet it had been mostly contained in the early decades of the Union, only to appear with sudden pent-up fury during the Missouri debates in Congress, proliferating from that point forward and becoming more contentious with each successive expansionist controversy. The expansionist tendency, prominent from the start in U.S. history, accelerated in the 1820s. Americans were a restless, mobile people, with no limit to their ambitions. It was an age of boundless energy, boundless territory, and boundless optimism that the future would be better than the past. Yet the political union that was the key to its great success grew increasingly fragile. For alongside Manifest Destiny's narrative of freedom and progress unfolded a counternarrative of acrimony and disunion that heralded a darker destiny drenched in blood.

EMPIRE OF COTTON

Any history of the antebellum American Empire between the end of the War of 1812 and the beginning of the Civil War must emphasize the critical importance of cotton. Cotton, and the activities related to its production and distribution, was both the single most important engine of national economic development during this time and a crucially important commodity in the emerging world economy. U.S. cotton exports, virtually nonexistent in the 1790s, by 1830 had reached $26 million per year and 40 percent of total exports, and by 1851, $112 million and 59 percent of exports.[2] This radical shift had been driven by advances both in the production of cotton (most notably the cotton "gin") and in the manufacture of cotton textiles and was given an unstoppable momentum by the endless demand for affordable machine-made cloth. Indeed, cotton exports did much to reduce the long-term negative trade balance of the United States during the era. Its importance was not confined to the South: Northern merchants, shippers, and insurers shared

---

[2] Brian Schoen, *The Fragile Fabric of Union: Cotton, Federal Politics, and the Global Origins of the Civil War* (Baltimore, 2009), 122–131. Based on Stuart Bruchey, *Cotton and the Growth of the American Economy* (New York, 1967).

the wealth generated by the fiber. With cotton by far the greatest single source of national wealth during this time, the slaves who produced it represented the single largest source of capital.

The global importance of American cotton to the textile revolution is hard to exaggerate. The cotton boom was a critical part of world history, a vital cog in the beginnings of the Industrial Revolution. Brian Schoen observes, "By the beginning of the 19th century, a vast and intricate web of commerce already had created a regional, national, and global interest grounded in the raw cotton of the lower South."[3] Traditional views of nineteenth-century (especially post-1820) American foreign policy as being minimally involved in world affairs underestimate the degree to which cotton – and the slave labor system that produced it – deeply involved the United States in a crucially important historic event of its time: the textile revolution. Along the same lines the explosion of cotton production by a slave labor system was not a manifestation of regional "backwardness" as is sometimes suggested, but rather it was irrefutable evidence of the engagement of the cotton South in some of the most critical trends on the road to the modern world. The cotton empire benefited both large landowners and small farmers, each of whom stood to profit from the fiber. Its sudden, rapid movement across the South made moot notions that freed slaves might be "diffused" into sparsely populated western territories or colonized in faraway lands. By 1830, slavery had demonstrated its critical role in both national and global prosperity.

The post–War of 1812 rapprochement with England had numerous aspects – cultural, strategic, and ideological – but more than any other factor, cotton thread bound the interests of the two states together. The United States went from supplying 0.16 percent of British cotton imports in the period 1786–90 to 53 percent by the period 1806–10, and 81 percent by the late 1840s.[4] One might think that the position held by the United States during this time – as, in essence, a neocolonial source of raw material for the British economic empire – would have elicited the same fears of being resubordinated that dominated Anglo-American relations prior to 1812, but the successes in the war

[3] Schoen, *Fragile Fabric of Union*, 49.
[4] Schoen, *Fragile Fabric of Union*, 47. From Thomas Ellison, *The Cotton Trade of Great Britain* (London, 1886).

and the fabulous wealth generated by the cotton trade muted such objections.

Progress in the form of the textile revolution and the wealth that it generated came at the cost of a greatly reinvigorated slave institution. Nearly matching the fertility of the white population, the 500,000 slaves of the 1790s became, by 1820, 1.5 million. The diminishing importance of slave labor to the tobacco, indigo, and rice trade dramatically reversed once it became clear that there existed an open-ended demand for cotton and the land to cultivate it. By the 1820s, many Southerners defended the institution of slavery as both morally right and economically invaluable. The profitability of cotton increased the value of slaves: By 1840, the price of an adult field hand approached $1,000 or more, a very large sum of money for the time. Even as the federal government dispatched the navy to suppress the slave trade, the importance of slavery increased. Once cotton became king, the issue of slavery was transformed from being a manageable, diminishing concern to the central controversy of the age. A rising tide of abolitionist agitation collided with a suddenly resurgent slave labor regime and an emerging proslavery ideology to match.

Domestically, the cotton boom accelerated the removal of Native Americans from their ancient homelands in the southeastern United States. In the years after the War of 1812, Andrew Jackson became a one-man removal force. At times acting on his own authority, between 1816 and 1818 Jackson negotiated five land cessions from the Cherokee, Choctaw, and Chickasaw peoples. This was in addition to the massive transfer of Creek lands contained in the 1814 Treaty of Fort Jackson. James Monroe's formal adoption in 1817 of a removal policy based on gaining the consent of the subject tribes seemed to offer the hope that the process would be done humanely. By the 1820s, however, many tribes would no longer consent to part with their lands, much to the consternation of the southern states. The discovery of gold in Georgia fueled the determination of locals to remove Indians by any means necessary. Those who defended the rights of Indians, be it the federal government or Christian missionaries, felt the outrage of Georgians angry over outsiders meddling in state affairs. In contrast to the administration of John Quincy Adams, Andrew Jackson's withdrew federal support of Indian treaty rights and made it clear that it would not let signed treaties stand in the way of removal. The ethnic cleansing of the southeast culminated in the Indian Removal Act of 1830 stipulating the forced removal of any tribes that refused to leave voluntarily.

The harshness of removal, particularly of tribes such as the Cherokees that had taken steps to become agriculturalists, panged the consciences of many Americans, and the Removal Act passed by only a one-vote margin in the Senate. Yet the rhetoric of progress trumped the reality of Native American suffering. Jackson gave expression to this in his second annual message to Congress in December 1830: Acknowledging that "humanity has often wept over the fate of the aborigines of the country," Jackson urged Congress to see the disappearance of the tribes in a positive light: "What good man would prefer a country covered with forests and ranged by a few thousand savages to our extensive Republic, studded with cities, towns, and prosperous farms, embellished with all the improvements which art can devise or industry execute, occupied by more than 12,000,000 happy people, and filled with all the blessings of liberty, civilization, and religion?" Jackson argued that removal was the only means for Indians to avoid extermination at the hands of expansionist whites, concluding that "the policy of the General Government toward the red man is not only liberal but generous" for it "kindly offers him a new home, and proposes to pay the whole expense of his removal and settlement."[5] Indian removal represented another major expansion of federal power into the realm of imperial population management. By 1840 approximately 125,000 Native Americans had been removed by the federal government to new lands in the Oklahoma territory. The rage for cotton cultivation transformed the states of the Deep South, utterly changing their character in little over a decade, as had occurred earlier in Ohio. Plantation agriculture spread through the woodland homelands of Native America, as large profits from the trade resulted in the creation of elegant estates designed to advertise the great wealth and prestige of their owners.

TECHNOLOGIES OF EMPIRE

The explosion of cotton production and its importance to national (and international) prosperity were boosted by revolutionary developments

---

[5] James D. Richardson, ed., *Messages and Papers of the President* (Washington, D.C., 1903), 3:521, 3:522.

in transportation and communication that both bound the Union more tightly into a single economic unit and made it more closely tied to global markets. The railroad proved the most important of these innovations. Although the first railroad was founded in England in 1825, by 1830 the Baltimore and Ohio Railroad had begun work on a route west roughly along that first surveyed by Washington more than seventy-five years earlier. Aided by English financiers and minimal right-of-way acquisition costs, American railroads exploded. By 1860, more than thirty thousand miles of track had been laid in the United States, more than in all of Europe combined. This caused a radical drop in the cost of transporting bulk goods, making formerly distant places quite accessible. This, in turn, made American goods on the world market more competitive. The railroad, one of the key elements in the global transition to the modern world, first achieved prominence in the United States. It transformed the edifice of union into a structure built of iron and steel.

Only slightly less important than the railroads was the development of the steamship. The first commercially viable river steamers emerged in the years after the War of 1812; by the 1820s hundreds of steam-powered vessels of varying degrees of safety navigated the nation's rivers. Oceangoing ships, not facing the necessity of navigating upstream, evolved more slowly, but by the 1850s a combination of American steamships and sailing vessels patrolled the world's oceans and carried its mail. As with the railroad, the impact of steam-powered vessels on American economic development is hard to exaggerate.

The period 1820–60 also saw a spate of canal building. Starting with virtually no man-made waterways in 1815, by 1860 the nation had approximately three thousand miles of canals, binding the Union into a single economic entity in much the same way railroads did. Spurred by the efforts of DeWitt Clinton, the state of New York built a 358-mile canal connecting Buffalo and Albany between 1817 and 1825. The project cost the then-enormous sum of $7 million, but it reduced freight rates between New York and the Great Lakes by 90 percent. A rapidly rising demand for transportation meant that by 1827 tolls had paid for most of the original construction cost. By facilitating access to the West via the Great Lakes, the Erie Canal cemented New York's position as the most important city in the Union, and a major world port.

American innovations in terms of ship technology did not stop with steam. The age of sail continued in the first half of the nineteenth century, and American sailors and shipbuilders remained the best in the world, having the easiest and most affordable access to the raw materials needed to build a sailing vessel. The most famous of these vessels was the clipper ship, a narrow-hulled vessel sporting enormously tall sails (with masts approaching 200 feet in some cases) to maximize its speed. During the golden age of the clipper ships, roughly 1843 to 1860, they set virtually every record for long-distance sailing.

Of all the revolutionary technological developments of the age, the invention of the magnetic telegraph had perhaps the greatest long-term impact. It was devised by Samuel F. B. Morse, a noted painter-turned-inventor and son of Jedidiah Morse, whose 1790 text *American Geography* endeavored to catalogue and publicize the vast spaces of North America even as it imagined all of it as part of the United States. It was the genius of his son, however, that shrank that geography to manageable size. In only a few decades, the United States went from a country where a message could travel no faster than by horseback to widespread communication over a wire at the speed of light. It represented the quantum leap in communications, making all future innovations mere refinements. Like the railroad, the telegraph first became pervasive in the United States. By 1860, nearly fifty thousand miles of telegraph wire added another layer of networks binding the Union together. It is worth noting as well that the federal government allocated $30,000 for construction of the first telegraph line between Baltimore and Washington, as private investors proved unwilling to take the risk on the novel technology. "What hath God wrought?" Morse famously wondered on the first telegraph message; it is a question that might well have been applied to this entire era of American history.[6]

The revolutions in transportation and communications shrank the vastness of the U.S. continental empire into an increasingly manageable space and linked them ever more tightly into the emerging global market. Railroads, steamships, canals, and telegraphs provided layers of integrated networks that proved critically important in the creation

---

[6] See Daniel Walker Howe, *"What Hath God Wrought?" The Transformation of America, 1815–1848* (New York, 2007).

of a unified nation. Although Jefferson doubted that the great expanse of the continent could be bound together as one nation, the technologies of steam and telegraphy made the creation of a national economic, information, and cultural entity more easily united than had been the thirteen colonies. Expansion might truly have no limit in an age of seemingly magical innovation. The promise of one large, internal market with rapid transport and communication capabilities gave the United States an enormous advantage in dealing with the world beyond its borders. William Gilpin, protégé of Jackson and one of the more prominent apostles of Manifest Destiny, reflected the optimism of the age when he wrote in 1846, "The *untransacted* destiny of the American people is to subdue the continent – to rush over this vast field to the Pacific Ocean ... to regenerate superannuated nations – ... to confirm the destiny of the human race – to carry the career of mankind to its culminating point – to cause a stagnant people to be reborn – ... to absolve the curse that weighs down humanity, and to shed blessings round the world!"[7]

All of these developments in transportation and communication occurred against a backdrop of an industrial "takeoff" period for American industry, which, if not the dramatic beginning it is sometimes thought to be, nevertheless marked a decisive acceleration of a preexisting process, putting the United States on a trajectory to be the workshop of the world by the 1870s. The period 1815–61 proved a critical moment both in U.S. history and in the history of the world, as the transformation occurring before everyone's eyes had no precedent in history.

EMPIRE OF THE SEAS

The annexation and absorption of the vast spaces of North America into a single continental empire were not the only way Americans expanded their civilization and their way of life in the nineteenth century. They also expanded into the world beyond the limits of North America. From colonial times, Americans had extensive commercial contacts with the Caribbean, Europe, and the Mediterranean. Beginning in the 1780s,

---

[7] Henry Nash Smith, *Virgin Land: The American West as Symbol and Myth* (Cambridge, Mass., 1950), 37.

they began to push into the Pacific and toward Asia, motivated by the same reasons that drove continental expansion – the search for new and abundant sources of wealth. American expansionism during the period 1815–61 encompassed a global expansionism along an undifferentiated frontier, for even though it surely took different tools to navigate the Pacific Ocean as opposed to the Oregon Trail, the search for new and accessible sources of wealth, be it territorial, commercial, mineral, or natural, drove both tendencies. Historian Frederick Jackson Turner's well-known "frontier thesis" helped to create the impression of American expansionism as a linear progression across the continent in the nineteenth century. However, this observation distorts the nature of expansionism by omitting the global aspects of that expansionist process, whose tentacles had begun reaching to the far corners of the globe almost from the start of the republic. American expansionism, far from being confined to the territories of North America, is best conceived of as proceeding across a variety of opportunity frontiers – some landed, some watery, but all of them in pursuit of gain, be it found in lush fields of grain, nuggets of gold, bolts of silk, the carcasses of whales, or the harvesting of souls. Americans expanded for all of these reasons, but in almost every case, they carried with them an ideology of progress and civilization and an unshakable sense of themselves and their civilization as the cutting edge of human endeavor. More than a mere "westward movement," it was a globalized expansionist process. The capitalist imperative for profit that lured Americans to the Ohio Country in the 1750s also took them to Hawaii, China, and beyond.

The brave, ambitious – and, at times, rapacious – merchants and mariners who put their lives and fortunes on the line in pursuit of their dreams served as the primary agents of the American market empire. Although the movement of American pioneers across North American frontier has long been celebrated – Frederick Jackson Turner thought that movement the key to understanding all of American history – it must be recalled that Americans demonstrated themselves to be even more capable on the sea than on the land. During the first half of the nineteenth century, the United States reigned as the leading commercial carrier in the world. Americans built the best and fastest vessels, commanded by the most daring and able commanders, and staffed by the most experienced crews. By the 1840s, the United States boasted a fleet of ten thousand vessels and an estimated 180,000 merchant sailors.

Much as Thomas Paine had envisioned in "Common Sense," this sea-going arm of the empire had an enormous impact on world commerce, reaching virtually everywhere there were profits to be made. It made the United States a formidable presence in the markets of the world.

The high profile of American merchants and mariners in the emerging global marketplace encouraged the rise of an American empire of the seas, a regime of law and practice modeled on American norms and designed to make the world's oceans into highways on which safe travel might be assured. From the start, American prosperity had hinged on making the oceans safe for commerce; both the Barbary Wars and the War of 1812 had been fought to defend that principle. Indeed, the myth of nineteenth-century America as an isolationist hermit kingdom concerned only with domestic affairs fails to take into account the extent to which the nation's integration into the world economy made the oceans an extension of American territory. Americans not only sailed on the world's oceans but also presumed to order them in the name of their idea of civilization, and they were willing to commit both their diplomatic and their naval power to defend those principles. As was the case with land acquisitions, Americans sought to explore, survey, map, and bring American notions of law and order to the global commons that is the world's oceans.

The creation of an American empire of commerce depended upon the creation of an American empire of the seas. Americans aimed not only to trade with foreign states but also to redefine the terms of commercial intercourse. Americans sought to open the markets of the world to trade, although not in order to push for "free trade" in the modern sense. The negotiation of commercial reciprocity treaties with foreign states functioned as the main tool to open markets available to American presidents; the Monroe, Adams, and Jackson administrations made particular use of it. The national government also made a sustained and ultimately successful effort to reopen the valuable British West Indies trade to American shipping. Closed at the time of the War of Independence and reopened only partially by the Jay Treaty, this trade was fully regained by Americans only in 1830.

In the mid-nineteenth century, William Henry Seward stood out as the greatest advocate of an American empire of the seas. Seward, a protégé of John Quincy Adams, noted abolitionist, and secretary of state under Lincoln and Grant, distinguished himself as an early and outspoken proponent of an American oceanic empire. His first speech to Congress as a U.S. senator reflected this sentiment: Marveling at the good fortune that placed the United States bestride North America, a sort of keystone arch between East and West, Seward concluded, "[T]he nation thus situated ... if endowed also with moral energies adequate to the achievement of great enterprises ... must command the empire of the seas, which alone is real empire."[8] Forty years before Alfred Thayer Mahan argued for the necessity of an enhanced American commercial empire backed up by naval might, Seward envisioned a rapidly expanding American market empire supported by timely and appropriate support by the national government.

THE WHALING FRONTIER

If the search for wealth drove overseas expansionism, the American whaling industry functioned as the tip of the spear of this process. Domination of this extractive industry represented another way Americans made their presence felt in the first half of the nineteenth century. Jay Dolin observes that even though it is little remembered today, of all the nations "none has a more fascinating whaling history than does the United States.... American whale oil lit the world."[9] Whales had been hunted for centuries to supply the wants of local populations. But the emergence of a global market for whale products necessitated an ongoing search for new fertile fishing grounds as traditional sources of supply were depleted. Sperm whales in particular were valued for the spermaceti – hundreds of gallons of it – contained in their skull casings. This gooey white substance had a variety of uses, being employed to make exceptionally clean-burning candles as well as functioning as a critical lubricant for industrial machinery before the advent of petroleum. Whalebone, the plastic of its time, was utilized to make implements of all sorts, most famously perhaps the hoops in the ubiquitous hoop skirts of the nineteenth century. Secretions in the whale's intestines made ambergris, a substance prized as the only fixative for perfume scents available before the invention of synthetic fixatives in the twentieth century. So rare and so valuable as to be worth more per

[8] Richard H. Immerman, *Empire for Liberty: A History of American Imperialism from Benjamin Franklin to Paul Wolfowitz* (Princeton, 2010), 108.
[9] Jay Dolin, *Leviathan: The History of American Whaling* (New York, 2007), 11, 12.

ounce than gold, ambergris reinforced the analogy of the whale hunt as a sort of watery gold rush.

American whaling reached the peak of its profitability in the 1850s, before new sources of lamp oil and the Civil War decimated the fleet. In the 1840s, more than seven hundred American whale ships sailed the seas, comprising roughly 80 percent of the world's total. Thousands of sailors staffed this impressive fleet, which killed whales in every ocean in the world. By the early to mid-nineteenth century, however, the not yet fully discovered Pacific and Southern Oceans yielded most of the catch. The exploits of the whalers provided valuable new knowledge about the world's oceans. Analogous to the fur traders, whalers roamed the high seas, explored distant lands, charted unknown waters, and went places no American (or in some cases, no person) had ever gone in pursuit of fertile hunting grounds. Whalers had been among the first Americans to visit the Hermit Kingdom of Japan and had provided Commodore Perry with valuable intelligence that he used on his mission to "open" Japan to the world. The whaling industry had been centered in colonial days on Nantucket Island off the coast of Massachusetts, but by the 1820s it had moved to New Bedford, Massachusetts.

The modern sailing vessels that comprised the whaling fleet employed the most traditional methods in hunting their prey. They relied on stalking the whale from a small boat, hooking it with a harpoon and rope, and then holding on for dear life until the whale expired from exhaustion. Laboriously rowing back to the mother ship, the crews hauled the carcass up alongside the boat, where its blubbery skin was peeled from its body and its skeleton scavenged for bone. A giant pot called the "try works" was then used to cook the blubber down to yield a fine oil, perfect for lamps or for lubricants. A dangerous and frequently cruel business, whaling remained mostly hidden from public view. Yet by the 1850s it had become the third-leading American industry by value, trailing only textiles and shoemaking.

The allure and adventure of a life at sea inspired young Americans as much as did the appeal of western lands. It launched the career of one of the nation's most noted authors, Herman Melville. Restless and lacking any immediate prospects for advancement, at age twenty-one Melville left his native New York in 1840 for the adventure of a two-year whaling voyage on the *Acushnet* out of New Bedford. Finding the harshness of shipboard life unbearable, Melville deserted, spending a few weeks on the island of Nuka Hiva in the Marquesas group, the same island that briefly had been annexed to the United States in 1813 by Commodore David Porter at the command of the USS *Essex*. The Madison administration quickly disavowed this first example in U.S. history of the annexation of noncontiguous territory. Now Nuka Hiva would be colonized in a literary sense, as the place where one of America's greatest novelists and interpreters would have his most formative experience, an encounter with a different type of freedom by a man from the land of the free. Melville's brief idyll of sexual and psychological liberation on Nuka Hiva left him saddened by the damage being wrought on Pacific Islanders by the Euro-American invasion, especially by the missionaries. This fostered in him the ambivalence about the Euro-American way of life that is reflected in much of his writing. Enlisting on board an American naval vessel as a means to return to the United States, he proceeded to write two novels of his adventures – *Typee* and *Omoo* – both of which sold well and did much to form the initial impression of the Pacific world and its people in the popular mind. In 1851, Melville published a more ambitious work, *Moby-Dick, or the Whale*. Unlike his earlier works, *Moby-Dick* did not sell well upon release – only about five hundred copies – and endured harsh reviews by critics who lacked an appreciation for Melville's ironic tale of Manifest Destiny and its contradictions set on the watery stage of the high seas. Melville centers the action on the whale ship the *Pequod* (named for the Indian tribe nearly exterminated by the Puritans in the seventeenth century), manned by a multiracial, multicultural crew commanded by white officers, a sort of floating plantation extracting wealth from the sea ruled by the imperious Captain Ahab. The *Pequod*'s three harpooners – and therefore the most important members of the hunt – are Polynesian, African, and Native American, whose traditional hunting skills are now being harnessed to the needs of the modern American mercantile empire. *Moby-Dick* is primarily a parable of Manifest Destiny afloat; its catastrophic ending is a foreshadowing of the disaster awaiting a civilization whose people will acknowledge no limit to their acquisitiveness.

THE MISSIONARY FRONTIER

Protestant missionaries loomed nearly as important as the whalers in the discovery and exploration of the Pacific Ocean's vast spaces.

These self-styled "fishers of men" spread, like the whalers, to the far reaches of the world (including the far reaches of North America) in an effort to spread the word of God, save the heathen from Hell, and revitalize Christianity at home. The origin of the American missionary movement is to be found in a prophetic vision experienced by a Massachusetts college student to spread the gospel to the world. This led in 1810 to the formation of the American Board of Commissioners for Foreign Missions (ABCFM), which became the vehicle for sending the first wave of missionaries abroad. Soon the Baptists became the first of many Christian sects to send their followers to foreign lands to do God's work. A major part of the nation's redemptionist mission, missionaries functioned as the spiritual tip of the American spear in much the same way that whalers served as the economic tip. Hundreds of dedicated and determined young men and women went forth to spread the Good News of Christ and American progress to a presumably benighted world. The certainty of their righteousness matched the intensity of their commitment. For the most part, American missionaries suffered none of the modern doubts regarding the virtues of progress or the superiority of Christianity over other faiths. They combined evangelical neo-Puritan Christianity with American nationalism in one neat package, and they spread it with a dedication and glad-heartedness reflected in their letters and diary entries.

American missionaries made their presence felt throughout the Pacific, although their actual success in propagating Christianity proved limited. China proved to be especially disappointing in this regard, where very few embraced the preaching of the gospel and most ignored it. Perhaps the most enduring impact of Christianity on China was via the personage of Hung Hsiu-chu'an, who for a time had studied under an American missionary and found inspiration in the idea of Jesus as a prophet of the oppressed. In 1851, Hung began to have visions of a peasant uprising to overthrow the Manchu dynasty. What became known as the Tai-Ping Rebellion stands as one of the greatest disasters in Chinese history, costing an estimated twenty million lives before finally being suppressed in the 1860s. It contributed immeasurably to the slide of China into anarchy and warlordism that would plague it for decades. The Western powers, at first sympathetic to a movement they hoped would further open China to them, soon came to fear the violence and anarchy of the revolt as a threat to commerce. The American commissioner Humphrey Marshall, rightly or wrongly, believed the British sought to weaken the Manchus in the name of colonizing China and took steps to support the emperor if only to assure continued U.S. commercial access. Thus was born the idea of America as China's "special friend," shielding it from the exploitative aims of Britain, Russia, and France.[10]

THE AMERICANIZATION OF HAWAII

One place American missionaries did enjoy conspicuous success was in Hawaii. Americans missionaries and whalers came together to secure the Hawaiian Islands as an American outpost. The Hawaiian archipelago had become known to the world only in the 1770s, thanks to the voyages of Captain James Cook of Great Britain. American whalers had been visiting the islands since the 1790s, eventually establishing Lahaina on the island of Maui as the center of the American Pacific whaling enterprise. However, the turning point occurred in 1819, when the first wave of American missionaries arrived in Hawaii led by Congregationalist minister Hiram Bingham. The missionaries soon established themselves in the role of protectors of the Hawaiians, including from the depredations of whalers on shore leave. The raucous and randy crews arrived ashore with money in their pockets and debauchery in their heads, and they devastated the remnants of the traditional Hawaiian culture that they encountered. One American missionary commented on how shore liberty became synonymous with licentiousness, to the catastrophe of native culture: "[T]he whole nation is rotten with licentiousness. Men hire out their wives & daughters without the least scruple."[11]

American missionaries made themselves trusted advisers of the Hawaiian royalty even as their primary loyalty remained to the United States and all it represented. The soft sell approach of the Americans proved decisive in edging out the British for control of the islands. The neo-Calvinist missionaries became some of the most artful agents of American empire, posing as special friends and mentors in the Hawaiians' quest for independence against a backdrop of their sudden integration into the developing world system after a thousand years

[10] See Warren Cohen, *America's Response to China* (New York, 1990), 18–20.
[11] Bradford Smith, *Yankees in Paradise* (Philadelphia, 1956), 280.

of near isolation. Especially noteworthy in this regard was the work of William Richards, a missionary who proved quite adept at skirting the boundaries of religious and secular, Hawaiian and American. Edward Crapol writes, "This loosely knit contingent of missionaries and merchants demonstrated the potency of non-state actors in antebellum American foreign relations."[12]

The American missionary community precipitated the circumstances leading to the establishment in 1842 of the de facto protectorate over the islands known as the Tyler Doctrine. Fears that France aimed to seize Hawaii for itself prompted this audacious extension of the Monroe Doctrine. The French threat arose in large part owing to the actions of the American missionaries, who in 1839 had urged King Kamehameha III to forbid the practice of Catholicism on the islands and stop further entry by priests. In response to this provocation, French warships on the scene blockaded Honolulu and threatened bombardment, ultimately compelling the king to sign a treaty protecting the Catholic faith and the rights of its French practitioners on the islands, as well as gaining favorable tariff treatment for French imports.

American missionaries sounded the alarm, petitioning both Congress and the Van Buren administration for help, but to no avail. When the avid expansionist John Tyler acceded to the presidency after the early death of William Henry Harrison, the American Board of Commissioners sent the Reverend Hiram Bingham to Washington to plead for protection of both Hawaii and the missionaries. Among the most respected members of the missionaries in Hawaii, Bingham gained personal audiences with both Secretary of State Daniel Webster and President Tyler to detail the threat posed to Hawaii by French and British incursions. Highlighting the threat posed by the British proved especially useful in getting government action, be the territory in question Hawaii or Texas. Webster was especially concerned about the threat to American missionaries in far-off lands, and he affirmed in 1842 that "[t]he United States ... are more interested in the fate of the islands and of their government than any other nation can be" and therefore demanded "that the Government of the Sandwich Islands ought to be respected; that no power ought either to take possession of the island as a conquest, or for the purpose of colonization, and that no power ought to seek for any undue control

[12] Edward P. Crapol, *John Tyler: The Accidental President* (Chapel Hill, 2006), 136.

of the existing Government, or any exclusive privileges in matters of commerce."[13] A follow-up mission in 1842 sent by King Kamehameha III – a mission consisting of an esteemed prince, Timoteo Haalilio, and American missionary and royal confidant William Richards – aimed to secure diplomatic recognition and a commercial treaty with the United States. Haalilio's dark skin made the Tyler administration reluctant to engage him publicly for fear of setting what it saw as the bad precedent of negotiating with black diplomats. Nevertheless, the lobbying of John Quincy Adams and others, combined with the tacit threat that if the United States did not lend its support then the Hawaiians would seek the protection of the British, ultimately prompted Tyler to act. In the end, the fear of British encroachment on the islands trumped Tyler's reluctance to receive a dark-skinned diplomat.

President Tyler, building on Webster's earlier statement, clarified the U.S. position on Hawaii in a special message to Congress in 1842. The mood was paternalistic: "Just emerging from a state of barbarism, the Government of the islands is as yet feeble, but its dispositions appear to be just and pacific." However, with 80 percent or more of the vessels visiting Hawaii being American, and given the strategic importance of the islands and the recent annexation of Tahiti by the French and New Zealand by the British, Tyler did not waffle. Claiming that the United States "seeks ... no peculiar advantages, no exclusive control over the Hawaiian government, but is content with its independent existence and anxiously wishes for its security and prosperity," Tyler warned other nations not to attempt to compromise its autonomy. Those who challenged this policy would face "a decided remonstrance."[14] In 1849, Secretary of State John Clayton echoed the determination to maintain a firm foothold on Hawaii: "The U.S. do [sic] not want the islands, but will not permit any other nation to have them."[15] From this affirmation of doctrine, application soon followed. In the 1840s and 1850s, the U.S. presence proliferated. At the urging of his American advisers, between 1845 and 1855 King Kamehameha III initiated the Mahele, converting the informal land tenure practices of Hawaii into the Anglo-American system of recorded fee simple holdings. Now foreign investors could feel secure about their investments. The result was that by the 1860s,

---

[13] Crapol, *John Tyler*, 153.

[14] Richardson, ed., *Messages and Papers of the Presidents*, 4:212.

[15] William Earl Weeks, *Building the Continental Empire* (Chicago, 1996), 68.

Americans owned much of the best agricultural lands, devoting them to plantation-style sugar cultivation for the mainland market. Long before Hawaii was formally annexed in 1898, it had been Americanized and brought into the U.S. sphere.

NATIONAL SUPPORT FOR COMMERCIAL EXPANSION

The national government gave critical assistance to the American commercial penetration of the Asia-Pacific world. Although the federal government was given explicit control of foreign affairs by the Constitution, the limits of its foreign policy power remained uncertain for decades. No one disputed the government's power to declare war and to make treaties, including commercial agreements, with other states. But how much of a role should Washington play in defending the personal interests of Americans abroad? Daniel Webster's guarantee of the safety of American missionaries, little noticed at the time, represented a significant expansion of national authority. Yet even under the Articles of Confederation, the central government took it upon itself to defend the rights of Americans abroad. This included efforts to recover private claims against foreign states for ship seizures and its ongoing campaign to garner compensation for slaves liberated by British forces in both the War of Independence and the War of 1812. From there it came to seem natural that Americans abroad might expect the support of their government in controversies with foreign states. This at times included the naval bombardment of locales deemed to have violated the rights of Americans, as occurred in the Sumatran town of Quallah Battoo in 1832. American naval commander Charles Wilkes, recognizing its importance to national prosperity, deemed whaling so important as to merit federal support. Insofar as the benefits of whaling "are spread through the whole union" it followed that it "would seem to recommend it to the especial protection and fostering care of the government."[16]

The systematic exploration and mapping of the still mostly uncharted waters of the Pacific Ocean are other ways in which the national government played a crucial role in fostering overseas commerce. Seemingly outside the limits of appropriate action by the national government,

[16] Herman J. Viola and Carolyn Margolis, eds., *Magnificent Voyagers: The U.S. Exploring Expedition, 1838–1842* (Washington, D.C., 1985), 141.

exploration and mapping actually should be viewed as the logical extension of the principle of commerce and exploration that motivated Jefferson to dispatch the Lewis and Clark Expedition in 1804. The federal role in exploration and mapping the great white spaces on the map is mostly forgotten today. Yet, contrary to the myth of a minimalist national government in the decades before the Civil War, both the army and the navy endeavored to map and explore the unknown places of the earth, be they in the Pacific, the Amazon Basin, Paraguay, or western North America.

The United States Exploring Expedition of 1838–42, commonly known as the Wilkes Expedition, was the most significant exploration of the Pacific Ocean. The initial push for a federal role in the exploration of the Pacific was, as in the case of Lewis and Clark, in part scientific and in part economic. The scientific part concerned an effort to confirm or deny the so-called holes in the poles theory of John Cleve Symmes of New Jersey. In 1818, Symmes hypothesized the existence of giant holes at the northern and southern poles, providing entry into the interior of the earth. Crackpot as it sounds today, Symmes's theory could not be rejected out of hand because of the minimal exploration to that time of the far southern and northern hemispheres. The economic push came from New England whaling interests, who wanted a systematic investigation of the Pacific to complement the informal voyages of exploration in search of the next big catch that marked the whaling industry. In 1828 the citizens of Nantucket petitioned Congress for an expedition to "explore and survey the islands and coasts of the Pacific seas" to better support the whaling industry and its investors.[17]

The U.S. Exploring Expedition proved to be one of the last and most successful of the Euro-American voyages of discovery, exploration, and mapping of the Pacific Ocean and Antarctica that occurred in the nineteenth century. Comprised of six ships and nearly 1,700 explorers, it also stands as one of the largest. Congressional penny-pinching and an inability to find competent leadership delayed its departure for ten years. Led by Charles Wilkes, a thirty-eight-year-old junior officer who lucked into the command owing to a lack of alternatives, the U.S. Ex Ex, as it became known, ran aground in controversy and was overshadowed by domestic politics when it returned home in 1842. Much of the

---

[17] Dolin, *Leviathan*, 140.

controversy centered on the conduct of the irascible Wilkes, who commanded it with an iron hand, so much so as to engender near mutinies of his crew. Unlike the leaders of the Lewis and Clark Expedition, known for their wise and humane leadership, Wilkes was dictatorial and cruel, leaving his crew members perpetually on the verge of revolt. In place of the spirit of friendliness and cooperation with Native Americans characteristic of Lewis and Clark, the Wilkes Expedition engaged in numerous incidents of hostility and violence with local tribes and, in at least one case, a massacre.

Although his instructions urged amicable ties with any peoples they met, Wilkes at times resorted to violence to punish and intimidate local residents. He also presumed to enforce American notions of justice wherever that appeared necessary. These two motives came together on the island of Fiji. Wilkes's investigation of the murder of ten American merchant seaman in 1834 resulted in the arrest of a Fijian man named Vendovi, who was to be taken back to the United States to stand trial for his alleged crimes. As one of Wilkes's officers later wrote, the Americans hoped to show the natives that "[t]o kill a white man was the very worst thing a Feegee man could do."[18] Imprisoned on board ship for two years, Vendovi died soon after the expedition's return to New York. Wilkes also dispensed swifter and more violent forms of justice. Shortly after Vendovi's arrest, a group of Fijians attacked a small party Wilkes had sent ashore to barter for food. The brief skirmish resulted in the deaths of two officers, one of whom was Wilkes's nephew. In retaliation, Wilkes attacked the small island where the assault occurred, leveling its two main towns and killing an estimated eighty Fijians.

The extent of Wilkes's achievement, however, astounds even today. He charted the hazardous shoals at the mouth of the Columbia River and eight hundred miles of the Northwest Coast. He claimed to be the first to sight the Antarctic continent and surveyed and charted fifteen hundred miles of its coastline with remarkable accuracy, along a region that still bears his name – Wilkes Land. He drew more than 180 maps and charts of what was still a mostly uncharted Pacific Ocean. These charts became the foundation of American knowledge of the Pacific Ocean; his map of Tarawa Atoll guided the marines' amphibious assault there in World War II. The precedent of oceanic exploration and

---

[18] Viola and Margolis, eds., *Magnificent Voyagers*, 20.

investigation set by the Wilkes Expedition ultimately led to the creation of the U.S. Hydrographic Office in 1871. Wilkes and his crew brought back tens of thousands of specimens of flora and fauna that became the basis of the new Smithsonian Museum collection. Ironically Vendovi's skull and later his death mask became a part of that collection.

CHINA

From the time of Columbus, access to the China trade had been the ultimate desire of the Western commercial world. "Westward the course of Empire takes it way" went the well-known stanza by Bishop Berkeley, and China represented the ultimate destination of that westward movement. For centuries Europeans, especially the English, French, Spanish, Portuguese, and Russians, had sought access to the spices, silks, porcelains, and teas of the Celestial Empire. All of them went to the East as supplicants, for an intense racism and a sense of cultural superiority led the Chinese to view all non-Chinese as barbarians or, in the case of Europeans, "foul-smelling, hairy barbarians." Foreigners would be given the privilege of trading with China, but only on terms of superior to inferior.

American interest in China, though predating the War of Independence, escalated in 1784 when the merchant ship *Empress of China,* sailing out of Boston, returned home with goods worth at least twice the value of those it departed with. From that time on, accessing China's wealth became the ultimate goal of American commerce; the tangible profits and seemingly limitless potential of the Chinese market fired the imaginations of well-connected individuals, including John Jacob Astor, Thomas H. Perkins, and John P. Cushing. By 1819 American trade with China ranked second only to that of Great Britain.

The U.S. advance into the Asia-Pacific world comprised only part of a larger European invasion into the region, a process greatly facilitated by the very same revolutions in transportation, communication, and military might that had transformed the internal development of those states. Since the 1500s, Europeans had been trading by sea with China, but on humiliating terms. The protocols of Manchu China required visitors to perform nine prostrations before the imperial throne, a humiliating ritual known as the kowtow, as a precondition for communication of any kind. Cultural ethnocentrism does not entirely explain Chinese assumptions of Western barbarism. The Chinese (like the Hawaiians) directly experienced that barbarism in the form of the drunken, riotous activities of Western sailors on shore leave. Their frequent rampages left violence, destruction, and jurisdictional issues in their wake. A notable example occurred in the Terranova case of 1821. Francis Terranova, an American merchant sailor of Italian origin, was arrested by Chinese authorities and, based on dubious evidence, charged with the murder of a Chinese woman. Although in theory Western traders acknowledged the right of the Chinese to pursue lawbreakers on their soil, in practice, Chinese notions of justice, evidence, and culpability often clashed with Euro-American traditions. In Terranova's case, the American merchant community, notwithstanding its concerns about his innocence, acquiesced in the man's arrest. To the horror of this community, the Chinese tried Terranova in secret and executed him by strangulation. The case of Terranova and others like it made Westerners reluctant to allow their nationals to be prosecuted in Chinese courts.

Finding a suitable item to trade other than the silver traditionally favored by the Chinese constituted the biggest difficulty in the development of trade with China. Although a few trade items experienced temporary success in the early nineteenth century, including furs, sandalwood, and ginseng, the emergence in the late eighteenth century of opium as a trade good revolutionized commercial ties. Within a very few years, merchants from both Europe and the United States began importing large quantities of the drug, although Americans tended to deny involvement in the trade. As a high-demand, high-value, easily transported commodity, opium was soon relied on heavily as a medium of exchange by Western merchants. The opium trade built numerous American fortunes, including that of Warren Delano, Franklin D. Roosevelt's maternal grandfather.[19]

The flood of opium into China proved enormously destructive to the social fabric of that nation. In spite of the obvious moral implications of continuing the trade, the Western empires resisted efforts to end its use. When public pressure led to nominal restrictions on the import of what was termed "foreign mud" they went mostly ignored, both by the Western nations and by the Chinese merchants who bribed port officials to allow the trade to continue. When the Qing dynasty attempted

[19] Crapol, *John Tyler*, 132.

to force Great Britain to suspend the noxious trade, London dispatched an expeditionary force of twenty-five warships and 10,000 troops to challenge the authority of the Chinese government. What became known, appropriately enough, as the Opium Wars of 1839–42 resulted in the imposition by Britain of the Treaty of Nanking, which for the first time opened ports other than Canton to foreign trade, set tariff rates on imported Western goods, eased restrictions on travel on the mainland, and, crucially, established the principle of extraterritoriality, whereby Westerners would not be subject to Chinese law. It represented a major turning point in world history, in that what had been the mightiest power in the world for centuries now found itself hostage to the firepower of faraway states and subject to increasing discontent domestically. The defeat of China by a handful of Western warships marked the beginning of what would be known as the "century of humiliation." China was drugged, bombarded, and ultimately rendered subservient to the Western powers.

Some Americans watched with great interest unfolding events in China. Although many condemned the attempt to force China to allow the importation of opium, others saw the matter in a broader context. To John Quincy Adams, the conflict was rooted in China's refusal to trade on terms of equality: He wrote in 1842, "[T]he cause of the war is the kow-tow, the arrogant pretension of the Chinese to cultural superiority." Adams saw commerce as "among the natural rights and duties of mankind," obligatory to all peoples. Nations might define the terms of their trade, but they must engage with the markets of the world. The refusal to do so Adams deemed as "churlish" and deserving of harsh rebuke. For Americans the ideology of commerce functioned as an extension of the natural rights doctrine at the heart of their global revolution. Adams therefore welcomed the chastisement of what he saw as Chinese arrogance by British firepower during the Opium Wars.

Americans did not stand idly by as these developments took place in China. A select group of merchants, missionaries, and whalers whose wealth and political connections made up in influence what it lacked in numbers had already been lobbying for action. In 1839, Dr. Peter Parker, a missionary and surgeon schooled at Yale, urged Secretary of State Webster to conceive of the United States as China's "special friend" and protector from the rapacious practices of the other Western powers. The decisive opening of the China market in the early 1840s happened to occur at a moment when the White House was occupied by a president disposed to gain advantages from the situation. John Tyler, who earlier had worked to secure the Hawaiian Islands in the American orbit, now acted to secure American rights in the new trade regime in China. Tyler feared that if Americans did not gain formal access to the China trade they might find themselves excluded by European imperial powers, each of which now looked to expand its access to China. Accordingly, in the same message in which he affirmed a de facto protectorate over Hawaii, Tyler called for Congress to allocate funds to send a minister to China to represent American interests and possibly secure a formal commercial treaty, an emissary "ready ... to address himself to the high functionaries of the Empire, or through them to the Emperor himself."[20]

After the much-admired Edward Everett turned the job down, Tyler turned to Caleb Cushing of Massachusetts. Cushing came from a prominent New England commercial family. His father, John P. Cushing, had been among the first Americans to get rich from the trade with China, and the elder Cushing impressed upon his son the utter necessity of expanding American trade relations throughout Asia. Caleb Cushing, recognized as one of the most well-read and erudite Americans of his era, eagerly embraced the mission as a means of enhancing his own stature and opening once and for all a potential market of 300 million people. After an initial period of awkward uncertainty as to whether he would be received by Chinese authorities, Cushing negotiated the landmark Treaty of Wanghia in 1844. Building on the British agreement, it secured five treaty ports for U.S. merchants, allowed the United States to set tariff rates for bilateral trade, and, most importantly, codified the principle of extraterritoriality for U.S. citizens in China. Americans, while they cultivated an image of themselves as China's special friend, nonetheless took full advantage of what British firepower had gained in China. Contending with the British in many areas of the world – including, at that time, Texas – in China Americans rode on the coattails of the British Empire.

OPENING JAPAN

With the rising importance of the China trade and the rapid advance of Britain, France, and Russia in acquiring control of strategic Pacific

[20] Crapol, *John Tyler,* 214.

Island groups, it is small wonder that, by the mid-1840s, opening Japan to the trade of the world became an important goal for some Americans. Characterized by Melville as the "double-bolted land," Japan had been almost entirely closed to foreign vessels and traders since 1638, when the Tokugawa shogunate cut off contact with the outside world in the name of preventing invasion. Since that time only the Dutch had been allowed direct access to Japan, being limited to one ship per year landing at the port of Nagasaki. That one yearly contact had the purpose of allowing the Japanese to learn about the outside world via the medium of the Dutch. All others who dared land on Japanese shores, including shipwrecked sailors, faced torture, imprisonment, or death. The imprisonment and abuse of American shipwrecked sailors from the whaler *Lagoda* by Japanese authorities inflamed public opinion and proved to be important in building support for an expedition to compel Japan's humane treatment of future castaways upon its shores.

Edmund Roberts, who in an official capacity went on two extended trips to Southeast Asia in the 1830s, has the distinction of being the first American to plan a mission to Japan. On his second mission, after having established relations with Thailand and what would become Vietnam, Roberts planned to journey to Japan and seek to open its trade to the world. But he contracted malaria and died before he could get there. In 1845, Commodore James Biddle sailed three American frigates into Edo (Tokyo) Bay, only to withdraw in the face of signs of imminent Japanese resistance. In 1847, the Japanese made a guest of Ranald Macdonald, an adventurer of highland Scot and Chinook Indian ancestry, who purposely beached his small boat on Japan's shores. His story did much to publicize the still-mysterious land.

However, Commodore Matthew C. "Old Bruin" Perry is the true motive force behind both the expedition to open Japan and the strategic vision that informed it. Brother of Oliver Hazard Perry (a naval hero of the Battle of Lake Erie during the War of 1812), Old Bruin had served the nation for forty years when he began to push for a large naval expedition to open Japan to the world. Perry aimed to beat the other European imperial powers to the punch on what seemed to be the next target for expansion of Western influence. However, Perry also saw access to Japan as part of a larger geopolitical strategy designed favorably to position the United States in an emerging global marketplace increasingly driven by coal-powered ships. Wilkes's explorations of the Northern Pacific had greatly enhanced the understanding of the geography of the region, and in 1847 Captain Matthew C. Maury (himself an explorer and surveyor of considerable achievement) sketched on a globe for Perry the Great Circle Route to Asia and the economies in distance it represented. This novel geographic insight offered the chance to cut in half the time required to voyage to Shanghai, potentially giving American commerce a tremendous advantage compared to their main rivals, the British. Running along the North Pacific from San Francisco to China, the Great Circle Route contained the island of Japan as a key stopping point, especially as a place to establish the coaling stations critical to the projection of naval power in the decades ahead.

Perry harbored no doubts as to the direction U.S. policymakers needed to go: "It is self-evident that the course of the events will ere long make it necessary for the United States to extend its territorial jurisdiction beyond the limits of the western continent, and I assume responsibility of urging the expediency of establishing a foothold in this quarter of the globe, as a measure of positive necessity to the sustainment of our maritime rights in the east." American leaders seized on the Japanese practice of brutalizing shipwrecked whaling crews in the name of maintaining the country's isolation as a wedge to legitimate their forcible entry into Japan. Yet as Perry urged Secretary of the Navy William Graham, "The real object of the expedition should be concealed from public view."[21]

Perry's impressive flotilla included four new steam-powered vessels nicknamed the Black Ships, whose belching smoke and tremendous firepower cowed the Japanese without firing a shot. Under the pretext of being required personally to deliver a letter to the Japanese emperor, on March 8, 1854, Perry landed the fleet at Yokohama with the actual mission of compelling Japan to open its doors to shipwrecked sailors and its markets to foreigners. Perry presented as gifts to his reluctant hosts an illustrated history of the Mexican War and scale models of a railroad and the telegraph, iconic technological symbols of the land he represented. After several weeks of intense negotiations, the Treaty of Kanagawa of March 31, 1854, designated Shimoda and Hakodadi as open ports where Americans could take on coal, water, and other

---

[21] Peter Booth Wiley, *Yankees in the Lands of the Gods: Commodore Perry and the Opening of Japan* (New York, 1990), 348, 72.

provisions. The agreement also allowed Americans to trade with Japan on a most-favored-nation basis and obligated the Japanese to assist shipwrecked sailors. Four years later, in 1858, American merchant and diplomat Townsend Harris signed a pact opening four more ports for trade, formally establishing Japanese-American diplomatic ties, providing for a fixed tariff regime, and introducing the principle of extraterritoriality. European states soon followed the American lead, and Japan was irrevocably opened to the world.

SIGNIFICANCE OF THE AMERICAN PACIFIC

Perry's historic mission to Japan met with little acclaim when he returned to the United States, overshadowed by the controversy engendered by the Kansas-Nebraska Act and the apathy of the Pierce administration, which proved to be unwilling to celebrate the achievement of a mission begun by the Whig president Millard Fillmore. Nevertheless, all of this American activity – commercial, extractive, exploratory, diplomatic, and naval – created a significant U.S. presence and interest in the Pacific. This interest then acted to influence the course of continental expansion by making the ports of California – San Francisco, San Diego, and Monterey – of much greater importance much sooner than they otherwise would have become. California, little known to most of the American public, by the mid-1840s had assumed a role of great strategic importance – more for its connections to and from Asia than as a destination for Americans traveling west. The discovery of gold in northern California in 1848 greatly accelerated the process of the creation of a trans-Pacific migratory and commercial community, but the vision of this possibility had predated the strike. From this perspective California, rather than the end point of the expansionist process, is better understood as a hinge on which a door swung that opened both westward toward Asia and the Pacific and eastward toward the rest of the country. By 1850, no nation in the world stood better positioned for future dominance than the United States.

6

EXPANSIONIST VISTAS

Canada, Oregon, California, and Texas

The present golden moment to obtain Texas must not be lost, or Texas might from necessity be thrown into the arms of England and forever lost to the United States.

President John Tyler, quoting Andrew Jackson, 1844

The rapidity and scale of expansion of the American federation during the first half of the nineteenth century were, and remain, unprecedented in world political history.

D. W. Meinig, *The Shaping of America: Continental America, 1800–1867*, 458

WHEN THE EAGLE SCREAMED

Antebellum American expansionism encompassed nearly the entire globe, influencing the course of continental expansionism by introducing global concerns into North American territorial questions. Americans pushed into the Atlantic, into the Mediterranean, and into Asia and the Pacific, and all of these expansionist impulses conditioned continental ambitions, especially in the case of California, whose capacious harbors at San Francisco, Monterey, and San Diego first became desirable as West Coast access points to America's burgeoning Pacific presence. The growth of the imperial republic during this period is best understood as an undifferentiated process that occurred on the world's oceans and islands as well as its continents and was commercial, oceanic, and ideological as much as it was territorial. The decentralized, popular, market-driven nature of this expansionist dynamic made it a much more effective engine of empire than some of the European empires of the age, whose tendency to overcentralize the command, control, and direction of their imperial program insufficiently relied on the ambitions and genius of the people, particularly the entrepreneurial class, as the prime movers of empire. The absence of an overarching imperial blueprint at the national level even as the central government provided essential support to the expansionist project rendered the American Empire superior to its European counterparts, as evidenced by the U.S. record of unrivaled imperial growth in the nineteenth century.

Even as Americans freed the seas and opened Japan to the world, they continued to expand the limits of their North American continental empire. From 1820 to 1860, Americans – diplomats and merchants, soldiers and missionaries, farmers and slave masters – pushed against the British presence in Canada and the Mexican presence in the Southwest to find out where their seemingly unstoppable expansionist momentum might be checked. At the same time, all across the imperial frontier the American Empire confronted the traditional obstacle of dozens of Native American tribes, who posed a major military, legal, and moral roadblock to expansionism. In essence, the imperial struggle to control North America that first had called forth the idea of the North American Union in the 1750s continued in the second quarter of the nineteenth century, except that France had dropped out of the imperial struggle and Spain had been replaced by the newly independent Republic of Mexico in 1821. The long line of expansionist thrusts whereby the United States had pushed halfway across North America had only created new contact points for expansionist pressures to create imperial controversies.

CANADA

In spite of the expansionist success of the United States, many Americans retained a sense of being boxed in by other imperial powers. To the north, the British Empire loomed and the boundary with British-ruled Canada remained ill defined. Although the Convention of 1818 had established the forty-ninth parallel as the boundary across the great expanse from the Lake of the Woods to the Rockies, both the northwestern and the northeastern limits were ambiguous. Against this backdrop of diplomatic uncertainty, cross-border efforts to revolutionize Upper Canada threatened to bring the two states to blows. In 1837 a failed uprising against British rule in Canada just across the border from Buffalo, New York, spilled over into the United States when some Americans began to aid the rebellious Canadians. The old dream of the conquest of Canada refused to die; locals began to enlist in the rebel cause, provide the fighters with supplies, and even arm them with weapons from American arsenals, as the few federal officials on the scene watched helplessly. The sinking of the American steamer *Caroline* on the U.S. side of the Niagara River by British troops for allegedly resupplying the rebels so inflamed passions that a war did seem a distinct possibility, at least to those caught up in the excitement of the moment. The big picture, as seen by the administration of Martin Van Buren, was that however outrageous these events might seem, the overriding interest of both nations was for continued peace. Congress soon passed new neutrality statutes providing for stiff penalties for Americans who crossed into Canada intent on revolution. Nevertheless, Americans along the Canadian border from Vermont to Michigan began to organize Hunters' Lodges, secret militias that aimed, as Thomas A. Bailey once described it, "to emancipate the British Colonies from British thralldom."[1] The Hunters' Lodges numbered an estimated 15,000–20,000 members, who saw themselves acting in the spirit of 1776. In early 1838, Van Buren dispatched General Winfield Scott to the scene to use his powers of persuasion and impressive physical presence to tamp down the conflict. Scott traveled hundreds of miles along the border, assuaging the raw feelings of zealous Americans but mainly asserting the supremacy of the central government over matters of war and peace. From the standpoint of the national government, the actions of the locals both exacerbated tensions with Great Britain and, more importantly, represented a direct challenge to its war powers. Scott's presence calmed some and intimidated others, and even though he was not wholly successful in restraining the insurrectionists – at least two examples of cross-border attack occurred in late 1838, both ending in quick failure – the effort to revolutionize Canada receded.

In the far northeast, a dispute over the Maine–New Brunswick boundary left over from the War of Independence threatened to turn hot in February 1839 when local Maine militia attacked a party of Canadian loggers in disputed territories along the Aroostook River. The Canadians soon counterattacked and took fifty men prisoner in the

---

[1] Thomas A. Bailey, *A Diplomatic History of the American People*, 8th ed., (New York, 1969), 201.

woodsy skirmish known as the Aroostook War. Responding to pleas from Massachusetts, Congress made plans to raise 50,000 troops and allocate $10 million to support them. Another war with Great Britain loomed. For a second time, General Winfield Scott was sent to assert the authority of the central government over the local Massachusetts militias that threatened to embroil the United States in a war that it did not want over territories of the most marginal importance to the national interest. Once again, the central government had shown that when it wanted to, it could restrain border elements from violating the sovereignty of other nations.

On the high seas, British and American interests collided in the controversy surrounding the handling of the American slave ship *Creole*. In November 1841, the 135 slaves on the ship being transported from Virginia to Louisiana mutinied and sought refuge in the British Bahamas. Once they arrived, British officials freed most of the slaves, much to the outrage of American owners of the human cargo; as they had after the British slave liberations of the War of Independence and War of 1812, the slave owners enlisted the central government in their efforts to be compensated for their loss. The *Creole* affair was only the latest in a long line of U.S. efforts to defend the institution of slavery just as it would any other material interest of its citizens. Although Congress had ended the international slave trade in 1807 and was nominally committed to cooperating with Great Britain in suppressing it, American political leaders would not allow British naval vessels the right to visit and search American ships for human contraband. It was too reminiscent of the British practices in searching for contraband of war. Throughout the antebellum, U.S. policy insisted that maintenance of the principle of freedom of the seas trumped efforts to suppress the slave trade.

These and other irritants might have added up to a serious crisis at an earlier period in Anglo-American relations. Now, however, the nexus of trade and investment was too great to allow these distractions to determine the course of events. Fate also intervened to make Anglophilic John Tyler of Virginia president in 1841. Tyler's anomalous ascent to power was made possible, first, by his changing of party affiliation in 1840 to run on the Whig ticket with William Henry Harrison ("Old Tippecanoe") and then by Harrison's death shortly after his inauguration in March 1841. A lifetime of exposure to deadly fire and to the elements did not prevent Harrison from contracting a severe cold on the day of his inauguration, from which he soon died. John Tyler then assumed the office of president, being the first man to accede to the presidency from the position of vice-president. Whigs viewed Tyler (derisively known as "His Accidency") with suspicion, and his former fellow Democrats saw him as a turncoat. This distinct lack of political allies made Tyler a one-term president but did not stop him from realizing a substantial portion of his expansionist ambitions while in the Oval Office.

Tyler wasted little time in seeking to implement his plans. He almost immediately convened talks between Secretary of State Daniel Webster and British emissary Alexander Baring, Lord Ashburton. Ashburton proved an ideal choice from the American perspective in that he headed the banking firm Baring Brothers, which was heavily invested in the United States, and was married to the daughter of an American senator. Ashburton thus had both economic and personal reasons to see the controversy resolved and proved willing to go to great lengths to maintain peaceful ties.

Moreover, the British imperial project had at that time increasingly little stomach for contending over faraway holdings of marginal importance. The Maine–New Brunswick boundary dispute was rooted in uncertainty about the exact location of the geographic features referenced in the Peace Treaty of 1783, encompassing an area of about twelve thousand square miles. Webster and Ashburton divided the disputed area roughly 60/40 in favor of the United States. Ashburton also made concessions on three other minor ambiguities along the U.S.-Canadian border, including one near the Lake of the Woods in present-day Minnesota that gave the U.S. possession of what would become the Mesabi Range, for a time one of the richest sources of iron ore in the world. Ashburton's conciliatory attitude on these minor boundary frictions reflected again his understanding that a few thousand acres of timberland counted for next to nothing as compared to the emerging Anglo-American axis of trade and finance. Of course, the central government had to sell to Maine and Massachusetts the idea of conceding even an acre of land; each had a stake in the outcome, and both had rejected earlier attempts at compromise on the issue. This time Webster won the states' acquiescence with $150,000 in cash payments and some dubious arguments about the validity of their maximum claims. Although it left the Oregon question unaddressed, the

Webster-Ashburton Treaty of 1842 stands as another major landmark in the course of Anglo-American imperial cooperation.

OREGON

In the Northwest, American imperial interest in the Oregon Country, a vast, ill-defined expanse bordering the Pacific Ocean between California and Alaska, collided once again with those of Great Britain and with the rights of the native peoples who lived there. On first glance, it might seem surprising that Americans took such an early and lively interest in an area so far from the center of the Union in 1830. That such a distant place assumed such importance so early speaks again to the remarkable expansionist energies of Americans. U.S. interest in the region dates to the voyages of Captain Robert Gray of Boston, who, at the helm of the *Columbia,* is credited with the discovery of the mouth of the river of the same name in 1792. Gray had been the first American to grasp the potential value of furs for the China market; soon a number of prominent entrepreneurs jumped at the opportunity, including John Jacob Astor and his American Fur Company; Astor established Astoria at the mouth of the Columbia in 1811 as a fur trading *entrepôt.* Here Astor's enterprise collided with the Hudson's Bay Company's attempts to extract the wealth of the Northwest Coast; in 1813, men under Astor's employ surrendered Astoria to British forces during the War of 1812. Astor's influence with powerful people, particularly President James Monroe, contributed mightily to the staking of the first formal claim to Oregon via the transcontinental boundary drawn in the Adams-Onis Treaty of 1819. Astor's backstage lobbying resulted in Secretary of State Adams dispatching in September 1817 the USS *Ontario,* commanded by Captain James Biddle, to sail to the Northwest Coast and "to assert there the claims of sovereignty in the name ... of the United States, by some symbolical or other appropriate mode of setting up a claim to national authority and dominion."[2] So the original American interest in the Oregon Country occurred from west to east, informed by Oregon's potential role in trans-Pacific commerce.

Popular knowledge of the region seems first to have been stimulated by the publication in 1817 of William Cullen Bryant's poem "Thanatopsis"

---

[2] William E. Weeks, *John Quincy Adams and American Global Empire* (Lexington, Ky., 1992), 55.

in the *North American Review,* the nation's premier literary magazine. A meditation on death as the great equalizer, "Thanatopsis" urges its readers to

> – Take the wings
> Of morning – and the Barcan desert pierce,
> Or lost thyself in the continuous woods
> Where rolls the Oregan, and hears no sound,
> Save his own dashings –

and tells the tale of a deathly idyll in a mythic land drained by a mighty river named the Oregan [sic]. Official interest in settlement of the region began with the publication of a congressionally authorized report in 1821 by Virginia representative and later governor Dr. John Floyd. Floyd had an outsized interest in western expansion and, along with his Senate colleague Thomas Hart Benton of Missouri, decried what he saw as the capitulation of U.S. interests in Oregon to Great Britain via the "free and open occupation" clause of the Convention of 1818. Floyd's report argued that "from the usage of all nations, previous and subsequent to the discovery of America, the title of the United States to a very large portion of the coast of the Pacific Ocean" was "well founded" and denied that "any other government than Spain has made any claim to any part of it, from Cape Horn to the sixtieth degree of North Latitude."[3] This disregarded the long-standing claims of both Britain and Russia to areas along the coast, not to mention the dozens of Indian tribes that inhabited these lands. Nonetheless, Floyd's report concludes that there can be no doubt "that an establishment made on the Pacific ... would give this country the advantage of all its own treasures, which otherwise must be lost forever, ... of more profit ... than the mines of Potosi," a reference to the fabled source of silver in Mexico. At Benton's urging, the report not only stakes a claim to the Oregon Country but also goes on to blame John Quincy Adams for giving up the American claim to Texas extending to the Rio Grande, the origins of later calls for the "reannexation" of that province. But Floyd's chief concern was Oregon, and he introduced legislation to allow Americans to build settlements along the Columbia River and the U.S. government to establish a customs house, regulate trade

[3] Samuel Flagg Bemis, *John Quincy Adams and the Union* (New York, 1949), 487.

with Indian tribes in the area, and license fur traders. Nothing came of this, because Congress's preoccupation with the Missouri question overshadowed all other issues.

Benton's role as a great expansionist visionary stimulating the march to Oregon should not be forgotten. A newspaperman, amateur historian, renowned lecturer, and for thirty years one of Missouri's first two senators, Benton made stentorian pronouncements about the promise of the West, giving his voice a special prominence. He devoted much of his energies to promoting an overland route to Oregon, an ambition that seems to have been sparked by Jefferson, whose own vision of a westward movement inspired Benton's. Indeed, Benton's son-in-law, John C. Fremont, described him as "a disciple of Jefferson," an appropriate characterization of the quasi-religious fervor with which Benton promoted Jefferson's vision. Benton's interest in history prompted a view that saw a succession of empires reaching back to antiquity, rising and falling as they came but heading ever westward. At the mouth of the Columbia he envisioned the establishment of a mercantile empire that would link the commerce of the United States with that of Asia. But could Astoria be easily accessed overland? His preliminary study of the still little-known American geography answered the question: "Happily, *Nature* has created such a route – one which lies through the heart of our dominions – and which may with justice be called "the American road to India."[4]

Benton's interest in an overland route focused on its potential as a sort of American Silk Road, an avenue of commerce more than settlement. He hoped that the rich products of the Northwest might be a good medium of exchange with the Chinese and thus reduce the drain of silver to the East. The desire to prevent the outflow of silver by finding a substitute for it in the China trade had informed the Monroe administration's interest in the Northwest; Benton now urged policymakers to follow up on that start and definitively assert U.S. hegemony in the region. Like Jefferson, Benton at times suggested that the nation he foresaw arising on the western slope of the continent might be a sister republic to the United States. Such comments were merely speculative and never had the slightest chance of becoming real. The American

---

[4] Tom Chaffin, *The Pathfinder: John Charles Fremont and the Course of American Empire* (New York, 2002), 81.

expansionist ethos would never have tolerated the establishment of a new state that could at some point be the dreaded roadblock to the West that had haunted the American imagination since at least the 1760s.

A distinct American interest in approaching Oregon from the sea complemented Benton's overland boosterism. American whalers and sea otter hunters working the offshore waters had stimulated the Monroe administration's strong response to the tsar's *ukase* reserving the Northwest Coast from the Bering Strait to 51 degrees north latitude solely for Russian subjects and banning the approach of foreign vessels to within one hundred miles of the shore. The claim represented a dramatic expansion of Russian influence aimed at preventing the "Bostonese" from encroaching northward in pursuit of whales and sea otters. Resistance to this move by Adams and Monroe resulted in the *ukase* being withdrawn, the first example of the successful application of the Monroe Doctrine's noncolonization clause. American activities in the offshore regions of the Northwest Coast had been secured. So an American interest in the Northwest Coast was formed, based in part on the lobbying of particular economic interests, in part on the assertion that Britain's and Russia's activities constituted an unacceptable challenge to the Monroe Doctrine's principle of noncolonization, and in part on Oregon's emerging role as the next great land of opportunity for the westward-looking American. In 1823 Adams, in instructions he drafted to Minister Henry Middleton in Russia, described the American claim to Oregon (at least to the forty-ninth parallel) as "unquestionable," making its acquisition a mere matter of time.

The Free and Open Occupation Treaty of 1818 (also known as the Convention of 1818) with Great Britain succeeded in putting off for ten years a decision about the Oregon Country. Yet the tide was ebbing for the British. In 1825, the Hudson's Bay Company pulled back to north of the Columbia River, essentially conceding the American claim to lands south of the river. North of there, the situation remained contentious. American claims to lands extending as far north as 54 degrees, 40 minutes collided with the British interests, whose rising economic importance had caught London's attention. As a result, Anglo-American negotiators chose to renew the Free and Open Occupation Treaty indefinitely, each nation needing to give one year's notice of an intention to withdraw from its strictures.

By the mid-1830s, evangelical aspirations also drove the rising interest in the Oregon Country. Reports of a group of Nez Perce Indians arriving in St. Louis searching for a black book they had heard would give them great power electrified the evangelical community. They took the journey of the Indians as a sure sign of the hungering for Christianity of the heathen tribes of the far west and soon began organizing missionary bands to settle in Oregon. By 1835 Jason Lee had established a Methodist mission in the Willamette Valley, and by 1837 Marcus Whitman and his wife, Narcissa, had planted a Presbyterian outpost at Wailapu, near present-day Walla Walla, Washington. Anglican and Catholic missions also were established to civilize the Indians, who in most cases showed little interest in conversion or civilization at least as defined by white people. Nevertheless, the missionary thrust into Oregon, like those before them into China and Hawaii, reinvigorated the evangelical movement domestically, suggesting that American-style Christianity, like the society as a whole, needed to expand in order to survive.

The Panic of 1837 and the subsequent hard times also served to increase the attractiveness of Oregon as a new land of opportunity. However, it was the endeavors of John C. Fremont of the U.S. Army Topographical Corps that unleashed what became known as "Oregon fever." Fremont's career epitomizes the possibilities inherent in nineteenth-century America. Born out of wedlock, the son of a French expatriate and the runaway wife of a much older man, Fremont exuded energy and ambition that caught the eye of Senator Benton and that of his talented and eligible daughter Jessie, whom in due course Fremont married.

Benton used his senatorial prerogatives to finance a topographical corps exploration of an overland route west with his son-in-law in command. With Benton as the visionary and Fremont as the "Pathfinder of Empire" (as the *Democratic Review* described him), the road west was surveyed and mapped. Fremont's first expedition in 1842 surveyed the route west from St. Louis to South Pass in the Rockies, by far the easiest path through the mountains. Going somewhat beyond his orders, Fremont took it upon himself to climb Mt. Snow (later renamed for him) in Wyoming's Wind River Range, where he dramatically planted an American flag on what he claimed (incorrectly) to be the highest peak in the Rockies. With the help of Jessie (a talented writer), Fremont, upon returning to Washington, published a report to Congress of his explorations. The narrative featured him in the role of dashing action hero and had an inestimable impact in fueling interest in the road west. These tales of a way west as blazed by the intrepid Fremont electrified the nation, stimulating the first great migration to Oregon in 1843, when a thousand Americans went to see for themselves the beautiful and fertile lands along the Willamette River. Soon, thousands more followed the Oregon Trail, carving wagon wheel ruts into the mountains and prairies that, in some places, are still visible today. These developments made the momentum toward annexation seem unstoppable. In June 1845, the *United States Magazine and Democratic Review* editorialized that "the tide of American emigration has lately set" in the direction of Oregon, "and nothing but a fatal misstep on our part, can prevent its habitable portions being occupied in a few years by our countrymen, and a vast trade thence carried on over all the Pacific."[5]

By the mid-1840s Oregon fever occupied a prominent place in the national imagination. An immense province inhabited by a handful of Americans suddenly became essential to the nation's future prosperity. Oregon seemed destined to be a part of the United States if only from the inevitable rapid population growth that would stem from the small colony of immigrants. British foreign secretary Lord Castlereagh had predicted to Americans as early as 1818 that "you will conquer Oregon in your bedchambers," and by the 1840s some members of Congress sought to bring that to pass. Rep. Andrew Kennedy of Indiana asked, "Where shall we find room for all of our people, unless we have Oregon? What shall we do with all those little white-headed boys and girls – God bless them! – that cover the Mississippi valley, as the flowers cover the western prairies?" Kennedy, in the tradition of Franklin, characterized the great fecundity of the American settlers as "the American multiplication table."[6] However much Americans may have desired Oregon, though, their claim to it was tenuous at best. John Quincy Adams addressed the legal shortcomings of the American position by affirming to Congress that the foundation of the claim rested on the biblical injunction to "be fruitful and multiply, and replenish the

5 *United States Magazine and Democratic Review,* vol. 16, 84:5.
6 Charles G. Sellers, *James Knox Polk, Continentalist,* 1843–1846 (Princeton, 1966), 384.

earth, and subdue it." To Adams, this was "the foundation not only to our title to Oregon but the foundation of all human title to all human possessions."[7]

John Tyler was nearly as staunch an advocate for Oregon as he was for Texas. In his special message to Congress marking the beginning of his presidency, he alluded to "the immense region" between the Rockies and the mouth of the Columbia, "about 770,000,000 acres, ceded and unceded, [that] still remain to be brought into market." Although the twenty million or so Americans at that time hardly seemed to require this distant land, Tyler sought to augment their numbers by extending "to the people of other countries an invitation to come and settle among us as members of our rapidly growing family.... No motive exists for foreign conquest; we desire but to reclaim our almost illimitable wildernesses and to introduce into their depths the lights of civilization."[8] Although Tyler seemed to hold out the promise of Oregon's being rapidly populated by people from around the world, in the early 1840s he did not want large numbers of American emigrants to enter the region for fear that it might complicate a diplomatic solution with Great Britain. Yet Benton and other staunch western expansionists pushed the expansionist tide, presenting Britain with a fait accompli of conquest by immigration that ultimately proved crucial in wresting the province from them. The rapid increase in the number of settlers in the region proved decisive in staking the claim of the American Empire.

CALIFORNIA

California represented another emerging expansionist vista for Americans. A keen taste for the needs of future millions motivated its acquisition, for, as with Oregon, Americans surely did not need its abundant resources in the 1840s. However, many recognized that California at some point would be a land of great opportunity and needed to be seized at the first chance that presented itself. California had come late under the white man's imperial gaze. Spanish imperial claims to the region dated to the voyages of Juan de Cabrillo in the 1630s, but for 150 years no effort was made to secure control of the area north of San

---

[7] Samuel Flagg Bemis, *John Quincy Adams and the Union* (New York, 1956), 490.
[8] James D. Richardson, ed., *Messages and Papers of the Presidents* (Washington, D.C., 1903), 4:40, 4:41.

Diego Bay, the unofficial beginning of what was called Alta California. Fearing the encroachment of Russia down the coast, in 1769 Jesuit missionaries began construction of twenty-one missions (or presidios) from San Diego to Sonoma, each a day apart and designed both to Christianize the numerous Indian tribes along the route and, if necessary, to enlist their services as soldiers in defending California. As it happened, the few regular Spanish troops in the province spent most of their energies pursuing Indians fleeing the forced labor regime and infectious diseases of the missions. The Indians of California did not respond well to their encounter with civilization; disease, overwork, and cultural dislocation reduced their numbers from an estimated 300,000 in 1769 to about half that by the 1840s.

Mexico's independence from Spain in 1821 resulted in California's increasing autonomy, and for a few years a small population of Californios lived a life of prosperity and relative ease, sustained by the oceanic tallow and hide trade derived from the large herds of cattle that grazed California's verdant fields. In the 1820s and 1830s, a few Americans established themselves as merchants and traders, most notably Thomas Larkin of Monterey. Mexican president Lopez de Santa Ana's attempt in 1835 to increase central control of California proved no more popular there than it had in Texas, but because Mexico City lacked the resources to make good on its new claim to authority, no revolt occurred as in Texas. California's irresistible allure captured the imagination of even Andrew Jackson, whom John Quincy Adams characterized as "wild" for the region.

By the mid-1840s and notwithstanding the distinctly dubious claims held to both places, California, like Oregon, seemed destined under the will of Heaven to become a part of the United States. To realize its vast potential required American energies. As an author in *Democratic Review* put it in the summer of 1845, "California will, probably, next fall ... The Anglo-Saxon foot is already on its borders. Already the advance guard of the irresistible army of the Anglo-Saxon emigration has begun to pour down upon it, armed with the plough and the rifle, and marking its trail with schools and colleges, courts and representative halls, mills and meeting-houses."[9] It is a candid and mostly accurate characterization of the nature of the American expansionist process.

---

[9] *United States Magazine and Democratic Review*, vol. 17, 85:9.

The American imperial juggernaut seemed poised to assume control of the entire continent. But how, exactly, would the transfer occur? In 1842, responding to false reports of a war breaking out with Mexico, American naval commander Thomas Ap Catesby Jones sailed his squadron into the central California port of Monterey and claimed the province for the United States. Jones just as hurriedly returned control to local authorities when he discovered that war had not broken out. Nevertheless, a point had been made: California could be conquered with a minimum of effort.

Fremont, so essential to bringing Oregon into the American sphere, also played a key role in facilitating the conquest of California. In 1846, on his fourth expedition to the West – ostensibly to explore and survey routes into California – Fremont met with and subtly encouraged (but at first refused openly to support) the growing American settler community in California, most of whom eagerly sought annexation to the United States. Upon receiving what he later characterized as implicit orders from President Polk to foment a revolution, Fremont freed his small force of soldiers to participate in the local uprising known as the Bear Flag Revolt, so-called because the image of a lone star and grizzly bear under the words "California Republic" became the standard of the rebels. Fremont's actions, while extraconstitutional to say the least, were in the tradition of Andrew Jackson, whose unhesitating takedown, without orders, of East Florida in 1818 remained an important precedent that Polk now relied upon. Fremont, conscious of the humiliation endured by Thomas Ap Catesby Jones for acting too precipitously and unaware of events along the Nueces River that would formally mark the beginning of the U.S.-Mexico War, only slowly recognized that the moment of annexation was at hand. Finally, Fremont joined with naval forces under Commodore Robert F. Stockton to create a U.S. military presence on land and sea, and after minimal fighting conquered both northern and southern California by January 1847.

TEXAS

Between 1820 and 1860, the United States pushed against the imperial limits that circumscribed it. In a great arc from the Maine boundary question, to the Oregon dispute, to the growing desire for California, the Americans defined and extended their claims with surprising ease.

Yet Texas – the last section of the arc – proved quite difficult to secure. A major part of the extensive borderlands between the United States and Hispanic America, Texas constituted a thinly populated area of indeterminate boundaries with tenuous ties to the capital in faraway Mexico City. U.S. claims to Texas were rooted in dubious assumptions about the boundaries of the Louisiana Purchase. It had been a part of the demands made on Spain during the protracted negotiations finally leading to the Adams-Onis Treaty of 1819. At that time, the claim to Texas seemed highly abstract, for relatively few Americans had even visited the province. At a crucial moment in the negotiations with Spain, Adams and Monroe decided to sacrifice the claim to Texas in exchange for the establishment of a transcontinental boundary dividing the United States from Mexico. James Monroe's concerns about the role of Texas as a possible new land for slavery explains this diplomatic sleight of hand that, in the celebratory mood that greeted the treaty, went mostly unnoticed at the time by the political classes. The western boundary of the Louisiana Purchase was set at the Sabine River, and the province of Texas gained independence in 1821 as the northernmost state of the Republic of Mexico.

Although diplomats drew a border that presumed to divide the United States and Mexico, ambitious Americans eager for the next big opportunity eyed Texas hungrily. The trickle of Americans crossing the Sabine and seeking wealth in Texas increased to a steady stream in 1823, when the central government in Mexico, eager to populate Texas as a means to better exert sovereignty over its vast extent, began to encourage Americans to emigrate there. Moses Austin, a newspaperman from Connecticut, led the first contingent of three hundred or so families to the new promised land of Texas; upon his death, his son Stephen F. Austin, whose economic hopes like those of his father had been dashed in the Panic of 1819, occupied the first land grant in 1823. The Mexican colonization scheme was generous: It offered parcels of 4,428 acres for a mere $200 that included with them the title of empresario. This made Texas land vastly more affordable than land in the United States, precipitating a flood of Anglo settlers – mostly young men on the make – into Texas in the 1820s and early 1830s.

Mexico's efforts to lure Anglo settlers into its distant province marked the beginning of the end of its hold on the region. Everything about the newcomers – their ethnicity, their Protestantism, their preexisting political loyalties – clashed with the reality of life in Old Spanish Texas. However, the first few years offered some hopes that the experiment in multicultural nation-building might work. The Texians (as they called themselves) began to employ the slaves many of them brought with them to grow cotton in the fertile, accessible lands along the Gulf Coast. Although required to swear allegiance to the Republic of Mexico, the Texians received assurances of the freedom to practice their Protestant religion in the otherwise Catholic country.

In spite of the hint of the possibility of peaceful coexistence, the situation on the Louisiana-Texas border did not bode well for future harmony. The lure of Texas became irresistible for a certain sort of young Americans, especially after Mexico began encouraging them to cross the river and settle. Texas became a place where those who had failed in business or in love or who were on the run from the law could go for a fresh start. It appealed to the imagination as a place where big dreams could come true. This is what drew the Austins and countless others like them to Texas in the coming decades. The policies of the Mexican government made Texas more attractive to remove to than the western imperial domain of the United States, and "the market" – the individual decisions of thousands of Americans seeking their fortune – responded accordingly by flocking there.

The society that took shape in Texas mostly resembled that of the emerging Deep South. Young, ambitious white men with an intense sense of honor, family, and faith – and a predisposition to settle disputes by force – dominated it. The proclivity of the Texas settlers for violence is legendary. Gary C. Anderson observes, "The vast majority of Anglos who came to Texas were capable with a rifle," often the Kentucky long rifle, which offered a significant advantage when matched against any other weapon currently in the province.[10] After about 1840, the introduction of the Colt six-shooter – the first revolver – augmented this firepower advantage. Modern technologies fueled the Texians' propensity for violence in ways that proved crucial to the region's political and cultural development.

The first wave of settlers who arrived with Stephen Austin for the most part sought to become loyal Mexican subjects and deal with the

---

[10] Gary C. Anderson, *The Conquest of Texas: Ethnic Cleansing in the Promised Land, 1820–1875* (Norman, Okla., 2005), 96.

Tejanos on conditions of equality, but, by the latter part of the 1820s, those who crossed the Sabine increasingly had in mind thoughts of future annexation by the United States. The first move toward independence had been the short-lived Fredonia Revolt of 1825, but the real impetus to rebellion occurred because of the limits on slavery imposed by the Mexican legislature beginning in 1828. This formed only one part of an attempt by the government in Mexico City and its new leader, Lopez de Santa Ana, to recentralize power under quasi-dictatorial rule. The formerly loose tie to Mexico City steadily tightened on a people unused to being closely governed. From that point on it would only be a matter of time before a revolt occurred.

The Texas Declaration of Independence, signed on March 2, 1836, by fifty-nine revolutionaries, most of them Anglos, justified the revolt by the alleged failure of the Mexican government to protect the lives and property of its citizens and for instigating Indian attacks on Texas settlements. It made no direct reference to the restrictions on slavery. The ragtag resistance, including some members of the Tejano community, seemed no match for Santa Ana's 5,000-strong expeditionary force sent to quash the revolt, and catastrophic losses at the Alamo and Goliad added to the sense of impending doom in the spring of 1836. Anglo settlers fearing retribution for treason fled by the thousands back across the Sabine River into Louisiana. Santa Ana's troops pursued one last remnant of the Texas revolutionary army to what looked like a final massacre of the sort that occurred at the Alamo and Goliad, in the latter case of several hundred Texian troops who had surrendered. But in near-miraculous fashion the Texians, led by War of 1812 veteran and Jackson protégé Sam Houston, destroyed the enemy force in a devastating surprise counterattack along the San Jacinto River in April 1836. After a short battle, the Texians took bloody revenge for their fallen comrades at the Alamo and Goliad, slaughtering hundreds of unresisting Mexican soldiers. The defeat of the Mexican expeditionary force meant the effective end of the war. With independence secured, the Texas Congress voted unanimously to petition for annexation to the United States. It seemed a prime candidate for admission into the Union. As an independent nation, Texas had adopted as its state flag a lone star against a red background, a design nearly identical to that adopted by the rebels in West Florida in their brief existence as an independent republic before Madison annexed the province in

1810, thereby securing the lands immediately to the east of Louisiana. Now the region immediately to the west of that state had been revolutionized in much the same manner and appeared ripe for absorption into the Union.

But fierce opposition greeted the prospect of Texas annexation. A broad cross section of Northerners, Whig party members, and abolitionists reacted with horror at the idea of another slave state being added to a republic founded on the idea of liberty. For as the cotton empire built on unfree labor grew immensely in the 1820s and 1830s, so did a rising opposition to slavery in both the United States and Britain. The abolition of slavery in the British Empire in 1833 had upped the stakes for many Americans, including John Quincy Adams, now a member of the House of Representatives from Massachusetts. Adams had long been one of the nation's most zealous expansionists and as president had made some minor efforts to purchase Texas from Mexico. He now represented only the people of Plymouth, Massachusetts, and the personal objections he had long held regarding slavery could openly be expressed. The writings of Quaker abolitionist Benjamin Lundy acted to spur Adams's conscience. Lundy, whose magnetic influence also drew William Lloyd Garrison to the abolitionist cause, had sought to establish a free-labor colony in Texas to demonstrate that economic success in the province did not necessarily depend on a slave labor regime. However, the dislocations caused by the Texas Revolution stymied his efforts. Lundy wrote of his struggles in "The Origins and True Causes of the Texas Revolution," detailing what he saw as a slaveholder plot to bring Texas into the Union as a first step toward the establishment of a slave labor–based Southern Confederacy. If the South did not remain in the Union, Northerners would face the prospect of inhabiting a country that both sanctioned and spread the institution of slavery. Adams now perceived the Union to be fracturing along free state–slave state lines and that at some point one side or the other would become dominant. If Texas entered with slaves, Cuba might soon follow; a worst-case scenario offered the prospect of an abolitionist Britain waging war to abolish the institution throughout the Western Hemisphere. Adams declared before the House that "it is my solemn belief that the annexation of an independent foreign power to this government would be ipso facto a dissolution of this Union" and that the United States would be "damned to 'everlasting fame' by the reinstitution of that detested system of slavery" after it had been abolished while Texas was a part of Mexico.[11]

In addition to the opposition of Adams and other Northern Whig political leaders to the prospect of Texas annexation, large numbers of citizens – estimated in the hundreds of thousands – deluged Congress with petitions in opposition to the move. Southerners in Congress prevented the petitions from being received and placed them in storage, where they have remained to this day. To get around Congress's denial of the sacred right of petition, Adams read an excerpt from a petition presented by the women of Plymouth, Massachusetts: "Thoroughly aware of the sinfulness of slavery, and the consequent impolicy and disastrous tendency of its extension in our country, we do most respectfully remonstrate, with all our souls, against the annexation of Texas to the United States."[12] Thanks to Adams and others sympathetic to the cause, the intensity of the anti–Texas annexation sentiment made itself felt in spite of efforts to gag it, as did a looming realization that annexation likely meant a war with Mexico. This grim possibility had stilled Jackson's hand in the waning days of his presidency; his successor, Martin Van Buren, fearing the collapse of the Northern wing of the Democratic party if Texas entered the Union, declined to submit the treaty of annexation to Congress.

The refusal to admit Texas into the Union over the question of slavery confirmed the breakdown of the expansionist consensus that had first appeared during the Missouri debates. It seems that only Americans themselves could stop the hitherto unstoppable expansionist juggernaut. Previous deals, such as Louisiana, had engendered some opposition but not enough to threaten their consummation. Now intense opposition to the annexation treaty prevented it from being submitted to the Senate, where it faced the imposing obstacle of a two-thirds majority needed for ratification. This logjam persisted through the remainder of the Van Buren administration and into the presidency of Whig party member and War of 1812 hero William Henry Harrison. Harrison almost certainly would not have acquired Texas. His unexpected demise opened the door to Tyler's fervent efforts to bring Texas into the Union. Tyler's states' rights politics put him at odds with Whig party principles, and as

[11] Bemis, *John Quincy Adams and the Union*, 362.
[12] Bemis, *John Quincy Adams and the Union*, 369.

president, he was embraced politically by almost no one. Nevertheless, Tyler proved a dynamic expansionist, establishing an American protectorate over Hawaii and improving commercial access to China. Yet he coveted Texas above all else. Like many Democrats, Tyler believed the imperial republic to be capable of virtually infinite expansionism; echoing Jefferson, he asserted to Congress his belief that "there exists nothing in the extension of our Empire ... to ignite the alarm of the patriot for the safety of our institutions. The federative system ... admits in safety of the greatest expansion."[13]

If the prospect of annexing Texas made the rising antislavery faction nearly apoplectic, the prospect of not annexing it disturbed proslavery Southerners even more. The refusal to absorb a population overwhelmingly Southern in its makeup and culture was insulting, but an even greater concern was what might happen to Texas outside the bonds of the Union. In particular, Southerners worried that Great Britain might see the reluctance of the United States to annex Texas as an invitation to bring it under its control by guaranteeing its independence and paying its debts in exchange for abolishing slavery. This scenario – not at all far-fetched – threatened the slave interest with the nightmare of seeing slavery's westward expansion blocked by Great Britain and the very existence of the "peculiar institution" challenged by an increasingly emboldened Northern antislavery sentiment. In 1843 Texas president Sam Houston, incensed that annexation had been blocked, subtly made known Texas's receptiveness to British offers of support if no better option presented itself. Playing the British card had prompted Tyler to act in the case of Hawaii, and it might work in the case of Texas. Yet, for the moment, President Tyler seemed to have no discernible path toward achieving Texas annexation.

Texas, meanwhile, left at the altar of annexation in 1837, pursued its own expansionist foreign policy as an independent republic while beating back Mexican efforts to subdue it and Comanche efforts to harass it. Driven by land speculation, in the late 1830s the Texans, under new president Mirabeau Lamar, waged unrelenting war on the Indian tribes of north central Texas, especially the Comanches, whose empire had bestrode the Great Plains for two centuries. A ferocious war of massacre and mutilation ensued against them in an attempt to eradicate what

---

[13] Richardson, ed., *Messages and Papers of the Presidents*, 4:42.

some whites termed "the wild cannibals of the woods."[14] This effort at the ethnic cleansing of Texas had as one of its aims bringing the United States into the conflict, which ranged back and forth across the ill-defined Texas-U.S. border. The presence of Indians recently removed to the vicinity from the east – Shawnees, Cherokees, and others – confused the already tense geopolitical situation in the region. President Lamar, lacking the sympathy for Native Americans that Houston retained from his close association with the Cherokees, pushed a campaign to conquer New Mexico and establish a claim all the way to the Pacific Ocean. The absurdity of this massive expansionist pretension by the relative handful of Anglos (fewer than forty thousand) who inhabited Texas at the time did not lessen its significance, for when the United States did go to war with Mexico over Texas its negotiating position was built on the claims established by Lamar and other expansionists.

The Texas question roiled American politics and American life, raising issues about the nature of the Union that threatened its future. Northerners in Congress, led by John Quincy Adams, proposed amending the Constitution to end the three-fifths clause (which inflated Southern political power in the House of Representatives), a move not calculated to ease Southern fears of becoming a permanent political minority. The fears of slaveholders mounted as they confronted what they saw as a rising abolitionist tide, both in the North and in Great Britain. On the annexation of Texas hung the question of whether slavery would live or die in North America, and yet there appeared no way a two-thirds majority in the Senate could be roused in support of it. In 1843, Mexico began negotiating with the Houston government the terms of permanent independence for Texas if it cooperated with Great Britain in emancipating its slaves. The rapidly ripening fruit of Texas dangled temptingly. The question remained, Who would pick it?

At this point Abel Upshur, Tyler's secretary of state and an uncompromising defender of slavery and the interests of the South as he saw them, began to push for another annexation treaty. An element of desperation drove his efforts, for in his mind, the South found itself nearly checkmated on the slave question. Upshur wrote to John C. Calhoun arguing that if slavery could not expand then it would die. An emancipated Texas would be both a refuge for runaway slaves and a barrier to

---

[14] Pekka Hamalainen, *The Comanche Empire* (New Haven, 2008), 215.

westward expansion. Slave owners must understand, Upshur pleaded, that the annexation of Texas was "indispensable to their security."[15] But could it be done in the face of so much opposition, both domestic and foreign? Yes, one step at a time.

Upshur first convinced President Houston to agree to a new annexation treaty by convincing him that it could reach the supermajority needed for ratification, enlisting former president Jackson, in one of his last acts, to write a letter to his old protégé Houston to that effect. Houston acquiesced to the pressure and speedily drafted a new treaty by April 1844. Prior to that, fate had stepped in by a bizarre and unexpected means. While a member of an official party witnessing the test-firing of a huge new gun – nicknamed "the Peacemaker" – on the USS *Princeton* in February 1844, Upshur and several others died when the weapon exploded on deck. The driving force behind a new annexation treaty was dead, but the momentum Upshur created for it lived on. New secretary of state John C. Calhoun, previously urged by Upshur to push for Texas, now embraced the expansionist cause with great fervor. So did Andrew Jackson, who in the waning days of his life took it upon himself to lobby against his former protégé Martin Van Buren as the Democratic nominee for president in 1844 owing to Van Buren's insufficient ardor for Texas. Mississippi senator Robert Walker produced tracts issuing dire warnings of slavery's imminent demise if Texas were not annexed, thereby denying slaveholders a place to "diffuse" their rising slave populations westward and "eventually get rid of an intolerable burden."[16] Slavery, like commerce, evangelical Christianity, and the Union itself, needed to expand in order to survive.

President Tyler lobbied the Senate hard for ratification. He argued for "reclaiming" Texas and cast it as a land of great promise: "To a soil of inexhaustible fertility it unites a genial and healthy climate and is destined at a day not distant to make large contributions to the commerce of the world." Besides, "the Southern and Southeastern States" would view annexation as "protection and security to their peace and tranquility, as well as against all domestic or foreign efforts to disturb them, thus consecrating anew the union of the States and holding out the promise of its perpetual duration." The president's zeal for Texas

[15] William Freehling, *The Road to Disunion: Secessionists at Bay, 1776–1854* (New York, 1990), 401.
[16] Freehling, *The Road to Disunion*, 426.

formed only one part of what Edward Crapol terms Tyler's "blind faith in the belief that endless territorial and commercial expansion could preserve the institution of slavery and maintain the Union as a slaveholding republic."[17]

By the time of the Democratic National Convention of 1844, the southern wing of the party demanded an uncompromisingly expansionist candidate. Its platform demanded the "reannexation" of Texas and the "reoccupation" of Oregon, all the way to the 54-degree, 40-minute border with Alaska. Moderate Northern Democrats found themselves marginalized, none more so than former president Van Buren. At the convention, anti–Van Buren elements in the party changed the number needed for nomination from a simple majority to a two-thirds majority, thereby derailing Van Buren's candidacy. On the third ballot the party nominated James K. Polk of Tennessee, another Jackson protégé and a former Speaker of the House of Representatives. "Young Hickory" held an expansive vision of American greatness, one that eyed expansion not only in Texas but also all the way to the Pacific and beyond to the markets of Asia. Although a slaveholder, Polk saw Texas annexation as important primarily for security reasons, and he eagerly sought to secure American control of the Oregon Country. The slave-owning faction in the Democratic party, despite its minority status within the party, had by decisive, unified action wrested the nomination from Van Buren and given it to a staunch supporter of their position.

Polk still faced an uphill battle against the Whigs, whose nominee, Henry Clay, had long opposed Texas annexation, as apparently did a majority of the country. But in two public letters on the question in April and July 1844, Clay waffled on his antislavery, anti-annexation stands in an effort to woo voters from the South. The strategy backfired, gaining Clay virtually no new supporters in the southern states and seriously compromising his support with Northern antislavery Whigs. His flirtation with proslavery annexationists prompted the tiny Liberty party to nominate an uncompromising antislavery candidate in the person of James K. Birney. Clay's waffling killed his chances for victory. Losing every state in the South, Clay likely would still have prevailed in the Electoral College had not Birney's candidacy cost him precious votes in New York and Michigan. In the face of a divided

[17] Edward P. Crapol, *John Tyler: The Accidental President* (Chapel Hill, 2006), 2.

majority electorate, Polk won the presidency by a 170–105 electoral margin. Polk's narrow victory by no means constituted a mandate for dramatic action, and yet lame duck president Tyler seized upon it in January 1845 to reintroduce the Texas question, this time in the form of admission as a new state. Annexation by a joint resolution of each congressional body required only a simple majority – an evasion of the troublesome two-thirds majority needed to ratify a treaty. A week before Polk's inauguration, the Senate voted 27–25 to admit Texas, following the lead of the House, which had given it a 120–98 victory. As Polk took the oath of office, Tyler sent a courier to Texas with the offer of statehood. On July 4, 1845, Texas representatives voted unanimously to accept the offer. Texas had been added to the Union.

Anti-annexationist forces reacted to this constitutionally dubious gambit with outrage. John Quincy Adams pronounced it "an apoplexy of the Constitution," signifying perhaps the death of the Union. A minority slave-owning faction had used a representational trick to inflate its political influence and then run roughshod over constitutional practice to impose its minority will on the majority. Mexico announced that it would refuse to recognize the annexation and prepared for a war that it could not win to avenge its sense of grievance. Yet if Northern anti-annexationist forces felt constitutionally wronged by the way in which Texas entered the Union, Southern sentiment sympathetic to slavery also perceived the integrity of the Constitution to be at risk by what seemed to be a reneging on the original constitutional bargain. The Union would never have been created without a compromise on slavery, what Adams termed the "odious bargain between freedom and slavery." Whatever one thought about that compromise, it had been part of the original plan. Now Adams and a few other mainstream political leaders, backed by a rising tide of Americans of all races and genders, began to advance the idea that slavery had no place in the American Union.

THE RISE OF POLK

James Knox Polk of Tennessee, like Tyler, was an unlikely occupant of the White House in an age of so many ambitious and accomplished individuals. Born in North Carolina, the descendant of Irish immigrants, he graduated from the University of North Carolina in 1816 with honors in mathematics and the classics at a time when few Americans had college degrees. A stint as a lawyer in the office of prominent Tennessee politician Felix Grundy positioned Polk to become a protégé of Andrew Jackson's and a staunch proponent of the Jacksonian program of expansionism and union. In 1825 Polk began a long career in the House as one of its youngest members, eventually becoming Speaker in 1835. Yet he never evinced a strong ambition to be president, never advanced himself as a candidate, and would never have been the Democratic nominee except for the rising expansionist tide within the party that denied the renomination of Martin Van Buren in 1844. Polk emerged as the first dark horse candidate in American presidential history, little known to many members of his own party. As had virtually every president before him, Polk in his inaugural address invoked "the aid of that Almighty Ruler of the Universe in whose hands are the destinies of nations." Frankly acknowledging his own youth (at forty-nine he was the youngest American president yet elected), he pledged his best efforts in administering an office critical to the nation's success "and in some degree the hopes and happiness of the whole human family."[18]

Thrust upon the biggest stage in American politics, Polk entered the presidency with one of the clearest agendas in American history. As a staunch Jacksonian, he was determined to preserve the Union, "the inestimable value of which" is "acknowledged by all." Avoiding use of the term "slavery," he called for Americans to respect the "compromises" on which the Union was built and decried those (presumably abolitionists) who "indulged in schemes and agitations whose object is the destruction of domestic institutions existing in other sections – institutions which existed at the adoption of the Constitution and were recognized and protected by it."[19] A slave owner and an advocate of expanding the institution, he emphasized his role as a staunch nationalist committed to the interests of all sections. Polk advocated the virtually unlimited expansion of a permanent American Union organized around a limited central government. He fervently believed in the Jacksonian notion of "expanding the area of freedom" by extending America's boundaries outward, possessed of a bedrock faith that the growth of the United States was synonymous with human progress. At the same time he also

---

[18] Richardson, ed., *Messages and Papers of the Presidents*, 4:373.
[19] Richardson, ed., *Messages and Papers of the Presidents*, 376–7.

advocated the Jacksonian program of expanding American trade to the markets of the world and affirming American principles of freedom of the seas.

Tyler's annexation of Texas by joint resolution, while constitutionally dubious, did make Polk's task of consummating the deal relatively easy. Lamenting that in 1819 Texas had been "unwisely ceded away to a foreign power," he warned Mexico, "I regard the question of annexation as belonging exclusively to the United States and Texas." He lauded the prospect of the further expansion of the imperial republic "not as the conquest of a nation seeking to extend her dominions by arms and violence but as the peaceful acquisition of a territory once her own," adding, "The world has nothing to fear from military ambition in our government." Polk framed annexation as a national security issue: "None can fail to see the danger to our safety and future peace if Texas remains an independent state or becomes an ally or dependency of some foreign nation more powerful than herself." He pointedly noted, "Whatever is good or evil in the local institutions of Texas will remain her own whether annexed to the United States or not" and that had "our forefathers" refused to admit slave-owning states it would have prevented the formation of "our present Union."[20]

With nearly equal fervor, Polk asserted American claims to Oregon. In his inaugural address, he quoted John Quincy Adams's instructions in 1823 to Henry Middleton asserting U.S. claims to the region as "'clear and unquestionable.'" Polk placed this claim in a larger context in his first annual message to Congress in December 1845. Proceeding from the position that "Oregon is a part of the North American continent, to which, it is confidently affirmed, the title of the United States is now the best in existence," the president called for Congress to increase the pressure on Great Britain by formally giving the year's notice required to end the Free and Open Occupation Treaty of 1828. He also urged the establishment of a line of forts between the Missouri River and the Rockies and insisted that "an adequate force of mounted riflemen be raised to guard and protect" American settlers heading west. Once again, the long arm of the central government reached out to defend the lives and interests of American settlers. Most importantly, Polk called for the United States to resist the encroachment of European imperial

[20] Richardson, ed., *Messages and Papers of the Presidents*, 4:379–80, 4:380, 4:381.

ambition in North America: "We must ever maintain the principle that the people of this continent alone have the right to decide their own destiny." In fact, Polk explicitly referenced Monroe's noncolonization principle articulated in his famous message of 1823 as the basis of his policy. Monroe's vision of a hemisphere free of further European meddling had indeed become sound doctrine in the hands of Polk, if modified to include only North America: "[I]t should be distinctly announced to the world as our settled policy that no future European colony or dominion" should be attempted "on any part of the North American continent."

Although somewhat overlooked by historians, Polk's first annual message remains one of the most significant such presidential addresses ever delivered, in part owing to the fact of Polk's subsequent determination to make good on its promises. Also significant is how much of it builds on the principles and perceived shortcomings of the Monroe administration, as the memory of that era continued to inform the expansionist politics of the 1840s. For if Monroe and Adams's statecraft merited praise for its affirmation of hemispheric superiority, it also deserved rebuke for "unwisely" ceding claims to Texas and Oregon.[21]

Polk's message is also significant for remaining silent on the institution of slavery. In fact, as was common for politicians of the time, he does not even mention it. Polk, like Tyler before him, denied that expansion threatened the Union, which he saw as capable of being "safely expanded to the utmost bounds of our territorial limits, and that as it shall be extended the bonds of our Union, so far from being weakened, will become stronger." A fierce critic of what he and many other Democrats perceived as the centralizing tendencies of the Whigs, Polk staunchly affirmed the Unionist and expansionist tradition of Jackson. Even as he decried interference in local matters by the central government, he charged anyone who contemplated the destruction of the Union as guilty of "moral treason."[22]

Polk first focused on acquiring Oregon, threatening the British with war if an agreement satisfactory to U.S. aspirations could not be worked out. Polk proceeded from the assumption that while the American legal position vis-à-vis Oregon might not be ironclad it still

---

[21] Richardson, ed., *Messages and Papers of the Presidents*, 4:396, 4:398, 4:399.
[22] Richardson, ed., *Messages and Papers of the Presidents*, 4:380, 4:379.

constituted the "best" claim, disregarding of course the claims of the Indian tribes to the region. This echoed a theme proving popular in the press, the notion that notwithstanding the claims and counterclaims of the various interested parties, "the true title" to Oregon belonged to Americans, ultimately coming from God in the name of progress. This attitude, a founding assumption of Manifest Destiny, guided Polk's Oregon diplomacy from the start. It received widest circulation via an editorial under the heading "The True Title" appearing in the *New York Morning News* on December 27, 1845:

> Away, away with all these cobweb issues of rights of discovery, exploration, settlement, contiguity, etc. To state the truth at once … we are free to say that were the respective cases … reversed – had England all ours, and we nothing but hers – our claim to Oregon would still be the best and strongest. And that claim is by the right of our manifest destiny to overspread and possess the whole of the continent which Providence has given us of the development of the great experiment of liberty and federated self-government entrusted to us.[23]

Perhaps no single paragraph better sums up the heads-we-win-tails-you-lose logic of the ideology of Manifest Destiny. Other voices in the emerging national print culture continued to beat the drum for Oregon. *De Bow's Review,* an important journal of commerce published in New Orleans, echoed the themes of Benton from a quarter-century earlier: "It seems to many chimerical to connect that country intimately with the commerce of the East Indies and the Pacific Ocean. But who shall prescribe bounds to national enterprise, and particularly to the enterprise of a nation like ours, so boundless in resources.... May not our commerce to … China … rival if not surpass that of any people on the earth?... Let an overland communication from ocean to ocean be established, and the Pacific coast will be of inestimable importance. Such a communication would give us a monopoly of the trade of the Pacific, and bring to us untold wealth."[24] As Oregon receded in importance to the British, it rose in importance to the Americans. Polk was determined to have Oregon, and California, too.

---

[23] Albert Weinberg, *Manifest Destiny* (Baltimore, 1935), 145.
[24] *De Bow's Review,* January 1, 1846, 69.

7

BULLYING BRITAIN, CONQUERING MEXICO, CLAIMING THE CANAL

There are now two great nations in the world which, starting from different points, seem to be advancing toward the same goal: The Russians and the Anglo-Americans.... Their point of departure is different and their paths diverse; nevertheless, each seems called by some secret design of Providence to one day hold in its hands the destinies of half the world.

Alexis de Tocqueville, *Democracy in America*,
vol. 1, 412–413

Throughout her history, right from her beginnings as a nation, America has been an *expansionary* power, with "expansion" being at least as important to her as the rather more celebrated ideal of "liberty."

Bernard Porter, *Empire and Superempire:*
Britain, America, and the World, 132

BULLYING BRITAIN, CONFRONTING MEXICO

Once fastened on to a goal, President James Polk was single-minded in its pursuit. He did not allow political opponents or constitutional objections to interfere with achieving his aims. His at times high-handed methods provoked controversy. To his critics, among them Alexander H. Stephens of Georgia, he was "Polk the mendacious," a president having an unparalleled capacity for "duplicity and equivocation."[1] There is evidence to support such a view, as Polk's intense sense of purpose at times prompted him to ride roughshod over the facts of a particular case. Yet he might equally be known as "Polk the audacious" for his outsized imperial ambitions as well as his get-it-done leadership style. Photographs of the Tennessean taken late in his life (photography being

---

[1] Frederick C. Merk, *Manifest Destiny and Mission in American History* (Cambridge, Mass., 1963), 106.

another one of the miraculous new technologies of the 1840s) reveal a visage that is as much a map to Polk's roughhewn character as are the more famous images of Abraham Lincoln made some years later.

Polk's Machiavellian duplicities offended the sensibilities of many of his contemporaries. However, it must be said that his mode of political and diplomatic operation fit well within the traditions and practices of American foreign policy to that point. The presidency of James Monroe in particular functioned as a foundational precedent for much of what Polk did as chief executive. Polk's commitment to the "reoccupation" of Oregon and the "reannexation" of Texas had the explicit aim of reversing the perceived bad precedent of compromising American claims to the territories even if it merely involved agreeing to a period of joint occupation, as was the case in Oregon. Polk artfully exploited the resentments of Southerners. Many demanded to know "Who lost Texas?," foreshadowing a political dynamic that would play out in twentieth-century American history over China policy. Polk, on the other hand, extended doctrinal status to the principles of noncolonization and nonintervention by reaffirming them in his 1845 annual message to Congress. At the same time, Polk absorbed the lessons of the Monroe administration regarding the use of war as an instrument of expansion; equally important, he learned how a vigorous defense of controversial foreign policy actions, combined with tight control over information about them, could intimidate and overwhelm domestic political opponents. Although he embraced his predecessor's foreign policy methods and principles, Polk did not share Monroe's fear that continued expansion into lands ripe for slavery might threaten the Union.

Faced with expansionist flashpoints on the northern and southern borders, Polk pushed a confrontation on both fronts. What others might have seen as problems, Polk saw as opportunities. He recognized that the fate of the western half of North America would be determined during his administration. He would not hesitate to use the apparatus of the state to achieve his expansionist aims. Bold action might secure the West for the United States; to be hesitant or indecisive would risk its being lost forever. Often seen as a mere tool of Southern slave expansionists, Polk was as eager, if not more so, to acquire California – more specifically its magnificent ports in San Francisco, San Diego, and Monterey – as he was Texas. He contended for Oregon spiritedly. He coveted the province of New Mexico in order to prevent its functioning as a foreign roadblock on the way to California. Polk's undoubted commitment to the institution of slavery and its spread should not obscure his commitment to a national expansionist program. His determination to meet the diverse expansionist ambitions of all sections in the name of union harked back to the original expansionist consensus on which it was founded.

Polk did not dally in pushing his ambitious agenda. At the outset of his administration he negotiated aggressively with Great Britain, ever ready to "twist the lion's tail" if necessary to let British foreign secretary Lord Aberdeen know that popular hostility toward Great Britain could be whipped up as necessary to support the administration's hard line. Britain sought to set the northern boundary at the Columbia River and to guarantee British vessels the right of passage along that stream. Given that few Americans lived north of the Columbia River at that time, it seemed a reasonable proposal. However, Polk wanted access to the harbor at Puget Sound, so he artfully used the rambunctiousness of the "54–40 or Fight" faction in the Democratic party to maneuver for his true goal: the establishment of the northern boundary at 49 degrees. He fomented Democrats from the Northwest such as Edward Hannegan of Indiana and William Allen of Ohio to demand all of Oregon, assuring them that he would never back down from the claim to 54–40 even though he planned all along to use their extreme claims to form the basis of a compromise at 49 degrees. He pushed Congress to vote to give the required year's notice of the intention to end the joint occupancy agreement in Oregon, apparently a step in the direction of confrontation. Here the president benefited from the demonstrated willingness of Americans to fight even when a lack of preparedness and plain common sense seemed to preclude that option, and indeed, the chest-thumping assertions of Hannegan, Allen, and others bore some resemblance to the War Hawks of 1812. Polk, unlike Madison, was not controlled by hotheads in Congress but rather used their threats to help extract a deal. He insisted that British settlements north of the forty-ninth parallel constituted a dangerous and unacceptable breech of the Monroe Doctrine's noncolonization clause forbidding further European settlement in the hemisphere, and in the early months of 1846 he threatened a third Anglo-American war over a territory peripheral to the immediate interests of both nations.

If Polk bluffed war and sought peace with Great Britain, it was very much the reverse as concerns the Republic of Mexico. From the time of Texas independence in 1836, successive governments in Mexico City had threatened war if the United States annexed Texas. This had not really delayed annexation – internal political divisions over slavery were largely responsible for that – but it had contributed to anxiety over the admission of Texas to the Union. Yet when Texas did enter the Union in July 1845, Mexican officials took no meaningful action other than to break off diplomatic relations. To Polk, this signified weakness and an invitation to increase the pressure, to provoke a confrontation forcing Mexico to defend its national honor and from which the United States could then attain its expansionist goals. First, he had to appear to try to resolve the differences with Mexico via negotiation. To that end, he dispatched John Slidell of Louisiana to Mexico City to negotiate the range of issues separating the two states. In truth, Slidell went not to negotiate but to dictate: He demanded that Mexico drop its protests against the annexation of Texas, recognize its boundary at the Rio Grande del Norte, and agree to sell California ($25 million) and New Mexico ($3 million) to the United States. In exchange for these extravagant demands, the Polk administration stood ready to assume the nearly $2 million in claims that American citizens held against the Mexican government for private property seized during the course of the numerous revolutions since 1821 (once again, the central government acted the part of the bill collector of last resort for American entrepreneurs abroad).

Polk had little confidence that Slidell would succeed in his mission; as it turned out, the chaotic political situation in Mexico City prevented Slidell's formal reception by the Mexican government. Slidell's rebuff probably did not matter. No regime could negotiate away territory to the Yankees and survive. Late in 1845 General Mariano Paredes y Arrilaga took power in a bloodless coup, making the army the de facto sovereign of the putative republic. Slidell remained unacknowledged, finally leaving Mexico City in March 1846 convinced that only force could bring Mexico to its senses. Although Polk hoped that annexation might be achieved peacefully, his reading of the Mexican political scene made him judge it as unlikely that an agreement of the sort he wanted could be obtained. The intransigence and chaos of the Mexican authorities played right into Polk's hands, for it opened the door to the war of conquest that he wanted. What national pride and political circumstance made impossible, the objective balance of forces between the two states made inevitable. Polk continued the American imperial tradition of feeding on the remains of the Spanish Empire, this time via the agency of one of Spain's successor empires, the Republic of Mexico.

Polk had been expecting and planning for a war (or possibly two) from the day of his inauguration as president. In July 1845, before annexation had even been finalized, he ordered General Zachary B. Taylor to advance a force of 4,000 troops to the south bank of the Nueces River. After Texas formally entered the Union in December, Polk ordered Taylor to take up a position in the north bank of the Rio Grande and launch a blockade – an act of war – against Matamoros at the mouth of the Nueces River. Equally important, Polk ordered the creation of a customs house, an unmistakable sign of national authority. The move to defend the Rio Grande is significant because it was evidence that the United States had annexed not only Texas but also Texas's imperial claims and now stood ready to assert them as its own. Just across the river, nearly 5,000 Mexican troops confronted the American presence.

In March 1846, Polk repeated his request to Congress for an increase in the size and preparedness of the army and navy, citing the "unusual and extraordinary armaments and warlike preparations, naval and military" by Great Britain in the vicinity of the Northwest Coast.[2] Yet, by that time, the talks with Great Britain verged on success; Polk wanted increased armaments to confront Mexico, not Great Britain. While the public fretted about the possibility of another war with Great Britain, Polk waited for circumstances to evolve with Mexico. Once an agreement with Britain on Oregon had been secured, and following the arrival of the news that Mexican officials had rebuffed Slidell, Polk acted. On Saturday, May 9, he convened his cabinet for a council of war. His diary entry on the meeting reveals that the members agreed that circumstances – on claims, Texas, and the insulting treatment of Slidell – justified an immediate declaration of war, all except for Secretary of the Navy George Bancroft, who argued that the United States should wait for Mexico to take some aggressive action so that it could plausibly be

---

[2] James D. Richardson, ed., *Messages and Papers of the Presidents* (Washington, D.C., 1903), 4:427.

blamed for starting the conflict. The president adjourned the meeting, having resolved to ask for war the following Tuesday. Yet, only hours later, news arrived that on April 24 a company of American dragoons patrolling the east bank of the Rio Grande had been attacked by a much larger Mexican force, killing sixteen U.S. troops and taking the rest prisoner. Polk now had his indisputable *casus belli*. He moved up his war message to Congress to Monday, May 11.

Polk's war message is one of the preeminent examples of the rhetoric and logic of Manifest Destiny. It builds on the nationalist themes and rhetorical devices of earlier American politicians and pundits even as it creates strong new precedents for future presidents contemplating war. Before a packed gallery, in a capital and a nation suddenly burning with war fever because of the news of the skirmish on the Rio Grande, Polk crafted a narrative of Mexican wrongdoing that made war seem to be reasonable, just, and inevitable. He predicated his message on "the strong desire" of the United States "to establish peace with Mexico on liberal and honest terms," emphasizing the harsh rebuke of Slidell's peace mission and Mexico's repeated threats of war if Texas was annexed. Consistent with the rhetoric of empire, Polk left no doubt that Mexico was the aggressor: "[A]fter a long-continued series of menaces ..." Mexico had "at last invaded our territory and shed the blood of our fellow citizens on our own soil." The bulk of the message crafted a narrative of a derelict and dictatorial Mexican regime incapable of maintaining order internally and unable or unwilling to honor its treaty commitments internationally. Polk cast Mexico as a rogue state that "has repeatedly threatened to make war upon us for the purpose of reconquering Texas." Hinting at the fact that war had been decided upon prior to the skirmishes along the Rio Grande, Polk marshaled a stunning indictment: "The cup of forbearance had been exhausted even before the recent information from the frontier of the Del Norte. But now, after reiterated menaces, Mexico has passed the boundary of the United States, has invaded our territory and shed American blood upon the American soil.... As war exists, and, notwithstanding all our efforts to avoid it, exists by the act of Mexico herself, we are called upon by every consideration of duty and patriotism to vindicate with decision the honor, the rights, and the interests of our country."[3]

---

[3] Richardson, ed., *Messages and Papers of the Presidents,* 4:438, 4:442.

Blood. Soil. Patriotism. Honor. Rights. Duty. Polk held a strong hand as he attempted to coax Congress into war notwithstanding widespread opposition to it. To ensure that the administration got the vote tally it wanted, Polk's congressional allies strictly limited debate on the measure, arguing that General Taylor's exposed position in Mexico allowed no time for discussion. The vote occurred after only two hours of debate in the Senate and only a little more than that in the House. Members of Congress had no time to examine the mass of documents submitted by the president in support of his case – documents that in any event had only a tangential relation to the arguments made by the president. Calhoun later claimed that had members been given a chance to scrutinize these documents, no more then ten would have voted yes. Yet Calhoun seems to have forgotten the circumstances surrounding the First Seminole War, when the Monroe administration had submitted a mass of documents that allegedly supported its case and that a later congressional investigative committee found to be largely irrelevant. As was the case in 1819, the rhetoric of American empire combined with the reality of American war dead overwhelmed facts at odds with the official narrative. In the end, Polk got his war, easily, as the House voted 179–14 in favor, and the Senate 40–2. Thirty-five members of the House abstained from voting, skeptical of Polk's rationale for war but too afraid to vote against the measure for fear of being labeled unpatriotic. Daniel Webster missed the vote. Polk called for "a large body of volunteers" to fly to arms to chastise the Mexicans and for all the resources needed to "prosecute the war with vigor."[4]

Why did Congress vote to commit the United States to war in the face of widespread resistance and an abundance of facts contradicting the administration's narrative of events? Frederick Merk writes, "The explanation is found in a momentary hysteria on the part of the public which Polk converted into a stampede ... This was a victory for stampede tactics."[5] Indeed, Polk's determination to frame the war as a response to Mexican aggression continued to stick in the throats of many for the remainder of the conflict. Charles Francis Adams, son of John Quincy and American minister to Great Britain during the Civil War, characterized it in print as "one of the grossest national lies that was

---

[4] Richardson, ed., *Messages and Papers of the Presidents*, 4:443.
[5] Samuel Eliot Morison, Frederick C. Merk, and Frank Friedel, *Dissent in Three American Wars* (Cambridge, Mass., 1970), 43, 39.

ever deliberately told."[6] Calhoun harped on the false premise justifying the war as a notorious and potentially fatal blow to the Constitution.

One of the strongest challenges to Polk's claims regarding the origins of the war came from first-term representative Abraham Lincoln of Illinois. Within weeks of taking his seat in 1847, Lincoln introduced a series of eight resolutions designed to interrogate the administration's claim that Mexico had started the war and more specifically to determine the exact "spot" on which it allegedly had "shed American blood upon the American soil." Lincoln feared that Polk, by manipulating the public to support his expansionist agenda, had opened the door to some future president using a similar ruse to unleash from congressional control the executive power to make war. Lincoln followed up his "spot resolutions" against the war by endorsing Rep. George Ashmun's January 1848 amendment asserting that the conflict had been "unnecessarily and unconstitutionally begun by the President." Finally, the first-term lawmaker made an hour-long speech to the House decrying the president's duplicity, characterizing his defense of the war as "the half-insane mumbling of a fever dream," and the president as "a bewildered, confounded, and miserably perplexed man." Yet while some observers cheered Lincoln's principled stand, others did not, including many in his home district. Newspaper editorialists contrasted Lincoln's "pathetic lamentations over the fate of those Mexicans" to his supposed "cold indifference in regard to our own slaughtered citizens." The Chicago *Times* alleged that Lincoln "made himself ridiculous and odious ... in giving aid and comfort to the Mexican enemy."[7] Ultimately, Lincoln learned from his one-man crusade against "Mr. Polk's War" that, once begun, a war could take on a life of its own and that the public had little interest in revisiting the details of how it began. Lincoln paid for his principled opposition to the war by being voted out of office in 1848.

To Polk, the fiction of Mexican aggression had to be staunchly maintained so as to justify a cession of territory as punishment. He spent the rest of the war affirming the thesis of Mexican aggression as the cause of the conflict. At times, his efforts to do so backfired. He nearly

---

[6] Morison et al., *Dissent in Three American Wars*, 40, from the *Boston Whig*, June 2, 1846.

[7] Michael Burlingame, *Abraham Lincoln: A Life* (Baltimore, 2008), 1:267, 1:266–7.

caused a revolt in the Senate by affixing a preamble to that effect to the actual congressional declaration of war. Some senators could not stomach signing off on what appeared to them to be an egregious falsehood. Polk well understood that the war needed to be seen as legitimate in its causes if he hoped to gain what he wanted as one of its consequences. Asserting Texas's claim to the Rio Grande del Norte is not as far-fetched as some historians have suggested. True, the Spanish imperial authorities in 1816 formally had defined the Texas boundary to be the Nueces; this was the claim now asserted by Mexico. But a Texas claim to the Rio Grande had first been staked via the terms of Santa Ana's surrender at San Jacinto in 1836; the fact that Santa Ana later renounced the agreement and that the Mexican legislature never ratified it meant not a whit to Texans – they had a signed treaty in hand and intended to assert its legitimacy by force, as did Polk. The claim to the Rio Grande del Norte was dubious at best, but no more so than other American expansionist claims, including that to Oregon. Wherever the first blood had been spilled, the matter proved moot once Congress validated Polk's narrative of events by voting for war. Once war had begun, no politically acceptable way existed to stop it without seeming to diminish support for the troops in the field. As a result, Congress regularly voted monies for a war that many members opposed.

Even as war with Mexico loomed, the diplomatic dance with Britain over Oregon reached its endgame. Polk reiterated the "unquestioned" American claim to all of Oregon in his December 1845 annual message and vowed never to retreat from this position, but not long after Congress voted to begin the countdown to abrogating the joint occupation agreement, he let it be known to British negotiators that he would consider a compromise at 49 degrees so long as the Senate agreed to the plan. Robert Peel's ministry, while outraged at the audacity of the Americans, calculated that the rapidly rising number of Americans in Oregon and the importance of maintaining good economic relations with the United States outweighed the insult to national honor and interest that compromise to some extent represented. Thus when a British compromise proposal drawing the boundary at 49 degrees as far as Puget Sound and limiting British navigation rights to the Columbia reached Washington in early June 1846, Polk presented it immediately for the Senate's advice, announcing that he formally would present it for ratification if supported by two-thirds of the Senate. By placing the onus on the Senate, Polk kept his pledge that he would not compromise on the Oregon question. Preoccupied with the war with Mexico, the Senate passed the Oregon Treaty on June 15 by a 41–14 vote.

Polk's bold policy of confronting two external challenges at once even as the domestic consensus for union rapidly frayed has led some historians to label him as reckless.[8] From a certain perspective, this is understandable. After all, Great Britain stood as by far the world's leading power at the time, and the government in Mexico City (still the largest city in the Western Hemisphere) ruled an emerging state with a landmass nearly as large as that of the United States. Peel's ministry had dispatched the compromise proposal only days before word had arrived in London of the outbreak of the war with Mexico. Had this information been available to them, it is possible that the British would have chosen war with a weakened and distracted United States. Yet Polk did not blink. Whatever the British stake in Oregon in the 1840s, he judged it highly unlikely they would test American military resolve a third time. If the Americans, against long odds, had been willing to take on the British Empire in 1776 and 1812, who could doubt that they might do it again? In the next showdown, the passion for Canada shown by the Hunters' Lodges on the northern border might be rekindled and supported, and not tamped down, by the central government. Then the conquest of Canada might truly be, as Jefferson had envisioned, "a mere matter of marching." Whatever their absolute advantage in ships, troops, and money, it made no sense for the British to confront a determined if weaker foe over some far-off claims, especially if that potential foe also had the role of your best trading partner. Polk lectured a member of Congress, "[T]he only way to treat John Bull was to look him straight in the eye; that I considered a bold and firm course on our part the pacific one; that if the Congress faltered or hesitated in their course, John Bull would immediately become arrogant and more grasping in his demands."[9] Polk the audacious had measured his opponent well. His bullying of John Bull had resulted in another American expansionist victory.

As for the Republic of Mexico, the facts strongly suggested that whatever seeming advantages it had in a showdown with the United States,

---

[8] See, for example, Daniel Walker Howe, *"What Hath God Wrought": The Transformation of America, 1815–1848* (New York, 2007), chapters 18, 19.

[9] Allan Nevins, ed., *Polk: The Diary of a President 1845–1849* (London, 1929), 42.

it ultimately would be no match for the armies of Manifest Destiny. Santa Ana's massive force had neither defeated the ragtag Texas rebels in 1836 nor challenged the Lone Star Republic's independence since then. What chance could it have against an American military machine led by a cadre of disciplined and experienced officers, soldiered largely by the militant sons of the South, equipped with the most modern firearms and field artillery, and supported by a navy capable of projecting power to the shores of Mexico in support of an invasion? Polk saw an imperialist opportunity of unprecedented proportions, and he did not allow the potential domestic political consequences – the further undermining of the increasingly fragile unionist consensus – to inhibit him. In this regard, his audacity and his recklessness exceeded that of his mentor and model, Jackson, who had carefully refrained as president from agitating sectional divisions.

The Mexican-American War had an unmistakable racial dimension. The assumption of Mexican inferiority – racial, religious, economic, political, cultural – informed discussion of the war even by those Americans opposed to it. By the 1840s, the liberal universalism of the revolutionary era had been supplanted by an early form of what later would be termed "social Darwinism." This outlook assumed human existence to be a grim struggle for survival in which the superior races (of which the Anglo-Saxon was considered the best) would thrive, and presumed inferiors, such as the mixed-race Mexican people, would be subordinated if not made extinct. In this manner, the war would have a salutary effect on human affairs, at least in the minds of some people. Early in the conflict the *Casket*, a Cincinnati publication, opined, "The Mexicans will be led by this war to think of their weakness and inferiority."[10] Tennessean and future president Andrew Johnson cast the war as God's punishment of Mexico's corrupt and uncivilized nature: "[T]he Anglo-Saxon race has been selected as the rod of her retribution."[11] The stark contrast between the revolutionary transformations occurring within the United States and the seeming backwardness of Mexico gave the war the appearance to some of being a humanitarian endeavor lifting Mexico out of darkness.

---

[10] Reginald Horsman, *Race and Manifest Destiny: The Origins of American Racial Anglo-Saxonism* (Cambridge, Mass., 1981), 236.

[11] Horsman, *Race and Manifest Destiny*, 237.

Yet it would be wrong to ascribe the origins of the war primarily to racial motivations. The U.S. ambition to take the next logical step in its expansionist process and acquire California and adjoining territories is the root cause of the war. The alleged racial and cultural inferiority of Mexicans served as a justification, and not a motive, for the conflict. Had the coveted lands been held by Great Britain (as was the case in Oregon), one can assume that nonracial justifications would have been duly trotted out. The insatiable land hunger of Americans brought on the Mexican-American war.

OPPOSITION TO THE WAR

Congress – caught in the whirlpool of excitement surrounding the events in Texas and Oregon and loath to seem weak when matters of national interest and honor arose – voted overwhelmingly for war, but the public stood divided over it, especially in the northern and western states. At the outset of the war some commentators – most notably the journalist Walt Whitman – welcomed the struggle as a means to redeem Mexico from its presumed backwardness. Whitman editorialized in the Brooklyn *Eagle,* "What has miserable, inefficient Mexico ... to do with the great mission of peopling the New World with a noble race?"[12] Yet most of the nation's literary elite (disproportionately it must be said from antiwar New England) was appalled at what appeared to be an act of naked aggression against a neighboring state. The annexation of Texas had been opposed by a popular majority but occurred anyway; now a popular majority opposed a war of aggression against Mexico but had to acquiesce in it, too.

Opposition began as soon as war was declared. On May 12, 1846, Horace Greeley editorialized in the *New York Tribune,* "People of the United States! Your rulers are precipitating you into a fathomless abyss of crime and calamity! Why sleep you thoughtless on its verge, as though this was not your business.... Awake and arrest the work of the butchery ere it shall be too late to preserve your souls from the guilt of wholesale slaughter!"[13] Ralph Waldo Emerson, perhaps the nation's

---

[12] Horsman, *Race and Manifest Destiny,* 35.
[13] Frederick C. Merk, *Manifest Destiny and Mission in American History* (Cambridge, Mass., 1963), 44, from the *New York Tribune,* May 12, 1846.

preeminent literary light, pronounced, "[T]he United States will conquer Mexico, but it will be as a man swallows arsenic, which brings him down in turn. Mexico will poison us."[14] William Lloyd Garrison, notorious as the publisher of the nation's foremost abolitionist newspaper the *Liberator*, characterized the war as transparently a slaveholder's conspiracy "waged for basest ends."[15] The poet James Russell Lowell gave expression to the same sentiment via a series of biting satires collectively known as the *Biglow Papers,* a lasting contribution to American literature. Henry David Thoreau made perhaps the most enduring protest against the war in his public address "Resistance to Civil Government." Although widely known as "Civil Disobedience," the original title better captures the ominous nature of Thoreau's protest in that he did not advocate the principled violation of the law in the name of social change as later did Gandhi and Martin Luther King, Jr. Rather, Thoreau urged individuals to withdraw their loyalty from a union that both protected slavery and sought to expand it by waging wars of aggression against its neighbors. Resistance in this scheme acted as a form of individualized secession. Thoreau's very public act of secession was matched in private by a growing number of other Americans whose consciences would not allow them to continue to rest easy in a union with slave holders.

The moral questions raised by the war precipitated a split in New England politics between the "conscience Whigs," who spoke with increasing fervor against slavery and its spread, and the "cotton Whigs" (such as Daniel Webster), who, for reasons of economic interest or the preservation of the Union, refused to challenge the dominance of the slave-holding faction.[16] John Quincy Adams stood out as the most outspoken of the conscience Whigs. He was one of fourteen House members to vote against the declaration of what he termed "this unrighteous war." In the waning months of his life he acted the part of an unrelenting prophet of the apocalyptic struggle he was certain would ensue as God's punishment for waging an unjust war.

---

[14] James Dunkerly, *Americana: The Americas in the World, Around 1850* (London, 2000), 24.
[15] Robert W. Johanssen, *To the Halls of the Montezumas: The Mexican War in the American Imagination* (New York, 1985), 215.
[16] See Kinley Brauer, *Cotton v. Conscience: Massachusetts Whig Politics and Southwestern Expansion* (Lexington, 1967).

If no one better personified the antiwar movement among the Northern Whig antislavery faction than did Adams, to many Southerners and some Northerners, he epitomized Yankee hypocrisy and faithlessness. After all, Adams's staunch opposition to Texas annexation did not lessen his zealous interest in acquiring Oregon. Even worse, his refusal to countenance the continued institution of slavery represented a de facto breach of the original constitutional bargain; had the framers held such radical views, no union would have been formed. Adams himself had as secretary of state (and against his own conscience) overseen the Union's expansion into lands suitable for slavery. It was Adams, more than anyone else, who had saved Jackson from congressional censure and disgrace by vigorously defending the latter's constitutionally dubious conquest of Florida. Now Adams affected outrage at Polk's similarly high-handed tactics and further boosted his role as the head of a new generation of Northerners who presumed unilaterally to renege on a crucial part of the constitutional bargain between the slave states and the free states.

Like the War of 1812, the Mexican-American War kindled intense divisions that threatened national unity. It intensified the abolitionist movement and radicalized many Northern antislavery Whigs by forcing them to acknowledge that slavery was not going to die a quiet death on the American political stage. While opposition to the war centered in the North and in the Whig party, some Democrats opposed it, perhaps most notably the old warhorse John C. Calhoun. As a Southerner and a slave owner, Calhoun might be expected to at least acquiesce in the war if not actively support it. But he spoke out against it with all his might: In February 1847 he said to Congress, "[E]very Senator knows that I was opposed to the war; but none knows but myself the depth of that opposition. With my conceptions of its character and consequences, it was impossible for me to vote for it ... I said to many of my friends that a deed had been done from which the country would not be able to recover for a long time, if ever ... it has closed the first volume of our political history under the constitution, and opened the second, and that no mortal could tell what would be written in it."[17] Not only writers and politicians opposed the war. Ulysses S. Grant, a recent graduate of West Point who served with distinction in the struggle, later wrote to

---

[17] Dunkerly, *Americana*, 491.

a friend, "I do not think there was ever a more wicked war ... I thought so at the time ... only I had not moral courage enough to resign.... I had the horror of the Mexican War, and I have always believed that it was on our part most unjust."[18]

Waging a war of aggression on a neighboring country based on a flimsy pretext greatly disturbed many Americans, especially those old enough to remember the revolutionary era. One of the most poignant protests of this sort came from Albert Gallatin, Democrat from western Pennsylvania, old-school Jeffersonian, and one of the most admired elder statesmen of his time. Gallatin published two pamphlets condemning the war as a gigantic overreaching of the sort that did violence to the traditions of the Founders. The second, titled "Peace With Mexico," decried the notion of expansion-by-conquest as fundamentally un-American and instead called for a more measured expansionist process by suggesting that noble growths are slow and that the United States should be a "model republic" to the world, and not a rapacious expansionist that wars on its neighbors to expand its domain. Polk and many other Democrats tended to see such arguments as absurd. In the first place, American expansion had never been "slow." U.S. diplomats had always grabbed for as much as they could, and far more than was needed at the time. Territorial expansion had always been about future, not present, needs. More to the point, circumstances did not allow Americans the luxury of a leisurely pace as concerned Texas, California, and Oregon. These regions had to be seized now or perhaps slip from the American grasp forever. In any case, Gallatin's pamphlet appeared near the end of the war, making its arguments moot and quickly forgotten.

A certain class of Americans opposed the war, but the combination of reflexive support for soldiers under fire, a string of stirring military victories, and a burgeoning national media market in which daily reports from the front were for the first time widely and affordably available, kindled a mass enthusiasm for the conflict especially in the early going. Large pro-war rallies – estimated at twenty thousand in Philadelphia and even larger in New York – inflamed the public mind with a vision of chivalrous American warriors in the tradition of Washington bringing

---

[18] Edmund Wilson, *Patriotic Gore: Studies in the Literature of the Civil War* (New York, 1962), 133–4.

freedom to a benighted people at the barrel of a gun. Popular writer George Lippard suggested a direct link between the victory at Bunker Hill and the "establishing in the valley of Mexico, a new dominion – THE EMPIRE OF FREEDOM."[19] Commodore Robert F. Stockton, who played a prominent role in the annexation of California, declared to an enthusiastic audience in Philadelphia in 1847 that "the glory of the achievements there ... is in the establishment of the first free press in California – in having built the first school house in California – in having established religious toleration as well as civil liberty in California." Stockton argued that the duty from which America "dare not shrink" was "redeeming Mexico from misrule and civil strife."[20] The creation of a new generation of American warriors suitable for "the hero worship" advocated by the popular contemporary English writer Thomas Carlyle functioned to allay anxieties about the rapid changes in ways of living being wrought by industrialization. Notwithstanding the moral and political objections of many to the war, the nationalist imperative to support American troops under fire limited dissent. Polk took direct aim at the war's critics. In his second annual message in December 1846 he accused those who questioned the war's origins of giving "aid and comfort" to Mexico (i.e., committing an act of treason), adding, "[A] more effectual means could not have been devised to encourage the enemy and protract the war than to advocate and adhere to their cause."[21]

TAYLOR'S ADVANCE

After the attack by Mexican forces on April 24, General Zachary Taylor took the initiative, not waiting for Washington formally to commence hostilities. Maneuvering against a force almost 50 percent larger than his, Taylor went on the offensive south of the Rio Grande. A veteran of the War of 1812 and the Second Seminole War, Taylor was yet another experienced, battle-hardened officer produced by the American military in spite of its practice of maintaining a skeletal force in time of peace. A slave owner from Mississippi, Taylor was a staunch unionist who inspired the devotion of his troops by being both plainspoken

---

[19] Johanssen, *To the Halls of the Montezumas*, 61.
[20] Armin Rappaport, *A History of American Diplomacy* (New York, 1975), 96.
[21] Richardson, ed., *Messages and Papers of the Presidents*, 4:473.

and casually dressed, shunning the feathered hats and epaulets worn by some generals. On May 8 and 9, Taylor's army won important victories at Palo Alto and Resaca de la Palma, in no small part owing to the effectiveness of the army's "flying artillery," units capable of devastating enemy ranks with deadly cannon fire and then rapidly redeploying to another position. The Mexican troops fled in panic across the Rio Grande, leaving Taylor and his army virtually unopposed along the northern border.

After taking control of Matamoros, Taylor led his army on a daring march deep into Mexican territory. Far removed from resupply or reinforcement, the American army lived off the land as it advanced, requisitioning supplies as needed from the mostly indigenous people in its path. By summer, Taylor and his troops stood before the imposing fortress at Monterey, taking it only after a bitter house-by-house struggle. The ornate architecture and exotic locale of Mexico prompted some American soldiers to regard themselves as latter-day knights-errant of the sort popularized by the novelist Sir Walter Scott. After taking Monterey, Taylor stopped his advance to await further diplomatic developments. As a Whig, he was reluctant to press his advantage so as to deprive Polk of leverage to make ever more outrageous claims on Mexico. Taylor's army of invasion made one last rendezvous with history when his force, composed largely of inexperienced volunteers and outnumbered between 2 and 3 to 1, held the line against a counterattacking Mexican army at the Battle of Buena Vista in February 1847. At that point, Taylor dug in to await a diplomatic end to the conflict.

Historians have long seen the Mexican-American War as a dress rehearsal for the Civil War, and for good reason: The war gave an entire generation of officers combat experience that proved critical to their service in the much larger war to follow, including Robert E. Lee, Ulysses Grant, Jefferson Davis, James Longstreet, George McClellan, and many more. West Point graduates comprised a substantial portion of the officer corps, validating Jefferson's establishment in 1802 of a national military academy. The naval blockade of Mexico's ports on both its Atlantic and its Pacific coasts prevented the Mexican army from being resupplied from abroad and previewed a strategy that would be critically important in the Civil War. Moreover, the mania for war news greatly accelerated the construction of telegraph lines along the East

Coast; by the end of the war, the telegraph wire connected cities from Boston to Charleston.

Although it is true that the Mexican-American War served to prepare the U.S. military for the coming conflagration, it must be noted that every American war, to one degree or another, has been a dress rehearsal for the next one. Even by the 1840s the American military tradition had built on a legacy of individual valor and institutional memory to create a fighting force that, man for man, arguably was the best in the world at that time. The Mexican-American War served notice to the European powers not to take American military might lightly, whatever the minuscule size of its peacetime force. The war did result in some distinct and crucial institutional knowledge: It gave the central government its first experience in conquering a foreign country. Heretofore, America's wars with other nation-states had been to defend its own territory, and with the exception of the numerous failed efforts to take Canada, it had not attempted the force projection necessary to invade and conquer a foreign state. The Mexican-American War changed that, and the national government emerged from the conflict much more capable of marshaling and projecting military power.

As Taylor plunged deep into Mexico, Colonel Stephen Watts Kearny and the army of the west, a well-supplied force of about 5,000 troops, marched quickly from Fort Leavenworth, Kansas, to conquer New Mexico. More populated than either California or Texas, New Mexico was important chiefly as a connecting route from Texas to the West Coast. Aided by the Mormon Battalion, a supply convoy sent west by Brigham Young to demonstrate his sect's loyalty to the United States, Kearny took Santa Fe in August with a minimum of bloodshed; the acting governor of the province went into exile along with the bribe money it is rumored he took in exchange for surrendering his outnumbered and outgunned command. From there, Kearny sent a small force to California to assist Fremont and Commodore John D. Sloat in securing the victory there and dispatched Colonel Alexander W. Doniphan and his Second Missouri Regiment overland to link up with Taylor in Monterey. The American military marched across the North American continent, and forces opposing it either suffered crushing defeats or melted away in the face of the advance. This thrust through the midsection of the continent also marked the extension and continuation of the Indian War; the Comanche Empire, dominant on the Plains for two centuries, now entered a period of decline culminating in total defeat by 1875.[22]

TO THE HALLS OF THE MONTEZUMAS

With Taylor stopped at Monterey and the Mexicans battered and bloodied but as yet unbowed, Polk conceived a plan to attack the Mexican capital via a landing at Vera Cruz. He reluctantly selected General Winfield Scott, army chief of staff, to head the invasion. In Polk's eyes, Scott's status as a Whig and likely presidential candidate diminished the latter's undoubted capacity for the command. Like Taylor, Scott had served in the War of 1812, emerging from that con-flict with only a little less prestige than did Jackson. Unlike Jackson, Scott remained in the army his entire professional career, resigning his commission in the early days of the Civil War. In contrast to Taylor, Scott was meticulous in appearance, earning himself the nickname "Old Fuss and Feathers." Yet his reputation is that of one of the fin-est military leaders in American history. Working with the navy, Scott designed a bold plan to surmount the heavily guarded entrance to Vera Cruz by an amphibious landing a few miles from the city. Scott helped to design a flotilla of flat-bottomed craft that effectively landed 10,000 soldiers quickly and safely, along with heavy naval cannons brought ashore to batter the fortresses that guarded Vera Cruz, the place where Cortes had launched the Spanish invasion of Mexico more than three centuries earlier.

It proved to be one of the first large-scale amphibious assaults in modern history and the largest in American history until World War II. In March 1847, Scott's cannons pounded the city of Vera Cruz and its inhabitants, both military and civilian, with six thousand shells, thereby reducing its stone architecture to rubble. Vera Cruz soon fell, an astound-ing triumph of planning, logistics, and courage. From there, Scott's army retraced the path of the conquistadors 250 miles to Mexico City, fighting and winning all of the numerous engagements it faced en route, including a decisive encounter at Cerro Gordo, a Mexican stronghold

---

[22] On the rise and fall of the Comanches, see Pekka Hamalainen, *The Comanche Empire* (New Haven, 2008).

in a rocky and steep mountain canyon. American troops disassembled their artillery pieces and hauled them by block and tackle up and down the steep canyon to positions behind the Mexican lines, surprising the enemy with deadly fire from the rear. Some 3,000 Mexican soldiers surrendered to Scott, who quickly disarmed and paroled them before resuming the march of the "Army of Conquest" inland.

The pathos of Mexican resistance found its ultimate expression in the Battle of Chapultepec, gateway to Mexico City. An imposing fortress on a six-hundred-foot hill, Chapultepec housed Mexico's military academy and was bravely defended by its occupants, among them child soldiers whose determined yet futile resistance has caused them to be remembered as *los niños héroes*. After several days of heavy fighting, American soldiers scaled the walls of Chapultepec with ladders and pickaxes, raising the American flag over "the halls of Montezuma" on September 13. The next day, Mexico City fell to American forces. Scott's march from Vera Cruz to the capital is remembered today as one of the boldest military campaigns in history. The United States had conquered the neighboring state of Mexico.

The Mexican-American War represented another example of the dynamic expandability of the American military. From a prewar force of about 8,000 troops, by war's end the army numbered approximately 120,000, some 73,000 of whom were volunteers. Many of these volunteers had previous military training, and most of them came from the southern states. A core of experienced and skilled officers allowed for the efficient and effective increase in the nation's forces in a short time. One authority has pronounced American artillery "the equal if not the superior" to any of its time.[23] The engineering skills of the officer corps had proven enormously valuable to the efficient projection of military force. It was an innovative approach, which avoided the massive cost of maintaining a permanently large military establishment without compromising the nation's security. By conventional assessments – the size of its standing military force – the United States did not pose much of a threat on the world stage. However, considering how quickly and effectively that small force could be expanded and deployed, and how minimal annual military expenditures meant huge savings related to the

[23] John S. D. Eisenhower, *So Far From God: The U.S. War with Mexico, 1846–1848* (New York, 1989), 379.

costs associated with maintaining a large force in readiness, even in the 1840s the United States ranked as a first-rate military power.

Anticipating a short war, Polk acted to extract a favorable settlement almost immediately after hostilities began. His first gambit sought to employ Lopez de Santa Ana – ousted as president in 1844 and currently in exile in Cuba – in a scheme to bring the old dictator back to power and then reward the United States for its help with hefty territorial concessions in a peace treaty. Santa Ana returned to Mexico from Cuba on a British warship and received special permission to cross the American blockade. Once back in Mexico City, however, Santa Ana betrayed Polk and vigorously sought both to energize the Mexican resistance and to restore himself to power. When word of this sordid scheme leaked out, critics lambasted it as a blow to America's integrity. It is true that Polk's audacity usually served him well as president, but in allowing himself to be gulled by Santa Ana, he overplayed his hand, to the detriment of his own and the nation's reputation.

Polk next initiated peace feelers with Mexico via the unusual path of designating *New York Sun* publisher Moses Y. Beach as his confidential agent empowered to explore possible peace proposals with the Mexican government. Acting in a semiofficial manner, Beach was accompanied on his mission by the journalist, speculator, and Manifest Destiny booster Jane McManus Storm, who served as his interpreter. Beach and Storm hoped to broker a peace deal, and Beach sought to collect a tidy commission on his handiwork in the form of a grant of control of the right of transit across Tehuantepec. Whatever slim chance of success Beach may have had evaporated when he and Storm backed a clerical revolt against the military government of Paredes in Mexico City. The revolt soon collapsed, forcing both Americans to flee for their lives to avoid being executed for their revolutionary exploits. For a second time, Polk's peacemaking efforts proved amateurish.

Although the war began as an attempt to punish Mexico for its presumed wrongdoing, few Americans had the stomach for the naked conquest of its territories. It just seemed too greedy. Secretary of State Buchanan went so far as to suggest to the president that the United States should issue a formal announcement to foreign governments signaling its intentions to refrain from conquest. Polk quickly quashed that idea, arguing that even though it was not a war for conquest, certain territories might need to be retained if only as compensation for the cost of the war. As those costs mounted, so did Polk's territorial demands.

In April 1847 he selected Nicholas P. Trist, the chief clerk in the Department of State, as a special envoy to attempt to persuade the Mexicans to make peace on American terms. In his youth Trist had been a protégé of Jefferson, and that, along with his long government service, made him a reasonable choice for this important mission. The terms of Mexico's capitulation were to include the unconditional recognition of Texas annexation, with a border at the Rio Grande, and the purchase of Alta California and New Mexico for no more than $20 million. In addition, Mexico would be required to pay the longstanding claims against it by American citizens. Once in Mexico, Trist revealed himself as a diplomat to be something of a free agent. Linking up with Scott in Vera Cruz, Trist soon took to feuding with the aged general over matters of authority and protocol to a point where the two men refused to speak to one another, communicating only by letter. It is said that a timely offer of guava marmalade from Trist to an ill Scott repaired relations between the two men, and the two began to work together to produce a deal with the Santa Ana government. In August, Scott halted his troops a few miles outside Mexico City while a brief armistice was declared to allow for talks. Mexican negotiators agreed to acknowledge the fact of Texas annexation but continued to claim the Nueces as the boundary and demanded that the United States pay the costs of the war. Scott then prepared his assault on Mexico City.

ALL OF MEXICO

Monitoring events in Washington, Polk fretted when he discovered that Trist and General Scott were working together to craft a deal. One of the purposes of sending Trist in the first place had been to deprive Scott, a staunch Whig and likely presidential contender in 1848, from getting the credit for winning both the war and the peace. In early 1847, California and New Mexico had seemed an adequate recompense for the war; by the fall, however, the lengthening list of American victories along with Mexico's obstinate refusal to yield seemed to suggest a need for further territorial concessions.

Polk's impulse to claim more territory occurred against a backdrop of a rising sentiment, found mostly in certain newspapers, for annexing all of Mexico. That such sentiment ever arose is indicative of the malleable nature of public opinion and shows how easily it can be influenced by a relatively few well-positioned individuals. The questionable manner in which the war began and the dissent it generated muted for a time annexationist sentiment in the press. Indeed, at the outset few understood that American war aims included large territorial gains. But as the war dragged on into a second year, its costs mounting and American presumptions of racial superiority and national destiny rising with each victory, the administration and some members of the public began to consider the annexation of all of Mexico as a possibly appropriate outcome of the struggle. The acquisition of California implied that, at the least, the province of New Mexico would have to be acquired if only to avoid the geographic and strategic awkwardness of an angular boundary in the Southwest. Now as American casualties mounted and the U.S. army moved to occupy Mexico City, it seemed at least plausible that Americans might need to establish an entirely new Mexican government, making Mexico a protectorate of the United States, especially if the Mexicans continued their stubborn resistance.

Yet punishment was not the sole reason advocated for total absorption. Some opinion makers began to push the idea of "All of Mexico" as a way to "regenerate" the Mexican people, redeeming them from political chaos and economic backwardness. In contrast to California, where a fertile land needed to be liberated from a backward government and redeemed in the name of progress, the All of Mexico faction idealistically urged the American people to take up what later would be called "the white man's burden" and absorb the presumed benighted population to the south. One of the most noted advocates for All of Mexico was Moses Y. Beach, failed peacemaker, whose *New York Sun* stood out as one of the most energetic voices of Manifest Destiny in the press and featured regular columns by John L. O'Sullivan. Beach rationalized that the Mexicans were "perfectly accustomed to being conquered, and the only new lesson we shall teach them is that our victories will give liberty, safety, and prosperity to the vanquished, if they know enough to profit by the appearance of our stars. To *liberate* and *ennoble* – not to *enslave* and *debase* – is our mission."[24] O'Sullivan, writing in the *Philadelphia Public Ledger* in December 1847, envisioned an institutional takeover of Mexico's government, its legal system, its revenue sources, and its schools. After that, "Our Yankee young fellows and the pretty senoritas will do the rest of the annexation, and Mexico will soon be Anglo-Saxonized, and prepared for the confederacy."[25] In this case, regeneration of a people seemed to imply its racial whitening, but what is astounding in the calls for All of Mexico is the unhesitating self-confidence that Yankees would be greeted as liberators by the masses of Mexican people and that the United States had it within its power to absorb and transform an entire nation, rebirthing it in its own image.

In spite of these and other voices calling for the absorption of all of Mexico, after an initial burst of enthusiasm public opinion seems to have cooled to the plan. In the first place, the notion of being a de facto foster parent to an entire nation was daunting to many Americans in terms of distance and logistics, even for a people given to extravagant projects. More importantly, the dominantly dark racial makeup of Mexico's eight million people represented to most white Americans an unbreachable barrier to closer national ties. At a time when notions of racial hierarchy became increasingly widespread, incorporating millions of new people of color into the Union proved unthinkable. O'Sullivan's notion that people of color annexed by the war could be whitened by intermarriage might have made sense in thinly populated California and New Mexico, but Mexico City was another matter.

In any case, Polk used the calls heard in the press and in Congress as a basis for new demands on Mexico. In October 1847, he recalled Trist to Washington as a preliminary to a new, tougher line. But Trist refused to be recalled. When the president's message arrived, Mexico City had fallen along with Santa Ana's latest regime, and a new government seemed eager to treat on Trist's original terms. With Scott's encouragement, Trist began talks with Mexican officials along the lines of his original instructions: Mexico to cede Alta California, New Mexico (comprising parts of half a dozen future states), and a Texas boundary at the Rio Grande, a total of approximately 500,000 square miles.

[24] Merk, *Manifest Destiny and Mission*, 122.
[25] Merk, *Manifest Destiny and Mission*, 125.

Mexico in exchange received $15 million, and the United States agreed to assume the claims held against it. Signed on February 2, 1848, the Treaty of Guadalupe-Hidalgo, named for the small village where it was negotiated, also promised to respect the civil rights of the Californios, Nuevo Mexicanos, and Tejanos, who inhabited the conquered territories – a clause of the treaty that in future years was for the most part ignored.

Trist's insubordination enraged Polk. When Trist returned to Washington with his treaty for ratification, Polk first contemplated not submitting it to Congress. He, along with a few rabidly expansionist Democrats in Congress, still harbored visions of a boundary as far south as Tampico on the Gulf of Mexico, with Baja California also included in an expanded concession package. However, insofar as the pact obtained virtually all of Polk's original aims, it proved impossible to bury it; a war-weary public was amazed at the extent of the territory the treaty had acquired and did not want to fight for more. In the name of expediency, Polk agreed to submit it to Congress. On March 10, 1848, the Senate voted to ratify the treaty 38–14. The "yes" voters included twelve Whigs, some of whom feared that rejecting the pact would lead to the absorption of another chunk of Mexico, as Polk desired. Six Democrats opposed the treaty for the opposite reason – that the treaty had not dispossessed Mexico of enough of its territory.

Polk, petulant to the end, showed his displeasure with Trist by refusing to compensate him for his expenses in Mexico. He also relieved General Scott of duty and charged him with malfeasance in command. The absurdity of bringing court martial charges against the architect of one of the greatest military campaigns in the nineteenth century soon brought an end to the prosecution, but not before it squashed any presidential aspirations Scott may have had.

GOLD!

Simultaneous with the arrival of the Treaty of Guadalupe-Hidalgo in Washington for its certain ratification, an event occurred in the newly conquered province of California of historic significance that seemed to many to confirm that some superintending power did indeed smile upon the United States. While exploring along the American River in northern California for a favorable spot to build a sawmill for his employer, Johan Sutter, James Marshall discovered nuggets of gold in the stream. From that small beginning, one of the great gold rushes in world history ensued. The lust for gold that had driven so much of the Spanish conquest of the New World had in California somehow eluded their eyes and the eyes of the Mexican successor state. Now, almost simultaneously with the transfer of California to the United States, the province literally turned out to be a gold mine. Although Marshall and Sutter initially sought to keep their discovery a secret, it proved to be impossible. A short while later Sam Brannan, a Mormon elder sent to establish a Mormon colony in California, paraded through the streets of Yerba Buena (as San Francisco was then known) holding aloft a vial of gold dust and shouting, "Gold! Gold from the American River!" The gold rush was on.

Yerba Buena was soon emptied of its able-bodied men, many of whom purchased picks, shovels, and other mining supplies from Brannan, who understood that the most reliable way to wealth was to sell picks to the would-be prospectors. When President Polk confirmed the strike in his final annual message of December 1848, the gold rush became national, even international in scope, attracting people from China, Sonora, Europe, and South America as well as the United States. Steamship companies advertised transportation to the "inexhaustible" gold mines of California, of great wealth to be had for the taking if only one could get there.[26]

In its timing and long-term consequence, the discovery of gold in California in the wake of its acquisition remains perhaps the single greatest piece of luck in American history. In a matter of months, California went from being a dream in the eye of expansionist visionaries to a key part of the American Empire, the ultimate land of opportunity in the land of opportunity. San Francisco almost immediately became a major Pacific emporium, a keystone between goods and people arriving from the East Coast and Europe and those coming from the Asian-Pacific region. By the early 1850s, tens of thousands of Chinese immigrants were coming by boat from Canton, lured to California by reports of a fabled "gold mountain" to be had. By 1860, approximately $500 million in gold had been extracted from the region; the

---

[26] See Kenneth Owens, ed., *Riches for All: The California Gold Rush and the World* (Lincoln, Neb., 2002).

establishment of the San Francisco mint in 1854 allowed the gold to be monetized into hard currency, providing a reliable and much-needed medium of exchange. Together with the increasing commercial penetration of China, the establishment of Hawaii as a de facto protectorate, and the subsequent "opening" of Japan, the gold rush marks the definitive beginning of the United States as a Pacific power.

CLAIMING THE CANAL

The discovery of gold in California gave a dramatic boost to what had been a slowly growing U.S. interest in a Central American isthmian crossing. The Isthmus of Panama had long seemed to be the most likely place for such a crossing, but engineers also eyed alternative possible routes in Honduras, Nicaragua, and across Tehuantepec in Mexico. Although an interoceanic canal remained a distant dream, by 1850 plans commenced to build a railroad connecting Atlantic and Pacific ports. Americans had been exploring the possibilities of an isthmian crossing since the 1820s; the acquisition of Oregon in 1846 heightened interest in what was the most strategic locale in the hemisphere south of the Rio Grande. As the imperial republic expanded westward toward Asia by land and by sea, the critical importance of Panama became undeniable. Recognizing this, the Polk administration moved to secure the American presence in Panama. In 1846, the Bidlack-Mallarmino Treaty with Colombia (then known as Nueva Granada) designated the United States as the guarantor both of Colombia's continued sovereignty and of the international right of transit across the isthmus. Little known today, the Bidlack Treaty marked another significant step in the creation of both a hemispheric and a global American Empire. It made a nice counterweight to the rising British influence over the coastal region of Nicaragua known as the Mosquito Coast. Once again Americans contended with the British for influence over a distant region.

Interest in a canal required a more vigorous U.S. role in the region than otherwise would have been the case. Relations with the nations of Latin America generally and Central America in particular had been marked by suspicion bordering on contempt from the time of the recognition controversy of 1817. The Monroe administration had made it clear that its proclamation of the principles of nonintervention and noncolonization did not necessarily imply a willingness to apply them multilaterally. Americans had no more desire to become "entangled" with other states in the hemisphere than they did with those in Europe. Southern members of Congress actively sought to limit diplomatic contacts with Latin America, quashing U.S. efforts to participate in the Panama Congress of 1826. Yet the existence of a clear and compelling interest, as in the case of an isthmian crossing, resulted in an active, if patronizing, policy toward the Central American nations.

Control of the Isthmus became of even greater importance when an alternative route across Mexico at Tehuantepec proved infeasible. A prospective Tehuantepec canal offered a much less mountainous but significantly longer crossing; transit rights for Americans across it were eyed as a potential benefit in an eventual peace treaty with defeated Mexico. Matthew C. Perry, who it has been noted was a fervent expansionist, surveyed the Tehuantepec route after taking part in the landing at Vera Cruz. An isthmian crossing played a key part in his schemes for a global American network of trade and communication. Much to his dismay, hazardous shallows and shifting sandbars at the mouth of the main river that would comprise part of the crossing made the plan unworkable. Nevertheless, in his report about his explorations to Secretary of the Navy John Y. Mason, Perry expressed his conviction that "if a Canal is ever to be opened across the Continent of North America, it should be executed by the government or people of the United States. Destiny has doubtless decided that the vast continent of North America from the Davis' Straits to the Isthmus of Darien shall in the course of time fall under the influence of the laws and institutions of the United States."[27]

Canal or no canal, Polk's confirmation of the discovery of gold in his annual message to Congress in December 1848 escalated the importance of Panama as the fastest way to California. Overland, immigrants faced a rugged journey along a cholera-pocked trail and extremes of heat and cold, usually taking about four months to go from St. Louis to the gold fields. The ocean voyage via the rough waters of Cape Horn was fourteen thousand miles and also took four to five months. The isthmian crossing, in contrast – involving two relatively short boat trips sandwiched around a three- to ten-day journey via foot and bongos, the canoelike vessels used for centuries to ferry people from one ocean

[27] Merk, *Manifest Destiny and Mission*, 141.

to the other – took six to eight weeks. As early as 1847, the U.S. Mail Steamship Company (headed by George Law) and the Pacific Mail Company (headed by William Aspinwall) established a privately owned and government-subsidized mail service to the West Coast via the isthmus. By the mid-1850s, Cornelius Vanderbilt had built a railroad line connecting the Atlantic and the Pacific.[28]

By 1849, the United States and Great Britain, having only recently averted a conflict over Oregon, found themselves in an emerging rivalry over who would control the canal they knew would eventually be built somewhere in Central America. It was obvious that if a canal were constructed, it would be of crucial importance in the emerging world economy. Neither nation wanted to concede the right to build and own a canal, but neither did they wish to fight over it. In 1850, Secretary of State John Clayton and British minister Sir Henry Lytton Bulwer negotiated an agreement in which both parties pledged never to make a bid for exclusive control of a future canal, to guarantee the neutrality of any canal, and to refrain from direct control over the Central American states in the region. Although the agreement did defuse Anglo-American tensions, it is anomalous in the history of American foreign relations in that it contained a self-denying ordinance of the sort that American statecraft tried to avoid as a cardinal principle. Yet in certain respects the Clayton-Bulwer Treaty merely reprised the joint occupation agreement over Oregon, affirming an American claim to the region without the need to directly confront Great Britain over it, at least at that time.

THE WILMOT PROVISO

The war on Mexico had gone better than Polk or anyone else could have anticipated. True, it had cost approximately twelve thousand American lives (the abysmal sanitary conditions, especially for the volunteers, meant that most of the deaths had been non–combat related); it had cost the U.S. Treasury approximately $100 million, plus the roughly $20 million in costs associated with the peace treaty. It had cost the

---

[28] On the U.S. encroachment in Panama, see Aims McGuinness, *Path to Empire: Panama and the California Gold Rush* (Ithaca, 2008).

lives of an estimated fifty thousand Mexicans – soldiers and civilians – along with the devastation of large portions of Mexico. The behavior of the invading American troops had been at times atrocious, and Mexico emerged from the war having lost half its territory and much of its sense of national dignity. However, the war had provided inestimable imperial benefits to the United States: In addition to the massive territorial gains, the war affirmed the undisputed superiority of the United States in the Western Hemisphere. The Monroe Doctrine had been invoked and applied for all to see; by themselves, the bonanza of the gold strike in California and the subsequent silver rush in Nevada justified the costs of the war, at least in material terms. The loud and principled opposition to the war fell mute in the peace, and the loudest opponent of them all, John Quincy Adams, could no longer be heard, having died from a stroke suffered in February 1848 while at his congressional desk.

The principled objections of Adams, Benton, Calhoun, and others paled in importance to the practical objections to the possible territorial acquisitions raised by David Wilmot, a Democrat House member from Pennsylvania. No friend of the abolitionists, Wilmot had voted for the war. But when in August 1846 Polk requested $2 million from Congress to pay for the "extraordinary expenses" incurred by the administration in dealing with foreign states (specifically the costs associated with bribing Mexican officials, starting with Santa Ana), Wilmot proposed to qualify the appropriation by adding to the House version a resolution barring slavery from any new lands acquired as a result of the war. Modeled along the lines of similar restrictions in the Northwest Ordinance of 1787, the resolution spoke not on behalf of slaves but on behalf of working-class white men, who could not successfully compete in a slave labor–based society and who did not want to inhabit a state with a large black population be it slave or free. For the survival of the Union, this represented an ominous turn of events. Wilmot championed the white working man who saw his opportunities foreshortened and the dignity of his labor impugned by the institution of slavery. This marked the birth of the Free Soil movement, a progenitor of the Republican party. Now the relatively few Americans who opposed slavery on principle would be joined by a mass of people who opposed it based on economic interest. What Wilmot himself called his

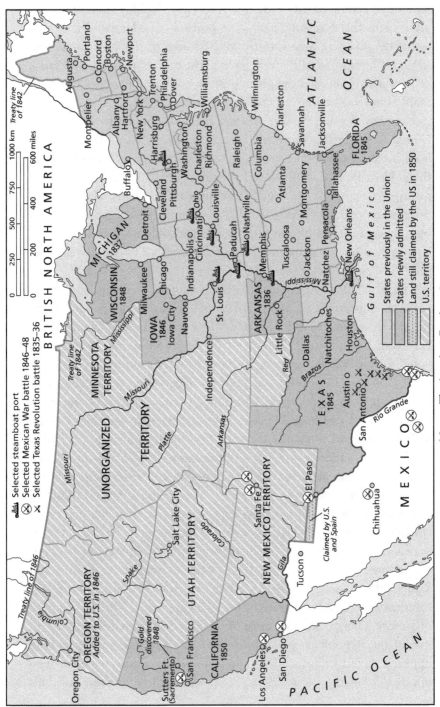

Map 5. The American Empire, 1850.

208

"White Man's Proviso" gave a mighty boost to those who sought to stop the further extension of slavery's domain.[29]

What became known as the Wilmot Proviso passed the House numerous times over the next year or so, failing in the Senate, where Southerners blocked its passage. But the proposal fired the imagination of Northern antislavery advocates. Horace Greeley deemed it "a solemn declaration of the United States against the further extension of Slavery."[30] In essence, the strategy of containing slavery where it currently existed seemed to offer a path both to preserving the West as "free soil" and to the gradual extinction of slavery. Like Thoreau's statement of principle in Concord that same year, Wilmot's proposal constituted an implicit act of secession against the Union as it was, and a vote for a Union that might be.

Politically, the Wilmot Proviso fractured the cross-sectional nature of political parties. Heretofore, both parties had northern and southern wings, thereby minimizing sectional strife even in the face of serious disagreements over things such as slavery and the tariff. Yet the Wilmot votes broke down almost entirely along sectional lines, as Northern Whigs joined Northern Democrats in voting for the measure, and Southern Whigs aligned themselves with Southern Democrats in opposition. In foreign policy terms, the expansionist consensus that had been one of the core reasons for the formation of the Union and that had largely held together in spite of increasing concerns about the future status of newly acquired lands was shattered beyond repair. The Wilmot Proviso and the fractures it caused in the foundations of the Union proved the greatest cost of the imperial conquest of Mexico.

[29] See Michael F. Holt, *The Fate of Their Country: Politicians, Slavery Expansion, and the Coming of the Civil War* (New York, 2004).
[30] Sean Wilentz, *The Rise of American Democracy: Jefferson to Lincoln* (New York, 2005), 598.

8

DISUNION

We are the peculiar chosen people – the Israel of our time; we bear the ark of the liberties of the world.

Herman Melville, *White Jacket*

Without the shedding of blood, there is no remission of sins.

John Brown, quoting Hebrews 9:22

THE REVOLUTIONS OF 1848

On July 4, 1848, a large contingent of dignitaries gathered in the capital to place the cornerstone of a new monument to honor the memory of George Washington. Located on a knoll not far from Capitol Hill, at a projected height of more than five hundred feet the marble obelisk when completed would be the tallest man-made structure in the world, casting an imposing shadow over the still mostly unbuilt landscape of the capital. In contrast to the Greco-Roman architecture characteristic of most other public buildings in the capital, the Washington Monument bowed in the direction of Egypt, another ancient empire renowned for its monumentalism. And even though the Washington Monument did not rival the Pyramids in scale, it, along with the U.S. Capitol Building then under construction, stands among the preeminent architectural accomplishments of its time, symbolizing not only the nation's preeminent founder but also the astounding energies and accomplishments of its people. The construction of the imposing spire vividly demonstrated the rising veneration Americans felt for Washington. Who knew what future American leader might merit a similar memorial?

The republican revolutions that broke out all across Europe that same year provided further evidence that the tide of world history flowed in an American direction. In dozens of European states, liberal democratic uprisings challenged the restorationist monarchical status quo. Americans attributed the upheaval in no small measure to their own democratic republican example. The European liberal revolutions so inspired some Americans as to prompt them to take part in the struggles, most famously the writer Margaret Fuller. Traveling to Rome in 1846 to cover the upheaval as a journalist, she soon married an Italian revolutionary, bore his child, and assumed a prominent role in the revolutionary movement. Only her journal survived her tragic death at sea in 1850 while she was returning home in the wake of the defeat of the revolutionary forces. Her colleague Thoreau later recovered this invaluable record from the wreckage of the ship off Long Island. Fuller's waterlogged journal provided the best American eyewitness account of the continent-wide upheavals of 1848. That most of these revolutions ultimately failed did not lessen their impact as what many Americans perceived as another step on the way to universal human emancipation.

A major turning point in European history, 1848 also proved significant in U.S. history. The Mexican-American War transformed the republic in many ways, among them being a greatly strengthened executive branch of government. James Polk became the first true commander in chief in U.S. history, the first president to assume close control of both the domestic and the foreign aspects of the struggle. He oversaw the domestic mobilization for war and had an unprecedented hands-on approach to the conduct of the war itself, thanks in large part to the enhanced communication offered by the telegraph, which allowed him to monitor and direct events on a daily basis. As the first American president to manage the conquest of a foreign state, Polk established a military government in Mexico, thereby pushing the limits of executive authority into new territory. On March 23, 1847, Polk had issued an executive order enabling American forces to take over Mexican customhouses and collect import duties to help defray the cost of the war. Polk justified this practice by what he termed the "right of the conqueror to levy contributions upon the enemy in their seaports, towns, or provinces."[1] The first U.S. experience in occupying a foreign nation resulted

---

[1] James D. Richardson, ed., *Messages and Papers of the Presidents* (Washington, D.C., 1903), 4:523.

in a significant increase in the centralized power of the national government and became a key precedent for future commanders in chief.

The tumultuous events of 1848 climaxed with Polk's official confirmation of the gold strike in newly acquired California. The mineral windfall of historic proportions seemingly provided further proof that God smiled on the American people. Polk's ambitions for ports on the Pacific now seemed remarkably prescient and not a bit premature. The United States stood poised to become a Pacific power. The president envisioned a dynamic future: "By the possession of the safe and capacious harbors on the California coast we shall have great advantages in securing the rich commerce of the East, and thus obtain for our products new and increased markets."[2] California's sudden emergence as a western terminus accelerated calls for the construction of a transcontinental railroad linking what had only a few years earlier been the seemingly unconquerable space between the oceans.

The nearly 500,000 square miles acquired via the Treaty of Guadalupe-Hidalgo did not slake Polk's expansionist desires. Nicholas Trist's handiwork, however well received by Congress and the public, did not go nearly far enough for Polk, whose expanded ambitions for Mexico had been for a border at Tampico and a guarantee of the transit rights across the Isthmus of Tehuantepec. As with the Oregon question, where Polk had used the cry of "54–40 or Fight" as leverage to gain a boundary at the forty-ninth parallel, he had wanted to use the extreme demands of the "all of Mexico" faction as a wedge to gain the lightly populated northern portion he really desired. Yet Trist's defiance had frustrated this aim. For a while it appeared that the United States might acquire almost the entire western edge of the Caribbean basin. In 1847, a Mayan Indian revolt against the Creole population of the Yucatan Peninsula seemed to present an opportunity for the annexation of that part of Mexico as well. Outnumbered by the native population and effectively abandoned by authorities in far-off Mexico City, in early 1847 the Creoles began seeking the protection of a foreign government. They petitioned Spain, Great Britain, and the United States for help against the uprising, the result of centuries of oppressive rule by a numerically tiny, light-skinned elite. Polk urged Congress to respond to this call, if only to prevent an expansion of European power in the

---

[2] Richardson, ed., *Messages and Papers of the Presidents*, 4:523.

hemisphere in violation of the Monroe Doctrine. By mid-1848, however, the native rebellion receded and with it the hope that the Yucatan peninsula might be annexed. Thus the southern boundary remained at the Rio Grande, and the dreams for acquiring still more of Mexico became a tantalizing "What if?" in the history of the American Empire.

COVETING CUBA

The territories acquired from Mexico did not lessen Polk's intense interest in the annexation of Cuba. Cuba had long been an object of North American imperial desire. As early as 1805, Jefferson had contemplated its acquisition, remarking, "I have ever looked upon it as the most interesting addition that could be made to our system of states." In 1823, John Quincy Adams had hypothesized a law of political gravity that destined Cuba to fall into the hands of the United States like a piece of rapidly ripening fruit. The island's strategic position at the mouth of the Gulf of Mexico made it seem a natural extension of the North American union, especially after the annexation of Florida in 1819. The tenuous to nonexistent grounds by which the United States claimed Cuba necessitated imaginative justifications for its annexation. One such view suggested that Cuba belonged to the United States insofar as the island was deemed to consist of the accumulated American soil deposited offshore by the Mississippi River.

Cuba's status as a Spanish colony kept its lucrative trade mostly closed to foreigners. However, the evolving geopolitical situation of the late eighteenth and early nineteenth centuries meant that Americans developed a thriving and highly profitable interchange with the island. Rum, sugar, and other high-value products fueled a triangular trade of great importance. The profitability of this trade had weighed heavily in the debate over the recognition of the revolting Latin American nations. Those, like Henry Clay, who trumpeted a potential trade bonanza with the newly independent states had to contend with the fact that recognition threatened the ongoing commercial relationship with still-colonized Cuba, whose trade exceeded that of any other Latin American market. For economic, strategic, and ideological reasons, the annexation of Cuba seemed to be only a matter of time, so long as American policy could prevent another European power from grabbing it.

The rising influence of the cultural phenomenon known as "Young America" also increased the desire for Cuba. Comprised of journalists and politicians, the movement had an activist political wing that included prominent Democrats John L. O'Sullivan, Stephen F. Douglas, and August Belmont. They gained renown as full-fledged spread-eagle expansionists and true believers in American republican ideology eager to "expand the area of freedom" (as Jackson put it in 1844) wherever impulse or opportunity beckoned. They had little patience for the cautious nationalism of older Jacksonians, whom they derided as old fogies. Taking their name from Ralph Waldo Emerson's 1844 essay "The Young American," this group waxed exuberant about the success of the United States and became intoxicated by contemplating the grand achievements that lay ahead. Senator Robert Stockton, who as a navy commodore had played a major role in the conquest of California, epitomized the attitude of the movement in a speech to Congress in 1852: "We are, in truth, the residuary legatees of all that the blood and treasure of mankind expended for four thousand years have accomplished in the cause of human freedom.... What course then, shall this government take to perpetuate our liberties and to diffuse our free institutions over the world?"[3]

Against this backdrop of intense ideological zeal, the acquisitions from Mexico merely whetted the expansionist appetite for more. As concerns Cuba, the expansionist desire to enlarge the area of freedom mixed with the desire to expand and defend the institution of slavery and the way of life it represented. The impetus for annexation came from elements in Cuba as well as the United States. Slave-owning elites in Cuba, like those in the American South, uneasily eyed the rising abolitionist tide around them. They feared that Britain aimed to take Cuba in order to abolish slavery, part of its effort to create a global free-labor system. Like their counterparts in the South, Cuban slave owners feared that international agitation against slavery might precipitate another revolt as occurred in Haiti, leading to the prospect of unspeakable acts of violence and retribution against the elite. By the 1840s, a de facto alliance of Cuban and Southern slave owners had coalesced into a political force.

[3] Yonatan Eyal, *The Young America Movement and the Transformation of the Democratic Party, 1828–1861* (Cambridge, 2008), 109.

In January 1847, O'Sullivan and New York newspaperman Moses Y. Beach had joined with members of the Club de la Habana, a clique of Cuba's wealthiest planters, to prepare a formal plan of annexation to be presented to President Polk. For several months, O'Sullivan and others personally lobbied the administration to back a plan to purchase Cuba for $100 million. The canny Polk showed little interest in the scheme, keeping his focus on the still-unresolved war with Mexico. By mid-1848, however, Polk sprang into action. On June 9, the same day he received confirmation that the Mexican legislature had ratified the Treaty of Guadalupe-Hidalgo, Polk prepared instructions to U.S. minister to Cuba Romulus Saunders authorizing him to offer Spain as much as $100 million for the island. Rumors that Cuba verged on revolt encouraged Polk to act. It seemed as if the old expansionist formula might work once more: A revolutionary party acts to seize power as a first step toward annexation by the United States. But Spain's representatives in Cuba flatly refused negotiations of any sort, loudly declaring that they "would rather see Cuba sunk in the ocean" than see it sold to the United States. Polk, his tumultuous time in office nearing an end, chose not to push the issue.

Official efforts to acquire Cuba ended with the accession to power of Zachary Taylor and the Whigs in 1849. As Polk had feared, Taylor's battlefield successes made him a formidable political candidate and led to an easy victory in the 1848 presidential election over Representative Lewis Cass of Michigan, whose zealous expansionism rang hollow when compared to the call by Taylor, the war hero, for restraint. Millard Fillmore continued taking this cautious attitude toward further expansionism after Taylor's death in office in 1850.

The change in presidential attitudes toward expansion prompted a change in tactics by the Cuban annexationist faction. The group now began to make plans for an invasion of the island to be led by the Venezuelan-born soldier of fortune Narciso Lopez. Lopez, almost forgotten today, for a while in the late 1840s and early 1850s dominated newspaper headlines with his various schemes to revolutionize Cuba in preparation for its admission to the Union. After arriving in New York in 1848 following an unsuccessful attempt to start a revolt in Cuba, Lopez joined with other Cuban annexationists (including O'Sullivan) to form the Junta Cubano. When the Club of Havana could not convince Mexican-American War general William Jenkins Worth to take command of an invasion force, Lopez had his opportunity. He became the public face of the annexationist clique: His long mustache and fancy uniformed attire met the public's expectation of what a Cuban freedom fighter should look like. Working with annexationist cells in New Orleans, New York, Baltimore, and other cities, and aided by a network of Masonic allies, many of whom were themselves staunch Cuban annexationists, Lopez very publicly raised his clandestine army. In the fall of 1848, U.S. navy patrols quarantined and eventually broke up an invasion force of approximately 600 men gathered on Round Island outside New Orleans. Undaunted, Lopez and his followers, including Ambrosio Gonzalez, a Cuban-born American citizen who functioned as Lopez's confidant and translator, continued to advertise for volunteers to join an invasion. In May 1850, Lopez landed an invasion force of about 500 men in the town of Cardenas. Flying the Lone Star flag that later would be the flag of an independent Cuba, Lopez's force engaged in fierce fighting with Spanish troops, momentarily taking the town of Cardenas before frantically fleeing back to Key West with a Spanish warship in hot pursuit.

Despite having twice failed to revolutionize Cuba, Lopez gained in celebrity upon his return to the United States. Attempts to prosecute him and his compatriots for violation of the neutrality statutes failed owing to the limited enforcement resources of the national government, the reluctance of local juries to convict a man widely seen as a hero, and by the emerging ability of the national press to create popular heroes in the name of selling papers. Tom Chaffin notes that "[b]y May 1850 Narciso Lopez's prominence in U.S. popular opinion owed as much to editors who simply wanted to sell more newspapers as to his ability to convince U.S. citizens of the righteousness of his cause."[4]

After friendly juries and judges stymied legal efforts to quash the Cuban invasion scheme, Lopez and his diminishing cadre of followers made one last stab at invading Cuba in August 1851. Prompted by reports of an uprising on the island, Lopez hoped that his tiny force of fewer than 500 men would gather supporters as they crossed Cuba. However, his army, including a regiment commanded by William L. Crittenden, the son of a U.S. senator, encountered indifference from

---

[4] Tom Chaffin, *Fatal Glory: The First U.S. Clandestine War against Cuba* (Charlottesville, 1996), 156.

the Cuban people and brutality from the Spanish troops massed to defeat it. Capturing the rebels after fierce fighting, Spanish authorities publicly garroted Lopez in Havana on September 1, 1851; their summary execution by firing squad of Crittenden and fifty men under his command elicited howls of outrage and calls for vengence from the North American press, but to no effect. This stilled, for the moment, the expansionist urge for Cuba.

THE AGE OF THE FILIBUSTERS

Lopez was not the last soldier of fortune who aimed to revolutionize foreign lands during the 1850s. The impulse toward expansion south into Mexico and the Caribbean gained strength throughout the decade, boosted by private armies that became known as filibusters, from the Dutch word *vribuiter,* or "pirate." These groups, often led by charismatic leaders of outsized ambitions, sought to conquer foreign lands without government sanction or support. For them, as Harris G. Warren memorably put it, "the sword was their passport." These groups aimed to revolutionize foreign lands in the name of American-style freedom and then seek quick annexation to the United States. Although use of the term in this context dates from 1850, the most successful filibuster expedition occurred in Texas in 1835, when large numbers of armed men crossed the Sabine River intent on gaining independence from Mexico. The Jackson administration, while officially frowning on these activities, did little to stop them. Lax enforcement of the various federal neutrality statutes (most notably the 1818 act), combined with the difficulties of getting local juries to convict men accused of violating the neutrality laws, had resulted in a de facto invasion by a rebel army that proved essential to the success of the Texas Revolution. Although the expansion of slavery lay at the heart of virtually every filibustering expedition, a mantle of republican freedom disguised this fact. Intoxicated by the rhetoric of Manifest Destiny and often driven by a personal economic interest, filibusters saw themselves as the vanguard of the republican revolution.

The most famous (or, perhaps, infamous) of these filibusters was William Walker of Tennessee, the so-called Gray Eyed Man of Destiny. Slightly built and lacking any special training as an empire builder, Walker had abandoned a career as a physician to assume a self-appointed role as an agent of Manifest Destiny. He framed himself as the tip of the spear of American expansionism, a bold adventurer willing to do the hard work of opening new lands to the republican revolution. Possessed of a penetrating gaze and a single-minded determination to achieve great things, Walker attracted small groups of mercenaries to support his schemes by promises of great wealth to be had. His first forays into Baja California and Sonora in the early 1850s proved abortive, because poor planning and limited resources forced him to abandon both expeditions within days of their launch. Like Narciso Lopez, Walker was undeterred by failure. In 1856, Walker and sixty men he styled as "the immortals" succeeded in revolutionizing Nicaragua in the name of a great Central American slave empire he envisioned springing up in the region. Newspapers across the country could not get enough of his exploits; his bold actions captivated readers and sold papers, even if many editors had serious doubts about the legitimacy of his aims.

Briefly installing himself as the president of Nicaragua, Walker might have succeeded in his improbable campaign had he any sense of justice and diplomacy as a leader. Instead, his dictatorial ways proved to be his downfall. Walker and his ragtag army soon retreated from Nicaragua, chased out not by locals but by forces in the employ of railroad magnate Cornelius Vanderbilt, who did not appreciate this upstart interfering with his plans to build a trans-isthmian railroad in Nicaragua. Evicted from Nicaragua, Walker returned home to a rapturous welcome by the many following his exploits in the papers. Refusing to be discouraged by his failures, Walker launched one more expedition against Nicaragua in 1860. With his tiny force facing annihilation by Honduran army units, Walker surrendered to a Royal navy schooner on patrol that he hoped would return him to the United States. Instead, the British handed him over to the Hondurans, who quickly stood him in front of a firing squad.

Filibustering expeditions proliferated dramatically during the 1850s. Robert May, perhaps the preeminent authority on filibustering, estimates that at any given time during the decade, at least two filibustering schemes were in the planning or execution stage. Although it was often true that the leaders of these schemes sought, like Walker, to expand slavery to new regions in the Caribbean and Mexico, it is not fair to attribute the movement as a whole to a "slave power conspiracy" directed from a single command. In the end, the filibusterers are best understood as another manifestation of the ceaseless American expansionist quest for new lands, new opportunities, and new sources of wealth. However, antislavery activists understandably tended to see the actions of Walker and others as part of a transparent campaign to spread the slave institution south of the border. Robert May suggests that the resurgence of filibustering played a key role both in kindling Southern secessionist sentiments and in creating Republican resistance to compromise on the eve of the Civil War: "[D]uring the late antebellum period, some Southerners became increasingly discouraged about slavery's future in the Union because of the filibusters' constant setbacks; and on the eve of the war, northern memories of filibusters helped to stymie a compromise that might have averted the conflict. Had Americans never filibustered, the Union might have weathered the storm."[5]

TEARING OFF THE SCAB: THE KANSAS-NEBRASKA ACT

Although Democratic politicians tended to oppose the actions of the filibusters as an unwarranted intrusion on the federal power to make foreign policy, this did not mean that they renounced further expansionism. Indeed, the hunger of Democrats, especially Southern ones, for expansion continued to increase. In 1848 Democrat standard bearer Lewis Cass proclaimed, "We want almost unlimited power of expansion. That is our safety valve."[6] The return of the Democrats to the White House in 1853 saw new president Franklin Pierce of New Hampshire decry "any timid forebodings about expansion." Pierce, a Mexican-American War veteran with a fondness for alcohol (his critics panned him as "the hero of many a bottle"), resumed efforts to acquire Cuba. In 1854, he instructed U.S. minister to Madrid Pierre Soulé to offer $130 million for Cuba and, if refused, to seek other ways "to detach the island from the Spanish dominion." A French expatriate and a fervent supporter of the Lopez efforts to revolutionize Cuba, Soulé engaged in outrageous behavior at the court of Madrid, stifling whatever small chance he had for success. Suitably rebuffed, Soulé rendezvoused with minister to France John Y. Mason and minister to Great Britain

[5] Robert E. May, *Manifest Destiny's Underworld: Filibustering in Antebellum America* (Chapel Hill, 2002), 279.
[6] Amy Greenberg, *Manifest Manhood and the Antebellum American Empire* (New York, 2005), 34.

James Buchanan in the Belgian city of Ostend. There they dispatched a secret report to Washington boldly calling for the seizing of Cuba and arguing that if Madrid continued to resist, "by every law, human and Divine, we shall be justified in wresting it from Spain."[7] When this confidential report (known as the Ostend Manifesto) was leaked to the press, it created a sensation. The boldness of the Cuban expansionist clique shocked Northern antislavery Democrats only slightly less than it did the European diplomatic corps. The ensuing contretemps forced President Pierce and Secretary of State William Marcy to repudiate the work of Soule, Mason, and Buchanan and, for the time being, give up on Cuban annexation schemes.

Amid all these schemes of imperial conquest, both official and unofficial, the domestic expansionist consensus continued to erode and, with it, the bonds of union holding it all together. Although Narciso Lopez draped the mantle of freedom and republicanism over his insurrectionist movement, the desire to defend the institution of slavery from the attacks on it that seemed to be proliferating in the early 1850s best explains his actions. Although the newspaper-reading public thrilled to the idea of American expansion into Cuba, the political system at home found itself still trying to recover from the schism created by the conquests of the Mexican-American War. If not for the determined efforts of Henry Clay and other senior lawmakers to cobble together eight contradictory resolutions collectively known as the Compromise of 1850, the Union might have collapsed then and there. The historic compromise admitted California as a free state, with the remaining territories acquired from Mexico left open as to the question of slavery, to be determined at some later date by their inhabitants. Although the compromise admitted no new slave states, it did strengthen the federal Fugitive Slave Law, much to the outrage of abolitionists. As compromises are prone to do, the settlement of 1850 satisfied no one but did succeed in preventing a civil war at that time.

From the time of the controversy over Texas annexation, a sizable and growing body of opinion, not all of it Northern Whigs, opposed annexing any potential slave states. Texas had been shoehorned in via the constitutionally dubious means of a joint resolution of Congress;

---

[7] See the text of the Ostend Manifesto at http://en.wikisource.org/wiki/Ostend_ Manifesto.

the lands seized from Mexico came as war booty and proved difficult to digest politically. Acquiring Cuba either by purchase from Spain or via the agency of a private army headed by the likes of Lopez seemed out of the question. In short, by the early 1850s the American expansionist juggernaut had effectively ground to a halt, stopped not by any external foe but by internal divisions over the meaning of the concept of freedom, the foundation stone of its empire.

Against this backdrop of the increasing effort of Southern Democrats and their Northern "doughface" allies to push new annexationist plans even in the face of a breakdown of the expansionist consensus, it is no wonder that the Kansas-Nebraska Act of 1854 shook the edifice of American union down to its foundation. The individual most responsible for the legislation was Stephen Douglas, a Young America devotee and senator from Illinois. One of the preeminent members of the new generation of political leaders, ambitious for higher office, and confident of his ability to navigate the turbulent waters of sectional differences, Douglas, as head of the Committee on Territories, in early January 1854 introduced legislation organizing the massive Nebraska territory (extending to the Canadian border) for future statehood. Previous efforts to do so had failed owing to disagreement over the status of slavery in the region. Douglas, desirous of securing a northern transcontinental railroad route and needing the votes of Southern senators to do so, presumed to solve the question of slavery in the territories by the device of popular sovereignty, leaving the slave question to be decided by the voters of the new state.

The possibility that such votes might be rigged by slaveholders disturbed antislavery politicians, but the repeal of the Missouri Compromise Line prohibiting slavery in all territories north of 36 degrees, 30 minutes proved the most controversial aspect of Douglas's bill. This had been an antislavery bulwark for more than thirty years, the line in the sand below which slavery could be contained; now all territories desiring statehood would henceforth decide whether they would be slave or free on the basis of popular sovereignty. In theory, this meant that slavery might now expand into any territory that sought or might in the future seek statehood. In practice, it demonstrated the limits of majority rule in an American political system that had fractured over the question of slavery. A precondition of any democratic state is that there be general agreement over first principles and that the various parties comprising a democratic system are willing to accept the electoral victory of other parties. But this was no longer the case. The antislavery impulse now refused to accept the victory of slavery anywhere.

This schism played out violently in the newly created territory of Kansas, where efforts to establish a territorial government resulted in the creation of two constitutions: one based on the principle of freedom, the other on the principle of slavery. By 1856, the two sides had commenced a conflict of rapidly escalating violence. The rampages of John Brown and his sons were the most notorious but by no means the only examples of violent confrontation, as groups from the North and the South sent arms, money, and men to support their side in what marks the true beginning of the Civil War. If the shelling of Fort Sumter in 1861 marks the breakup of the American union, the violence in Kansas in 1856 signifies the collapse of the American nation and the expansionist consensus on which it was built. Once the nation had shattered, the political union could not long survive. The sectional balancing act that had sustained the Union since 1787 had now come apart, with dire, unforeseeable consequences.

The collapse of the Whigs, who could no longer maintain the fiction of being a national political party, represented the most prominent manifestation of this new disunionist reality. Their dissolution in 1854 opened the door to the rise of the Republicans, the first explicitly antislavery major party in U.S. history. The Union had always contained at least two distinct visions of American freedom: one based on slave labor, and the other one based on free labor. Tolerance of that difference within a strong union had been the key to all the achievements since 1787. Now a political party existed that judged the Southern way of life to be a hideous blot on the fabric of the American idea, a stain that gave the lie to everything Americans advertised themselves to the world to be.

The celebrated visit in 1852 of Hungarian patriot and émigré Louis Kossuth had dramatized this tension. Kossuth was the living symbol of the republican ideal, but his uncompromising appeals to universal liberty rang hollow in a nation where one-sixth of the population lived in bondage. Americans had handled this awkward contradiction in the way they usually did when dealing with the slave question – by agreeing not to talk about it. Kossuth soon learned that it was best that he, too, make no mention of it. But now a faction had arisen that would remain silent and acquiescent no longer.

BUCHANAN

The collapse of the Whigs and the newness of the Republican party allowed Pennsylvanian James Buchanan to defeat Republican nominee John C. Fremont in 1856 and enter the White House as another in a series of staunchly expansionist Northern Democrats. Buchanan's expansionist ambitions rivaled those of Polk, but Buchanan faced far more intense political opposition then did his Tennessean predecessor. Many Northern Democrats and all Republicans unequivocally opposed any expansionist scheme that threatened to add potential new slave states to the Union. Buchanan was undaunted by this sentiment. Like Polk before him, he sought to achieve his goals in the face of what he knew to be strong opposition. Misreading the depth of the objections to slavery, he naïvely asserted in his inaugural address that the Kansas-Nebraska Act had solved the dispute over the future of the territories by affirming "the will of the majority shall govern ... the settlement of the question of domestic slavery in the territories!"

Buchanan was a typical Jacksonian: a committed Unionist but within the context of a national government with very limited powers, especially as regards the issue of slavery, which he extravagantly defined as being "beyond the reach of any human power except that of the respective states wherein it exists." Buchanan called for "the agitation" over the slavery question to cease before it endangered "the personal safety of a large portion of our countrymen where the institution exists." He warned that the "loss of peace and domestic security around the family altar" occasioned by the antislavery agitation outweighed the manifest advantages of union and threatened to chase Southerners into secession.[8] Here Buchanan touches on an underappreciated factor leading to the Civil War: the South's rising fear of an abolitionist-inspired slave revolt. The specters of Haiti, Denmark Vesey, and Nat Turner hung over the white South, uniting all whites, slave owners or not, in a mutual and not unreasonable fear of racial vengeance.

---

[8] Richardson, ed., *Messages and Papers of the Presidents,* 5:431–2.

As a faithful Jacksonian, Buchanan's notions of limited government led him to oppose most internal improvements as pork barrel projects that served only a portion of Americans while being paid for by all. He vigorously opposed homestead legislation that would have given land to Americans for a nominal fee as beyond the power of Congress and patently unfair to Americans who previously had purchased public lands. However, this philosophy of limited government in domestic affairs did not inhibit his efforts to commit the national government to buying Cuba. In 1859 Senator John Slidell of Louisiana introduced the so-called $30 Million Bill, seeking an appropriation that would form the basis of a purchase offer for the island. The Senate debate on the matter that February attracted a great deal of attention, with press coverage of the issue rivaling that of the murder trial of Representative Daniel Sickles of New York, accused of killing his wife's lover. In the end, this latest failed bid for Cuba inspired even more antislavery sentiment.

Throughout his often-criticized presidency, Buchanan advocated uncompromising support for the Union in the context of territorial popular sovereignty and diminished antislavery agitation. It spite of the criticism he has endured as allegedly one of America's worst presidents, Buchanan in fact sought a reasonable compromise (as he saw it) between all the parties involved in the name of preserving the Union. The president, however, confronted an antislavery tendency that was both increasingly unwilling to compromise on the matter of slavery and increasingly willing to risk all in the name of moving the nation in the direction of freedom. Buchanan never seemed to grasp this fact.

Buchanan presided over a fractious and fracturing empire. In addition to the shocking violence in Kansas, the national government confronted a challenge to its authority in the Utah territory. There, a Mormon colony led by Brigham Young, having fled Illinois in response to efforts to exterminate it, again found itself a part of the United States as a result of the Mexican-American War cession. Resistance to the imposition of American rule during the Utah War had led to the Mountain Meadows Massacre of 1857, in which Mormon militia had killed more than one hundred members of an emigrant wagon train en route to California. Buchanan now sought gentler means to gain the submission of Young and the rest of the Latter-Day Saints.

Along the southern border, relations with Mexico remained tense. The fluid situation extending from the mouth of the Rio Grande to

Arizona created security concerns. Ongoing clashes with Native Americans and Mexican bandits led the president to declare the border region a zone of anarchy that Buchanan tried to quell by seeking (unsuccessfully as it turned out) congressional permission to establish an American protectorate over the northern parts of Chihuahua and Sonora. The president also aimed to establish the right to protect the isthmian transit rights across Tehuantepec. Sounding very much like Polk, Buchanan railed against the Mexican government as incompetent and derelict and sought strong measures to vindicate the rights of Americans whose rights and or property had been violated. Pursuant to this end, he pleaded for the authority to dispatch American naval vessels to defend U.S. shipping in the Gulf of Mexico, yet another exercise of federal authority on behalf of a specific private interest.

RISE OF THE REPUBLICAN PARTY

If Brigham Young and the Mormons challenged federal authority in the Far West, the emerging Republican party represented an even greater threat to the Buchanan administration. Concerns about the spread of slavery and its negative impact on America's image abroad and on the economic prospects of non–slave-owning whites pushed the Republicans to seek to make Buchanan fail, creating the conditions for the election of a Republican to the presidency and a showdown over slavery. In the name of freedom and in the name of America, Republicans declared war on a Southern way of life built on bondage and inequality. Meanwhile, the Southern share of representation in Congress diminished because of increasing immigration to the Upper Midwest in the 1850s and by the admission to the Union of Oregon in 1859 and Kansas in 1860.

Opposition to a union with slaveholders had begun at the time of the drafting of the Constitution and grown slowly until exploding in the Missouri Debates of 1819–21. After that cataclysmic political eruption antislavery sentiment quieted for a time, only to be rekindled in the 1830s with the rise of the first abolitionist parties, the Texas controversy, and the imposition of the hated "gag rule" banning congressional debate on slavery. Insofar as abolitionism was synonymous with political extremism, mainstream politicians avoided describing themselves that way, but as time passed a growing number of them felt a rising revulsion for what slavery meant for the societies where it existed.

After making several trips to the South, Senator William H. Seward of New York condemned what he saw as slavery's evil effects on society, including bad roads, lopsided economic development, and the general torpor characteristic of a slave labor society. Slavery seemed to be a curse that blighted an entire society. As a charter member of the Republican party, Seward helped define the new organization as explicitly opposed to the "privileged classes" of the South, who, like other reactionary cliques in history, were presumed to be incapable of reform.[9] Republican party members almost without exception saw the Northern free-labor model as economically, politically, and morally superior to that of the slave South and were increasingly unwilling to have the reputation of the United States tarred by the inclusion of what they deemed to be a regressive social system.

Free-labor ideology comprehensively critiqued what Southerners admitted was a "peculiar institution." Slavery degraded masters by making them contemptuous of labor and prone to sexual exploitation of those they owned, degraded poor whites by limiting their opportunities to advance economically, and degraded slaves by depriving them of the incentives that were the basis of industry. If blacks were lazy, as the master class claimed, it was only because the institution of slavery denied them any motive to work hard. Staunch antislavery advocate Horace Greeley summarized it this way: "Enslave a man and you destroy his ambition, his enterprise, his capacity."[10]

The Republicans, while often claiming to intend to leave slavery alone in the states where it existed, in fact had no intention of doing so, although they did not necessarily see the federal government as the means to effect change. They hoped to elect a president as a springboard to establishing Republican party organizational cells in the South, and then to invade the South with an army of Northerners who would bring New England's work ethic to the region along with a repugnance for slavery. From there, slavery would end with the consent of Southerners themselves. In short, Republican plans to "reconstruct" the Southern wing of the edifice of Union have their origins in the 1850s, not the 1860s. It was a variation on the Jacksonian idea of

---

[9] Eric Foner, *Free Soil, Free Labor, Free Men: The Ideology of the Republican Party before the Civil War* (London, 1970), 65.
[10] Foner, *Free Soil, Free Labor, Free Men*, 46.

"extending the area of freedom," applied in this case to regions within the United States itself.

The rising antislavery tide was international in scope. The creation of the Republican party signifies not so much the origins of this phenomenon as it does its institutional expression in the realm of domestic American politics. Abolitionist agitation by free blacks and sympathetic whites, by women, by international antislavery organizations, and by the actions of the slaves on their own behalf had forced consideration of the legitimacy of an institution that seemed unchallengeable. Ultimately, the Southern slave-owning oligarchy found itself confronted by the gathering forces of freedom in an Age of Emancipation. The continued existence of slavery in an Age of Emancipation mocked America's pretensions to being the leader of the emerging free world. This fact greatly disturbed many Americans, most especially Abraham Lincoln and the Republicans.

Although he had only limited direct experience with slavery, Lincoln had long opposed it on moral grounds. His main objection to it, however, was rooted in his conception of the role of labor in society. The free-labor ideology that formed the founding principle of the Republican party also functioned as the cornerstone of Lincoln's political sentiments. Efforts in the 1850s to preserve and expand slavery rekindled the political ambitions of the successful Illinois attorney insofar as they constituted a direct threat to the happiness and success of people like him, white men from humble backgrounds. Whatever ambivalence he held regarding the social and political equality of blacks, Lincoln staunchly affirmed the principle that workers of any color had a right to the fruits of their labor. Historians at times underestimate the intensity of the free-labor sentiments that formed the basis of Lincoln's hostility to slavery. In his first annual message to Congress in December 1861, Lincoln reaffirmed this idea in terms that were a distillation of his views: "Labor is prior to and independent of capital. Capital is only the fruit of labor, and could never have existed if labor had not first existed. Labor is the superior of capital and deserves much the higher consideration." Most importantly, Lincoln vehemently denied "there is any such thing as a free man fixed for life in the condition of a hired laborer ... Many independent men everywhere in these States a few years back in their lives were hired laborers.... No men living are more worthy to be trusted than those

who toil up from poverty.... Let them beware of surrendering a political power which they already possess, and which if surrendered will
surely be used to close the doors of advancement against such as they,
and fix new disabilities and burdens upon them till all of our liberty
shall be lost."[11] Perhaps no single passage better sums up Lincoln's
staunch free-labor ideology or better explains why he saw slavery as
a threat to it. Lincoln's passionate attachment to the laboring classes
bears some similarity to Jefferson's ideas regarding yeoman farmers,
as a sort of chosen people of God upon whose continued existence the
survival of American liberty depended. Having no doubt that freedom
was indivisible, Lincoln keenly understood that to take it away from
one group of people was to invite its removal from another.

The Kansas-Nebraska Act had shocked Lincoln enough to prompt
his return to politics, from which he had retired after his one term in the
House. Perhaps no one felt more deeply affected by its empire-changing
implications than did Lincoln. He saw repeal of the Missouri
Compromise Line limiting slavery to the territories south of 36 degrees,
30 minutes as a major change in the structure of the edifice of the
Union, a blueprint for a new America quite at odds with the intentions
of the Founders, at least as Lincoln understood them. "We were thun-
derstruck and stunned; and we reeled and fell in utter confusion," he
said right after passage of the bill, and before long he began to emerge
as one of the leading critics of the new regime.

In an October 1854 speech in Peoria, Illinois, Lincoln hinted at what
the future held. He characterized slavery as a "monstrous injustice" that
"deprives our republican example of its just influence in the world –
enables the enemies of free institutions, with plausibility, to taunt us
as hypocrites.... Our republican robe is soiled, and trailed in the dust.
Let us repurify it. Let us turn and wash it white, in the spirit, if not
the blood, of the Revolution."[12] The reconstruction of American liberty
was essential if the United States was to recover its place as the world's
beacon of freedom. His public remarks for the remainder of his life
rested on the bedrock assumption that slavery was an enormous wrong
in need of being put right: "I am naturally anti-slavery. If slavery is not
wrong, nothing is wrong. I can not remember a time when I did not

---

[11] Richardson, ed., *Messages and Papers of the Presidents*, 5:57, 5:58.
[12] James McPherson, *Abraham Lincoln* (New York, 2009), 17.

so think and feel."[13] To an audience in Chicago in 1859, he observed, "Never forget that we have before us this whole matter of right and wrong of slavery in this Union, though the immediate question is as to its spreading out into new Territories and States."[14]

Committed to preventing the expansion of slavery, as a strict constitutionalist Lincoln strongly opposed using the national government to act against it in the states where it existed. He seized upon nonextension as a constitutionally acceptable means of containing slavery. From the time of the Kansas-Nebraska Act, Lincoln advocated placing slavery back on "a course to its ultimate extinction" via a policy of nonextension. James McPherson notes that between 1854 and 1860, Lincoln gave a total of 175 speeches with this as its main point. He ran for the presidency with this as his overriding goal. Yet he well knew that politically the road to doing so was fraught with obstacles: Success required that a major change in course occur in such a way as to gain the assent of antislavery advocates while not raising constitutional qualms or inflaming white racial anxieties.

Although Lincoln did not believe that the Constitution allowed the national government to interfere with slavery in the states where it existed, he did assert its jurisdiction over it in the territories, the traditional sphere of federal authority and control. A policy of nonextension offered a promising path to this end by effectively containing slavery in the states where it existed. Slavery, like the Union itself, needed to expand in order to live; if prevented from expanding it would soon wither and die. No federal intervention would be required, as local opinion aided by an infusion of Northern sentiment would abolish slavery without external coercion.

Lincoln's antislavery sentiments arose from his own experience. Lincoln's family epitomized the expansionist process at the heart of American history. His father had arrived in Kentucky in 1782 from Virginia and had found the challenges of farming a small plot without slaves made harder by the immense confusions created by the shoddy recording of deeds. Indeed, Lincoln's father lost three farms to bad claims and more generally suffered the ignominy of being a poor white farmer in a county where property in slaves constituted the only real

---

[13] Eric Foner, *The Fiery Trial: Abraham Lincoln and American Slavery* (New York, 2010), 3.
[14] Foner, *Fiery Trial*, 311.

visible sign of wealth and prestige. Crossing the Ohio River in 1816 when Abe was seven, the Lincolns found clear and secure land titles and no slave labor in the newly created state of Indiana (both thanks to the Northwest Ordinance of 1787) and an absence of hostile Indians, thanks to the campaigns of the War of 1812. Lincoln's visceral dislike of slavery was combined with his firsthand understanding of how the institution tainted everything in the societies where it existed. Most importantly, he learned that slavery limited the prospects of white men who did not own them.

The Kansas-Nebraska Act greatly augmented fears that a "slave power conspiracy" was scheming to take over the Union, and subsequent events added to that perception. The antislavery faction began to fear slavery's march not only into new lands to the west and to the south but also into the northern states as well. Although the banning of slavery by individual northern states seemed to preclude this possibility, the Dred Scott case of 1857, which held that the status of a slave did not change by bringing him or her into a free state and that masters had the same right to bring their slaves into free states as they did any other piece of personal property, aroused this fear in the minds of many Republicans, Lincoln included. What was to stop a slave owner from bringing a thousand slaves into a free state? The imposition in 1836 of the gag rule banning congressional debate on slavery was seen in retrospect as the first in a long line of steps by the South to infringe on the freedom of the North. Now the Dred Scott decision seemed to open the door to a second decision by the Taney court invalidating a ban on holding property in slaves anywhere in the Union.

THE UNION DISSOLVES

While Republicans correctly perceived that slave owners sought to make slavery a permanent part of the American union, slave owners and their allies feared the intention of the abolitionist and antislavery tendency to impose its idea on the South. In other words, the fears of both sides were justified. This fact suggests that the looming split over the issue was, as John Adams had said of the War of Independence, a revolution that occurred in people's minds long before it happened in the world. An accurate account of the origins of the Civil War must acknowledge that the split was mutual, as much the result of the rise of an uncompromising Northern abolitionist and antislavery sentiment as it was the consequence of Southern secessionist agitation.

By the late 1850s, many Northerners and almost all Republicans saw the slave South as another country, one that was unfit for inclusion in the great temple of liberty they presumed the Union to be. Although the spread of the institution had long been opposed, there now emerged a sizable minority committed to ending it, one way or another. William Seward, the leader of the Republican party, attracted headlines in 1858 when he announced the existence of "an irrepressible conflict between opposing and enduring forces, and it means that the United States must and will, sooner or later, become either entirely a slave-holding nation, or entirely a free-labor nation." Opponents of slavery, in language reminiscent of the 1840s, began to echo the outlook of the "All of Mexico" faction, arguing that the people of the South were in need of civilizational regeneration in much the same way as the Mexicans had been. The New York *Tribune* made this point: "It is only by the abolition of slavery and the cessation of the slaveholding and the slave trade, followed by an emigration of Northern capitalists, manufacturers, and merchants, that the practical regeneration of Virginia can be effected."[15]

The seriousness of the impending crisis radically escalated as a result of John Brown's abortive attempt in October 1859 to seize the federal armory in Harper's Ferry, Virginia, arm slaves, and launch an uprising in Virginia. Brown's fanaticism and his flawed plan of revolt doomed his efforts to failure. However, the sheer audacity of Brown's actions and his near-canonization by some Northerners in the aftermath of his trial and execution rattled Southern nerves. How could anyone, of any view on slavery, countenance a replay of Nat Turner's campaign of terror and vengeance? In December 1859, Buchanan decried the "sad and bloody occurrences at Harper's Ferry" as yet another provocation against the interests of the South, more "symptoms of an incurable disease in the public mind, which may break out in still more dangerous outrages and terminate at last in an open war by the North to abolish slavery in the South." He reiterated his view and that of others that the net result of all abolitionist and antislavery agitation had been to threaten "the peace and domestic fireside" of the fifteen slave states,

---

[15] Foner, *Free Soil, Free Labor, Free Men*, 53.

shaking the mothers of "this extensive region," who might "not be able to rest at night without suffering dreadful apprehensions of what may be their own fate and that of their children before morning."[16]

Nina Silber, in a perceptive work on gender and the causes of the Civil War that poses the question, "What makes men fight?" has shown that Southern white men, in contrast to their Yankee counterparts, most often fought "for the protection of home, families, and women.... Confederates placed domestic commitments central to their wartime enterprise."[17] James McPherson agrees: "[T]he conviction that they fought for their homes and women gave many Confederates remarkable staying power in the face of adversity."[18] Government propaganda does not explain this resistance; rather, a legitimate fear that home, hearth, and family were at risk led many white Southerners to fight. One did not need to be a slave owner to have a stake in preventing the potentially catastrophic overthrow of the slave oligarchy. Under such a state of fear, appeals to the advantages of maintaining the Union could fall only on deaf ears.

Buchanan repeated his plaintive appeal for Union in his last message to Congress in December 1860. Although the country had been "eminently prosperous," disunion now loomed. Although Northern efforts to exclude slavery from the territories and the refusal of some northern states to enforce the Fugitive Slave Act provoked controversy, Buchanan claimed that "the immediate peril" stemmed from "the incessant and violent agitation of the slavery question throughout the North for the last quarter century," an action that had "produced its malign influence on the slaves and inspired them with vague notions of freedom. Hence a sense of security no longer exists around the family altar. This feeling of peace at home has given place to apprehensions of servile insurrections." In the face of such fears, "Self-preservation ... the first law of nature" would overrule all the practical advantages of union and prompt secession. Buchanan practically begged Northerners to let Southerners handle the slave question in their own way. "As sovereign States, they, and they alone, are responsible before God and the world for the slavery existing among them." Northerners had no more right

[16] Richardson, ed., *Messages and Papers of the Presidents*, 5:553, 554.
[17] Nina Silber, *Gender and the Sectional Conflict* (Chapel Hill, 2008), 3, 13.
[18] Silber, *Gender and the Sectional Conflict*, 14.

to interfere with it, Buchanan claimed, "than with similar institutions in Russia or in Brazil."[19]

At the same time, Buchanan continued to deny the right of the South to leave the Union – "Secession is neither more nor less than Revolution" – but at the same time denied the right of the national government to wage a war to keep the southern states in the Union. The national government had no constitutional right to use force against a state, and, more practically, an effort to do so would itself make future reconciliation "impossible." He went on to say, "[O]ur Union rests upon public opinion, and can never be cemented by the blood of its citizens shed in civil war. If it can not live in the affections of the people, it must one day perish." He urged all parties to pause before they acted "to destroy this the grandest temple which has ever been dedicated to human freedom since the world began.... Consecrated by the blood of our fathers, by the glories of the past, and by the hopes of the future." In words that anticipate those later used by Lincoln at Gettysburg, Buchanan observed that "[t]he Union has already made us the most prosperous, and ere long will ... render us the most powerful nation on the face of the earth." If it was torn asunder, "the hopes of the friends of freedom throughout the world would be destroyed, and a long night of leaden despotism would enshroud the nations. Our example for more than eighty years would not only be lost, but it would be quoted as conclusive proof that man is unfit for self-government."

THE RISE OF LINCOLN

Lincoln's emergence as the Republican nominee in 1860 was unexpected; the presumptive nominee, Seward, had made too many enemies during his long career in public life to garner a majority of the votes at the 1860 Republican convention in Chicago, thus opening the door to the lesser-known lawyer from Illinois. Like Polk before him, Lincoln was a dark horse candidate whose chief attribute was as everyone's second choice. A one-term congressional representative and defeated senatorial aspirant, Lincoln seemed ill prepared for the task before him. Self-educated and self-effacing, Lincoln did not impress as someone able to lead a crusade to end slavery.

[19] Richardson, ed., *Messages and Papers of the Presidents*, 5:636, 5:637.

In this case, appearances deceived, for beneath a rather awkward and homely exterior resided a commitment to the American Union, the American Empire, and, above all, to American freedom, as intense (if not more so) as that of any spread-eagle advocate of Manifest Destiny. Almost as if channeling a higher power, Lincoln gave pitch-perfect voice to the cause of freedom and union. Although more measured and more reasonable on the stump than the firebrand Seward, Lincoln gave a surface appearance of moderation that disguised an iron-willed determination to act against slavery, a determination that was far greater than that of the more famous New Yorker. Seward's passion for freedom was constrained, as had been the case with many Northern politicians before him, by a fear of the potentially cataclysmic consequences of pushing his views too hard. In contrast to his more famous rival, on the stump Lincoln systematically sought to tamp down the heated emotions about slavery. Yet Lincoln's intentions were clear to those who knew him well. The writer Lydia Maria Child described him as "an honest, independent man, and sincerely a friend to freedom." Radical abolitionist Gerrit Smith, a public critic of Lincoln, speculated privately, "I feel confident that he is in his heart an abolitionist." Meanwhile, the proslavery *New York Herald* claimed that Lincoln was "as rabid an abolitionist as John Brown, but without the old man's courage."[20]

Critics were right to perceive in the humble and self-effacing Lincoln a man with a profound sense of personal destiny. From young adulthood he had adhered to what he called "the Doctrine of Necessity," the belief that "the human mind is impelled to action, or held in rest, by some power over which the mind itself has no control."[21] He also seems to have been motivated by a conviction that he was destined to play a reconstructive role in U.S. history. In an 1838 address titled "The Perpetuation of Our Political Institutions" delivered to the Young Men's Lyceum of Springfield, Lincoln speculated on the meaningful part his generation might have to play in the ongoing creation of American nationality: "The question then is, can that gratification be found in supporting and maintaining an edifice that has been erected by others? Most certainly, it cannot … Towering genius disdains a beaten path. …

---

[20] Michael Burlingame, *Abraham Lincoln: A Life* (Baltimore, 2008), 1:634, 1:635, 1:631.
[21] Edmund Wilson, *Patriotic Gore: Studies in the Literature of the American Civil War* (New York, 1963), 101.

It scorns to tread in the footsteps of any predecessor, however illustrious. It thirsts and burns for distinction; and if possible will have it, whether at the expense of emancipating slaves or enslaving freemen. Is it unreasonable then to expect that some man possessed of lofty genius, coupled with ambition sufficient to push it to its utmost stretch, will, at some time, spring up among us?"[22] In these remarks, Lincoln envisioned his transformative role in the remodeling and reconstruction of the edifice of the Union.

Lincoln is a singular phenomenon in U.S. history, a leader of unparalleled moral insight and rhetorical power. As early as 1820, John Quincy Adams had longed for "but one man" who "could arise with the genius capable of comprehending, a heart capable of supporting, and an utterance capable of communicating those eternal truths" regarding slavery, "to lay bare in all its nakedness that outrage upon the goodness of God" that the institution symbolized. Such a man, Adams asserted, "would perform the duties of an angel upon earth!"[23] In 1856, Walt Whitman had mused, "I would be much pleased to see some heroic, shrewd, fully-informed, healthy-bodied, middle-aged, beard-faced American blacksmith or boatman come down from the West across the Alleghenies, and walk into the Presidency, dressed in a clean suit of working attire, and with the tan all over his face, breast, and arms; I would certainly vote for that sort of man ... before any other candidate."[24] Now that man had emerged in the person of Lincoln, a mountaintop visionary with the political genius to act in the world. Lincoln sought a legal, constitutional, and nonviolent resolution to slavery if possible, but above all he sought a resolution. Until now, antislavery advocates had always backed down in the face of Southern threats or bullying. In Lincoln, they now had a candidate who would not back down under any circumstances.

Lincoln's "House Divided" speech, made during his debates with Stephen Douglas in 1858, is further evidence of his single-minded determination to confront slavery in the temple of Union no matter the cost. The ringing phrase, "a house divided against itself cannot stand" seemed to leave little room for compromise. Yet it is by no means clear

---

[22] Wilson, *Patriotic Gore*, 107.

[23] Charles Francis Adams, ed., *Memoirs of John Quincy Adams* (Philadelphia, 1874–7), 4:424–5.

[24] *New York Times*, December 15, 2010.

that Lincoln, Seward, and other Republicans who adhered to this view were correct. Most Southerners appeared willing to extend the status quo of part-free, part-slave indefinitely, if only because it was part of the original constitutional compact. It was the Republicans, and the abolitionist and antislavery tendency that they represented, that could not imagine such a future. When during the speech Lincoln states, "a house divided against itself cannot stand," what he really meant was "not in my house."

Notwithstanding his supposed moderation vis-à-vis the abolitionists or the so-called Black Republicans, Lincoln's candidacy took direct aim at the Southern way of life. If his rhetorical bobbing and weaving on the stump at times tended to disguise this fact, the Cooper Union speech of 1860 removed all doubt as to the intensity of his convictions. In that address – noted both then and since as one of his most significant – Lincoln picked up on ideas first developed by zealous antislavery advocate Salmon P. Chase. In a tour de force that constituted his introduction to the New York political scene, Lincoln assumed the guises of constitutional scholar, skilled attorney, and messianic leader in demonstrating that the Framers of the Constitution did not intend to sanction slavery in any area subject to the jurisdiction of the central government, that is, anywhere outside the limits of the states, either on land or sea. In this address, he characterized slavery as a local, not a national, institution, with no long-term claim to either legitimacy or security. Lincoln condemned efforts to quiet the rising antislavery agitation and reaffirmed the morality of his side: "Let us have faith that might makes right, and in that faith, let us, to the end, dare to do our duty as we understand it."[25] This bold rhetoric effectively declaring war on slavery inspired Republicans and their allies as much as it terrified the South.

Lincoln continuously affirmed the principles of the Declaration of Independence even as he refused to speculate as to what black freedom might mean socially and politically. His uncompromising commitment to ending slavery matched that of John Brown's, but, unlike Brown, he strove to end it in a legal and constitutional manner. Slavery had to be put back on "the road to its ultimate extinction" as Lincoln believed

[25] Burlingame, *Lincoln: A Life*, 1:586.

the Founders had intended; the Missouri Compromise had appeared to establish a path to its eventual demise, but its sudden repeal along with the intensifying drive for a Southern slave empire in Mexico and the Caribbean now offered the real possibility that slavery might be expanded both north and south. Hence the rising importance that it be challenged now.

Armed with a deep-seated conviction that he was destined to put slavery back on a course to extinction, Lincoln became a master of dodging the treacherous shoals of American presidential politics that threatened to sink his campaign. It is important to grasp that Lincoln's primary ambition was not to get elected president but rather to put slavery back on "course to its ultimate extinction" and that he saw the presidency as the best means to accomplish this end. Thus, he learned to say both less and more than people thought they had just heard, to dodge efforts to make him speculate on the long-term consequences of his plan, and to resist efforts to race-bait him into politically suicidal statements defending race mixing even as he framed a program pointing inescapably in that direction. Nonetheless, he endured volleys of criticism from both North and South. The *Illinois State Register* opined that if its favorite son should win the presidency "we shall have the nigger at the polls, the nigger on our juries, the nigger in the legislature." The Cleveland *Campaign Plain Dealer* warned that Lincoln's advocacy of the "practical equality of all men" as his "central idea" would lead to "the central idea of a common mulattodom."[26]

Lincoln's perceived moderation on the slavery question was a device to get elected. Southerners correctly discerned that beneath the folksy humor and roughhewn eloquence beat the heart of an unrelenting foe of slavery and their very way of life. The Texas *Register* warned that the mere prospect of Lincoln's election raised the specter of "poisoned wells," infants "brained" against trees, and "stalwart men" seizing white women and "after perpetrating outrages too horrible to relate, mutilated with fiendish cruelty."[27] Such fears were whipped up to foster secessionist sentiments, but it would be wrong to deny the reality of the fears of many white Southerners about the consequences of

[26] Burlingame, *Lincoln: A Life*, 1:632.
[27] Burlingame, *Lincoln: A Life*, 1:675.

a postslavery society. Lincoln was coming for their slaves, directly or indirectly, and the slaves knew it. Excluded from direct knowledge of political developments, slaves realized that the master's great upset at the mere mention of the name "Lincoln" revealed that the man who soon would become the next president might be their emancipator.

9

THE IMPERIAL CRISIS

Your country has a right to your services in sustaining the glories of her position.... You cannot decline the burdens of empire and still expect to share its honors. You should remember also that what you are fighting against is not merely slavery ... but the loss of empire...."

Thucydides, History of the Peloponnesian War, 94

In the second respect in which the Civil War has been viewed as a revolution – its achievement of the abolition of slavery – Lincoln fits the pattern of a revolutionary.

James McPherson, Abraham Lincoln and
the Second American Revolution, 35

Mine eyes have seen the glory of the coming of the Lord.

Julia Ward Howe, "The Battle Hymn of the Republic," 1862

THE SECESSION CRISIS

The dual elections of the 1860 presidential campaign signified the political dissolution of the Union. Heretofore, political party loyalties had crossed sectional boundaries. Now the widening chasm over slavery meant that Democratic nominee Stephen Douglas, a man with a long record of successfully straddling the sectional divide, received minimal support in the southern states. This failure of the political system any longer to contain the slave question followed the failure of the judiciary to do so, as symbolized in the Dred Scott decision of 1857. No inherent flaw or human shortcoming explains the failure of the institutions binding the Union together. Rather, the institutional failure of the Union resulted from the breakdown of the national ideological consensus on which the institutions rested.

Lincoln's victory at the polls initiated a process of secession by the states of the Deep South, beginning with South Carolina on December 20. Although historians often characterize this as an overreaction to the electoral outcome, such views underestimate the asphyxiating nature of Lincoln's bedrock principle of nonextension. The slave system, like the American Empire generally, needed to expand in order to survive. Intensive, slave labor–based cash crop agriculture rapidly exhausted the soil, leading to declining profitability and diminishing the value of the capital investment in slaves. Fertile lands in potential new slave territory to the west and south promised to maintain a high price for slaves into the foreseeable future. This is the process by which thousands of slaves had been sold in the Deep South from Virginia and Maryland. But without the oxygen of future expansion, and confined to the states in which it already existed, slavery would soon whither and die.

In this regard nonextension should be seen as a form of gradualism, a policy of putting slavery in the United States back on "a course to its ultimate extinction," as Lincoln was sure the Founders intended and that more than a few members of his generation demanded. Lincoln's determined advocacy of the nonextension of slavery in the name of American-style freedom is a precursor to the twentieth-century policy aimed at containing communism. Both policies counterposed a notion of freedom to that of slavery; and both aimed for freedom to prevail not by challenging slavery directly but by containing its further spread, to put it on a path to extinction.

Proslavery Southerners correctly perceived Lincoln and his principle of nonextension as a mortal threat to their way of life that required an immediate challenge before the new president could consolidate his power and that of the Republican party. Southern opposition to Lincoln and his party is best measured by the fact that he received about 2 percent of the vote in the region. To secessionists, Lincoln's victory was roughly equivalent to what the Kansas-Nebraska Act had been to the antislavery faction: a completely unacceptable turn of events requiring a radical response. White Southerners feared for their property in slaves, and, increasingly, they feared for the safety of their families. The time for desperate measures had arrived.

The secession crisis cast in high relief the two distinct and incompatible versions of union existing at that time. One version, centered in the southern states but by no means confined only to them, saw the

Union as a consensual community of states, loosely bound together, in which one's primary loyalty remained to one's state. A second version, articulated by Lincoln and others, framed the Union as prior to and above the states, a permanent political entity in which the whole constituted more than the sum of its parts.[1] This division dated back to the ambiguous representations propagated during the ratification debates of the Constitution, and it had never been fully addressed or resolved. It might not have needed to be resolved but for the massive chasm that had opened over slavery. Yet the chasm that had opened brought to the surface the fundamental dispute over the very nature of the Union. In this respect, both sides plausibly saw themselves as inheritors of the revolutionary tradition. The key difference was that the emerging Confederate ideology, while claiming the revolutionary heritage as its own, explicitly rejected the promise in the Declaration of Independence of universal human equality in favor of an edifice dedicated to racial inequality, in which the white person's freedom was made real by the black person's bondage. Newly installed Confederate vice-president Alexander H. Stephens of Georgia, a moderate who almost until the last minute opposed secession, evidenced this view in February 1861 when he declared the Confederacy's "corner-stone rests upon the great truth that the negro is not the equal of the white man; that slavery – subordination to the superior race – is his natural and normal condition. This, our new government, is the first, in the history of the world, based upon this great physical, philosophical, and moral truth."[2]

Although President-elect Lincoln continued to reassure Southerners that he did not aim to interfere with slavery directly, he evinced a clear determination to affirm federal authority. He informed one Tennessean, "[T]o execute the laws is all that I shall attempt to do. This, however, I will do to the utmost." While secession loomed during the critical moment between his election and inauguration, Lincoln spent most of the time in Springfield, making no public statements regarding the crisis. He claimed that he had made his position clear and that further comment would only serve to make more fragile the political coalition

[1] On this see Sean Wilentz, *The Rise of American Democracy: Jefferson to Lincoln* (New York, 2005), chapter 25.

[2] Alexander Stephens, Cornerstone Speech, 1861, http://teachingamericanhistory.org/library/index.asp?documentprint=76.

he struggled to hold together. He rebuffed one plea for compromise by allegedly stating that he "would rather go out into his backyard & hang himself."[3] In any case, Lincoln and the Republicans never contemplated allowing the South to go forward with its plans for secession. No American president could acquiesce in the creation of an independent, powerful new neighbor on the nation's southern border. It would have been the ultimate violation of the Monroe Doctrine.

By late January intense feelings of melancholia came over the president-elect as he pondered the likely future course of events. One historian has recently written, "[I]t is not clear if Lincoln fully understood the severity of the crisis before his inauguration."[4] Such a claim underestimates Lincoln's luminous intelligence. Like a chess grand master, he had the ability to see, many moves in advance, where a particular gambit might lead. In this case, he recognized that his steadfast refusal to make meaningful compromises on the principle of nonextension likely would precipitate secession by the states of the Deep South and probably most of the Upper South as well, and that the critical border states of Maryland, Kentucky, and Missouri might go with them, depending on how the crisis was handled. While politicians in Washington furiously sought a last-minute compromise to avert a split, Lincoln calculated how he could affirm federal authority without either appearing to run roughshod over the Constitution or seeming like the aggressor in the conflict.

Lincoln's secretary of state designate, William Seward, frantically tried to find a way out of the crisis in the weeks leading up to the inauguration. In late March he thought he had found one. Spain, in what constituted the first attempt by a European power to take advantage of the secessionist crisis, had accepted the voluntary transfer of the sovereignty of Santo Domingo from its hapless political leadership. Spain's attempt to expand its influence in the Western Hemisphere, a clear violation of the Monroe Doctrine, created great concern in Washington, concern that grew substantially following reports that France intended to assume sovereign control of neighboring Haiti. In a confidential proposal in early April, Seward urged the president to demand an

3 Michael Burlingame, *Abraham Lincoln: A Life* (Baltimore, 2008), 1:692, 1:703.
4 Eric Foner, *The Fiery Trial: Abraham Lincoln and American Slavery* (New York, 2010), 150.

explanation for these actions and, if no satisfactory response proved forthcoming, to declare war.

Some historians have since characterized as slightly absurd Seward's desperate attempt to save the Union by provoking a foreign war. This view underestimates the power of warfare as a national cultural bonding agent. Seward's idea, though fraught with risks, may have represented the best chance for averting a split in 1861. A vigorous assertion of the Monroe Doctrine in the name of American greatness no doubt would have made at least some border state secessionists reconsider, especially if it could be shown that the intervention might benefit the South and slavery in some demonstrable way.[5] Lincoln, however, had the enemy he wanted. Although the panicky actions of Seward and other prominent Republicans during this time may have given secessionists the impression that their threats and bluster once again might work to compel the antislavery forces to back down, they could not have imagined the president-elect's implacable resolve to stay the course no matter the cost. This put Lincoln one move ahead of his Southern adversaries during these critical moments. He did not get elected to compromise. His seeming passivity at this crucial time was calculated to allow the confrontation that he saw as inevitable to begin. As he wrote to his old political colleague Lyman Trumbull in an often-quoted line, "The tug has come, & better now, than anytime hereafter." He later bid farewell to his loyal supporters in Springfield by acknowledging that he felt a sense of responsibility "greater than Washington," a clear indicator of the magnitude of the challenge he thought himself to be facing.[6]

THE CRITTENDEN COMPROMISE

As the secession crisis worsened, key members of Congress worked to construct a compromise that could stave off disunion, at least temporarily. In early December a special Senate Committee of Thirteen – including Seward, Douglas, Benjamin Wade, and Jefferson Davis – introduced the most famous of these plans, named for Senator John Crittenden of Kentucky. It consisted of six constitutional amendments effectively barring the national government from interfering with slavery in any

[5] On this point see Lawrence M. Denton, *William Henry Seward and the Secession Crisis: The Effort to Prevent Civil War* (Jefferson, N.C., 2009).
[6] Burlingame, *Lincoln: A Life*, 1:709, 1:759.

way, including banning abolition in the District of Columbia or on any federal property. It also prevented federal interference in the interstate slave trade and resurrected and extended the Missouri Compromise Line to the Pacific Ocean, designating as future slave states any territories south of that line as well as any territories acquired in the future. Stephen A. Douglas added to this plan restrictions prohibiting states from extending the franchise to free blacks and allocating federal aid to any state seeking to colonize its free black populations. Most onerously, Douglas proposed to make public criticism of slavery, either verbal or written, illegal. The Crittenden-Douglas "compromise" amounted to an utter capitulation to the slave oligarchy and a de facto nullification of the presidential election of 1860 by making unconstitutional the main policy principle of the winning candidate.

William Seward, while not publicly endorsing the Crittenden plan, privately praised it and offered his own suggestions for staving off disunion, including a constitutional amendment denying Congress any power over slavery in the states. At this crucial moment, Seward the firebrand, who had pronounced the free labor–slave labor controversy an "irrepressible conflict" in 1858, shied away from confrontation over slavery and sought a means to repress it one more time in the name of preserving the Union. Yet Lincoln, with the support of most Republicans, rejected any concessions implying that slavery was a national institution. At least some Republicans had judged war preferable to capitulation. Rep. Sydney Edgerton of Ohio saw an opportunity in the looming crisis: "The standard of revolt will be the signal of emancipation."[7] Such comments revealed the degree to which the views of the abolitionists had, over several decades, migrated into the mainstream. As early as 1840, some of them had called for "no Union with slaveholders." From that point, it was easy to conclude, as did the Massachusetts Anti-Slavery Society in 1844, that "the dissolution of the Union is the dissolution of slavery."[8] Some secessionists also understood the potentially revolutionary effect a war might have on the institution. Even as he reluctantly supported his state in joining the Confederacy, former North Carolina senator and secretary of the navy

[7] Foner, *Fiery Trial*, 149.
[8] John L. Thomas, ed., *Slavery Attacked: The Abolitionist Crusade* (Englewood Cliffs, N.J., 1965), 91.

George E. Badger predicted that secession would be "the death knell of slavery."[9]

Lincoln saw any a priori compromise limiting his options as president as a slippery slope inevitably resulting in more demands. The only hint of compromise he made during this critical time was a half-hearted offer to allow New Mexico in as a slave state as part of an agreement banning it in all other territories. This went nowhere. The president-elect viewed the Crittenden Compromise as especially toxic in that its guarantee of slavery south of the Missouri Compromise Line opened the door to the expansion of slavery in Mexico and the Caribbean. He had not run on a platform of containing the spread of slavery only to compromise away the power to do so and preside over its spread into places it had previously been ended. He made clear the extent of his commitment to freedom to a crowd in Independence Hall, Philadelphia, shortly before the inauguration: "I have never had a feeling politically that did not spring from the Declaration of Independence.... But, if this country cannot be saved without giving up that principle – I was about to say I would rather be assassinated on the spot than to surrender it."[10]

BAITING THE SOUTH INTO WAR

Lincoln finally arrived in Washington, D.C., in the early morning of February 23, sneaking into town in the dead of night so as to foil a rumored assassination plot against him in Baltimore. Continued reticence had marked his long, leisurely eleven-day journey by rail from Springfield to Washington. Met by large and enthusiastic crowds almost everywhere along the route, Lincoln remained mostly tight-lipped and inarticulate in talking about the crisis. Always a man of multiple aspects, the Lincoln revealed to curious onlookers and well-wishers was a country bumpkin given to wearing ill-fitting suits and telling off-color stories. One observer commented that the president-elect was "making an ass of himself," finding it "disgusting and exceedingly humiliating ... that we have become so degenerate, as to forward an obscure ignoramus ... to the highest position in the known world."[11] Many of those

[9] Gregory P. Downs, "The Death Knell of Slavery," *New York Times*, May 25, 2011.
[10] Howard Jones, *Abraham Lincoln and a New Birth of Freedom* (Lincoln, Neb., 2003), 32.
[11] Burlingame, *Lincoln: A Life*, 2:30.

around him in those early days felt he was in over his head. Charles Francis Adams chimed in: "The impression I have received is that the course of the President is drifting the country into war, by its want of decision.... For my part I see nothing but incompetency in the head. The man is not equal to the hour."[12]

Lincoln's critics did not grasp that he had placed himself in the hands of a larger destiny that dictated confrontation. He had been working on his inaugural address since the time of his election, and he used it not so much to prevent secession (which despite verbal feints to the contrary he assumed to be a foregone conclusion) but to position his administration on the moral high ground for the struggle to come. His address on March 4 reiterated his conviction that the Union was "perpetual" and therefore secession was unlawful, but he vowed not to use violence to resolve the crisis "unless it be forced upon the national authority.... You can have no conflict without being yourselves the aggressors." The address denied both the correctness and the practicality of secession, but Lincoln did note that he had "no objection" to an amendment championed by Thomas Corwin, Charles Francis Adams, and Seward that would have permanently banned federal interference with slavery in the states where it already existed. This was less a concession than is sometimes thought: Lincoln was firm in his conviction that the Constitution did not allow and that he would not use (under normal conditions) federal power to limit slavery in the states. The amendment thus appeared to him to be unnecessary, but if others found it reassuring, he would not prevent its adoption. At Seward's suggestion, Lincoln added a final paragraph affirming that "we are not enemies, but friends" and memorably appealing to "the better angels of our nature" to resolve the crisis.[13]

However, no amount of poetic phrasemaking could forestall the crisis, and Lincoln did not intend it to do so. As Eric Foner observes, "Lincoln's refusal to recognize the legitimacy of secession and his insistence on retaining control of federal property in the seceded states amounted to a decision for confrontation."[14] Lincoln's primary audience for the address was not the secessionist South, which he viewed as beyond acceptable compromise, but rather the citizens of the uncommitted

[12] Denton, *Seward and Secession Crisis*, 141.
[13] James D. Richardson, ed., *Messages and Papers of the Presidents* (Washington, D.C., 1903), 6:5–12.
[14] Foner, *Fiery Trial*, 160.

upper south and border states, whom he hoped to persuade to stay loyal to the Union. Lincoln also aimed the message at European governments, especially Great Britain and France, whose response to the unfolding conflict would be key to its outcome.

Committed to confronting the slave power, Lincoln nonetheless understood that he had to act with caution in responding to the secession crisis. Political reasons made a direct attack out of the question. The national government could not appear to be bullying the South. As war approached, Lincoln acutely understood that the way the war began would be critical both in gaining widespread Northern support and in constructing a narrative justifying federal action. At this crucial moment, he relied on Polk's example as a guide. Polk had shown how easily the public could be galvanized for war by casting a particular incident as an unprovoked attack on American soil and the American flag. Much to Lincoln's disgust, in an effort to avert war Buchanan had abandoned federal installations across the South to the secessionists. Lincoln now determined to hold the remaining federal forts in the South – Fort Pickens in Pensacola, Florida, and Fort Sumter in Charleston – because he knew these were the two main "spots" where his authority to act was unquestionable. Whereas Polk had to send Taylor and his army into the disputed territory in order to provoke the attack he wanted, Lincoln need only wait for the South to fire the first shot on a preexisting installation. Then he would have an instant broad consensus in the North for defensive measures to secure federal property. The forts would function as ideal pawns in an opening gambit designed to lure the South into a vulnerable position. Even former president Buchanan had acknowledged the inherent right of the federal government to protect its property.

In the first weeks of his presidency, Lincoln cagily maneuvered the South Carolinians into firing the first shot. When they finally did so on April 14 in response to the anticipated arrival of a Union resupply vessel, Lincoln had the moral and constitutional high ground he so desperately needed. The fact that no soldiers died in the siege (the shelling did result in the death of a horse) deprived the president of the grounds to claim that, as had Polk, American blood had been shed on American soil. Nevertheless, the seizure of the fort functioned as the *casus belli* necessary to launch a full-scale war on the South in the name of defending federal property.

Although the war began as a narrowly construed effort to defend
federal property and thereby preserve the Union, Lincoln's intention
never wavered from putting slavery on a course "to its ultimate extinction." He recognized that, at the outset, Northern public opinion would
not support a war for freedom, but he also knew from Polk's example
that wars can start in the name of one cause and, once begun, evolve
into struggles for something quite different. So he carefully concealed
his ultimate purpose while building initial support for a war on the narrow grounds of the necessity to protect federal property.

THE IMPERIAL WAR PRESIDENT

With Congress out of session (it would remain so until July), Lincoln
assumed unprecedented executive power and began to manage the war
in an almost dictatorial fashion. On April 15, he issued a proclamation
calling for 75,000 volunteers to repossess the federal facilities seized by
the secessionists. Four days later, he issued another proclamation order-
ing the navy to blockade the entrances to ports of the rebellious states,
an act of war under international law that belied the fiction that the
conflict was a police action. On April 27, he called for another 80,000
officers, soldiers, and sailors to be enlisted in the Union forces. By April
1862, the federal military establishment had grown to 627,000 from a
pre-war force of approximately 16,000.

Lincoln soon followed up these measures by suspending the right to
habeas corpus in the state of Maryland; to prevent that crucial border state
from seceding, Lincoln arrested the entire state legislature. Confronted
with a massive rebellion and operating in uncharted waters in terms of an
appropriate response to the crisis, Lincoln neither hesitated nor equivo-
cated. If secession were to succeed, it would not be the result of half-way
measures to stop it taken by the president. From the start, Lincoln was
entirely committed to the cause, even if many in the North, including
some of his leading generals, were not. Although Lincoln had long advertised his preeminent admiration of Henry Clay, "the great compromiser,"
as president he responded to the crisis of the Union with a decisiveness
more reminiscent of Andrew Jackson and James Polk.[15]

[15] On Lincoln's little-appreciated Jacksonian side, see Sean Wilentz, "Lincoln and Jacksonian
Democracy," in Eric Foner, ed., *Our Lincoln: New Perspectives on Lincoln and His World*
(New York, 2008).

Although the administration's official line cast the war as an internal rebellion that denied the autonomy of the Confederacy, in practice Lincoln conducted the struggle as if he were at war with a foreign state. To a considerable degree, it was a foreign war. The Confederates had declared their independence, formed a union and a government, and were rapidly building a nation. In many respects, secession made real the de facto dual unions of the 1850s. The regional nature of the separation lent a binational aspect to the strife in a manner lacking in many civil wars in which both sides occupy the same political space. And while historians may differ as to what degree the North and the South existed as different countries by 1860, it is clear that Lincoln and the Republicans considered that the case, and acted accordingly.

Historians have recently shown how both the War of Independence and the War of 1812 were, to some extent, civil wars. It may be that the Civil War, rather than being primarily an internal conflict, is best understood as a foreign war against a breakaway confederation. The only "civil war" occurred between Confederates and pro-unionist factions in the South itself.[16] By the spring of 1861, the Confederate States of America had achieved a degree of independence and institutional autonomy characteristic of a nation-state. It had transcended mere insurgency. Though controversial, perhaps the most accurate name for the struggle is the War of Southern Independence.

Lincoln faced a three-front war. On the Southern battlefront he evolved a plan to starve the economy of the Confederacy via a blockade and to conquer it by multiple invading armies. On the European diplomatic front, he aggressively resisted efforts by the European powers (chiefly Britain, France, and Spain) to intervene in any way in the struggle, even at the level of offering mediation. On the rhetorical front, Lincoln repeatedly gave voice to what the war was about and what it meant both to Americans and to the world. This third front may have been the most important in that the war could not have been sustained for very long domestically or tolerated internationally without a clear and public justification.

The assault on the Confederacy, ostensibly a police action in the name of defending federal property, represented an unprecedented military

---

[16] See Victoria E. Bynum, *The Long Shadow of the Civil War: Southern Dissent and Its Legacies* (Chapel Hill, 2010).

and logistical challenge. It seemed an impossible task. The Confederacy occupied an extensive territory peopled by nine million whites, many of whom were armed and most of whom could be relied on to defend their land and their homes with great tenacity, if only in the name of repelling a foreign invasion. It was difficult to imagine the North being able to sustain popular support for a war to keep a resistant populace in the Union. However, the recent campaign against Mexico, in which a coordinated land and sea assault had resulted in the conquest of a nation roughly the same geographic size and population as the Confederacy, made the task more plausible. Northern factories were significantly more productive in 1861 than they had been in the 1840s, and an integrated national rail network now encompassed most of the northern states. Also important, the northern states had seen a 41 percent increase in population during the 1850s as compared to a 27 percent rise in the South. States such as Wisconsin and Minnesota, which had been minimally occupied in 1850, now had large and growing populations capable of making significant contributions to a national army. So it was not inconceivable that the national government could marshal the requisite troops and materiel and then project this great power to conquer the South. The question remained, Could it muster and maintain the political will to do so?

Reminiscent of the strategy employed to defeat Mexico, Lincoln's plan counted on the navy's near total control of the seas to make possible a blockade of the South, thereby cutting it off from world trade and resupply. Rapidly evolving naval technologies, along with a cadre of experienced naval officers, made feasible the imposing task of blockading an extensive coastline having dozens of rivers, bays, and harbors.[17] The hastily erected naval blockade compelled the European powers to respect its strictures by not challenging it. Early in the war the governments of Great Britain, France, and Spain announced their neutrality in the conflict, promising to respect the blockade and recognizing Southern belligerency but not independence. Lincoln and Seward, eager to maintain the fiction that the war was an internal police action, objected to the recognition of southern belligerent status even as, in private, they were relieved that the Europeans had gone no further. The issue of European intervention would hang fire for most of the war.

---

[17] On the Union naval effort, see Craig Symonds, *The Civil War at Sea* (Santa Barbara, 2009).

In contrast to the able and enthusiastic support of his blockade strategy shown by the navy's leadership, an inability early in the war to find army commanders fully committed to victory hindered Lincoln's plans to invade the South and decisively defeat the Confederates on the battlefield. Many were like General George McClellan, who harbored an ambivalence about the legitimacy of the war and who seemed content to engage the enemy in a limited way – as if the war was an elaborate duel aimed not so much to defeat the Confederates as to assure that the honor of both sides had been protected – and then withdraw.

Lincoln, notwithstanding his near-complete lack of military experience, instinctively recognized that victory required that the North use its advantage in troops and materiel to put continual pressure on the enemy at multiple points simultaneously. In this way, the Confederates could be denied the advantages of interior lines of support giving them the capacity to rapidly shift troops to wherever they were most needed. In addition, Lincoln recognized better than his commanders that the goal was to defeat the enemy's armies, not to capture its cities or capitals. T. Harry Williams, one of the most renowned of military historians of the war, thought enough of the president's wartime leadership to assert, "Lincoln stands out as a great war president, probably the greatest in our history, and a great natural strategist, a better one than any of his generals."[18] James McPherson emphasizes that Lincoln had an instinctive Clausewitzian grasp of the fact that "[t]he political objective is the goal, war is the means of reaching it, and means can never be considered in isolation from their purpose.... War should never be thought of as something autonomous but always as an instrument of policy."[19]

Lincoln assembled a war cabinet made up of many illustrious and powerful personages, some of whom had been more famous than Lincoln and had more experience in national affairs than did he. In addition to the well-known Seward in the Department of State, this evolving "team of rivals" included at various times the prominent abolitionist Salmon P. Chase at Treasury, Edwin P. Stanton at the War Department, and Gideon Welles as secretary of the Navy. Although historians have lauded the president for his courage in selecting this diverse and accomplished group as advisers and department heads, it is actually another

[18] James McPherson, "A. Lincoln," in Foner, ed., *Our Lincoln: New Perspectives*, 20.
[19] McPherson, "A. Lincoln," 23.

indication of his political shrewdness. In the tradition of the Chinese military strategist Sun Tzu, the president understood that it is best to keep your friends close and your rivals closer, if only to co-opt them as political opponents. Lincoln aimed to keep an eye on their attitudes while relying on the force of his magnetic personality to cultivate and sustain their support. It proved a winning political strategy.

The European diplomatic front loomed only slightly less important than the Southern battlefront. As was the case in the War of Independence, Southern hopes for victory hinged on gaining the support of a major European power that could provide it with military supplies, money, and, ideally, troops. Some form of European intervention seemed inevitable at the outset of the conflict. Great Britain, France, and Spain each had geopolitical and ideological reasons to welcome the breakup of the United States: Such an outcome would check the rising economic and military power of the upstart New World state as well as cast doubt on the durability of a republican system of government. From the time of the Treaty of Paris in 1783, Europeans had anticipated the breakup of the Union. Formal diplomatic recognition of the Confederacy appeared unavoidable, and more active support down the road seemed likely. "I cannot but feel," wrote U.S. minister to France William L. Dayton, "that all these governments are disposed to take an advantage of the present distracted condition of the United States."[20]

Lincoln and Seward took a tough line to head off the catastrophic prospect of European intervention. Simultaneous threats to the Union from internal and external foes had been the greatest fear of American leaders from the time of independence, and the administration unambiguously signaled that any foreign interference (even in the form of mediation) would not be tolerated. Ministers Charles Francis Adams in London and Dayton in Paris informed their host governments that support for the Confederate cause would result in a war with what remained of the United States. With an audacity as great or greater than that of Polk when he simultaneously threatened war against Britain and Mexico, Lincoln evinced a steely determination to confront any nation that intervened in the struggle no matter how overextended federal forces might be, thereby letting the Europeans know that their efforts to aid the Confederacy would come at a steep cost. For Great

[20] Jones, *Lincoln and a New Birth of Freedom*, 70.

Britain, that cost might include Canada, ever hostage to an American invasion. This alone proved sufficient to stay London's hand. Lincoln made it clear he would take the Union down in flames rather than meekly acquiesce in European meddling in what he defined, in this context at least, as an internal quarrel. The United States, though in no position to contemplate another war while preoccupied with the South, staved off foreign intervention by its previously demonstrated willingness to take on its enemies no matter how difficult the circumstances. The nation's well-established reputation for truculence gave pause to the Confederacy's possible allies. Neither Lincoln nor Seward publicly uttered the term "Monroe Doctrine" during their time in office together, but their determined efforts to resist European interference in the Civil War contributed to its elevation to a type of Holy Writ. In the 1860s, as Jay Sexton observes, the Monroe Doctrine "became a nationalist symbol, a permanent feature of the political and diplomatic landscape."[21]

The Union blockade of the Southern coastline and the sea-lanes approaching it constituted a radical reversal of the traditional U.S. policy of freedom of the seas. Having only about ninety ships available at the outset of the war to blockade 3,600 miles of coastline meant that an "efficient" blockade – stationing ships at the entrance of every Southern port – was out of the question. Instead, the administration opted for "flying squadrons" empowered to intercept foreign ships on the high seas and the positioning of warships at the entrances of neutral ports in the Caribbean and British Isles. These practices violated international law and the American principles so vehemently contended for during the Napoleonic Wars. Nevertheless, Lincoln and Seward shamelessly employed them in the name of national survival. With the fate of the Union hanging in the balance, neutral rights suddenly seemed less sacred than previously had been the case.

The Union blockade, a bold and provocative move designed to starve the South into submission, risked precipitating the greatly feared foreign intervention. Such action almost occurred in November 1861, when the USS *San Jacinto*, commanded by Charles Wilkes of U.S. Exploring Expedition fame, intercepted the British mail steamer *Trent* in international waters about three hundred miles east of Havana.

---

[21] Jay Sexton, *The Monroe Doctrine: Empire and Nation in Nineteenth-Century America* (New York, 2011), 153.

Wilkes, twenty years older and no less irascible than when he had sailed the world, instead of taking the captured vessel to a prize court for adjudication, chose to arrest two Confederate envoys on board – John Y. Mason and John Slidell – who had been sent as ministers to London and Paris, respectively. Deeming the two diplomats "the embodiment of dispatches," Wilkes declared them contraband and carried them off to be imprisoned. The British government and press expressed outraged at this latter-day example of impressment on the high seas, the violation that more than any other factor had caused the War of 1812. A third Anglo-American war loomed. Minister to the United States Lord Lyons worried that if war broke out, a desperate Lincoln might unleash a slave revolt: "British subjects may have their throats cut in a servile insurrection."[22] In January 1862, after several weeks of tense diplomacy, Seward, wisely ignoring the popular support Wilkes's actions had generated in the North, agreed to release the two Confederates. This bit of confrontational diplomacy had the unexpected benefit of getting Great Britain to renounce once and for all the practice of impressment.

The American war received a mixed response in Great Britain. Political conservatives tended to view with glee the imminent collapse of the experiment in republican government. The arrogant, upstart Americans were getting their comeuppance, and not a moment too soon. Manufacturers and merchants, as well, were generally inclined toward a Confederate victory that they expected would lead to an enhanced and freer cotton trade. Almost everyone hoped for a speedy end to the war, whose scale and horror shocked Europeans amid the relative peace of the mid-nineteenth century. At the same time the abolitionist tendency remained strong in Britain. All recognized that to aid the South in effect reinforced an institution outlawed in the British Empire in 1834. The working classes expressed strong solidarity with the Unionist cause, understanding their freedom to be in some sense connected to that of the slave. However, for the first year and a half of the war, British intervention of some sort seemed inescapable. Prime Minister Palmerston and Foreign Minister Lord John Russell waited for the right moment to act, for word of a Confederate victory comparable to that won by the Patriots at Saratoga in 1778. Precipitous

---

[22] Jones, *Lincoln and a New Birth of Freedom,* 57.

action in the short run risked provoking a bloody spat with the United States that no one wanted.[23]

The Confederacy's incompetent diplomacy increased the Union's chances for staving off European intervention. This was especially true as concerns the use of cotton as a tool of economic coercion. Cotton's rising importance in the economy of the Western world led South Carolina senator James Hammond memorably to proclaim in 1856, "[N]o power on Earth dare make war on it ... Cotton is king." When the war began, the Confederate government believed it could force the British and French into helping its cause by threatening to embargo new shipments of the fiber, thereby crippling the textile industry, which was critical to prosperity and social peace in both countries. Accordingly, President Jefferson Davis declared an embargo on all cotton exports in an effort to coerce European support. It seems odd that the Confederate leadership placed so much confidence in this new attempt at economic coercion given what a disaster Jefferson's embargo had been in forcing concessions from the Europeans. In spite of this history, the Confederate government vigorously enforced an embargo, going so far as to burn 2.5 million bales of cotton during the course of the struggle to keep it off world markets. The Confederates did not grasp that their heavy-handed efforts might have the effect of lessening support for their cause in Britain and France and, more importantly, prompting those nations to seek new sources of cotton from India and Egypt. In the short run, they did not even have to do that, because a bumper crop of cotton exports in 1860 supplied British mills with enough of the fiber to keep factories humming, at least for a while. Only in the latter part of 1862 did cotton shortages begin to occur in the textile mills of Lancashire. The crucial delay in making a cotton embargo effective combined with the blundering diplomacy of Slidell in Paris and Mason in London mostly negated the diplomatic advantages held by the Confederacy at the outset of the war.

Imperial France had its own agenda vis-à-vis the American conflict. To Napoleon III, the schism offered an irresistible opportunity to realize a longtime ambition: the reestablishment of a French colonial foothold in the Americas. A tripartite agreement with Spain and

[23] On British opinion about the war, see R. J. M. Blackett, *Divided Hearts: Britain and the American Civil War* (Baton Rouge, 2001).

Great Britain empowered the three states forcibly to collect debts owed them by Mexico. The controversy over the *Trent* affair gave Napoleon the opening he wanted. With Washington preoccupied with rebellion and averting war with Great Britain, Napoleon moved to land French troops in Mexico and install Prince Maximilian on the throne. Defying the Monroe Doctrine was a bold move, predicated on the assumption of a Confederate victory that would establish a strong buffer state between the United States and the restored French New World Empire. What began as a joint Anglo-French-Spanish beachhead in the name of debt collection evolved into a platform to revolutionize Mexico in the name of monarchy, to the consternation of the Lincoln administration. In the end, the artful diplomacy of Seward and Charles Francis Adams in London thwarted Napoleon III's ambitions. Their combination of bluff, bluster, and retreat worked to prevent Palmerston from committing Britain to the Confederate cause. With British power stayed, France and Spain ultimately proved unwilling to make any move without support of the British navy. To some extent, Seward's diplomacy reprised that of John Quincy Adams in fending off European intervention in the hemisphere by ensuring that British power remained sidelined. This rendered French ambitions much less realizable. Howard Jones observes, "The threat of war with the Union ... acted as a decisive restraint on Napoleon."[24]

Russia was the one major power that unambiguously supported the Union cause. In geopolitical terms Russia did not want to see the United States disappear as a counterweight to the British, whose victory in the Crimean War threatened Russian security. At the same time Tsar Alexander II, who on the day before Lincoln's inauguration issued a proclamation announcing his plans to free twenty million serfs, correctly saw the Civil War as another chapter in the Age of Emancipation, and Lincoln as a fellow emancipator. To Lincoln and Seward's delight, Russia neither recognized Southern belligerency nor received Confederate diplomatic envoys. Russia also refused to participate in Anglo-French mediation efforts. Russia's pro-Union stance bolstered the U.S. diplomatic position in Europe, significantly reducing the chances of intervention.

[24] Jones, *Lincoln and a New Birth of Freedom*, 183.

THE RHETORICAL FRONT

Lincoln's third and most challenging scene of engagement as commander in chief was on the rhetorical front, where he had to explain and justify the war, define its aims, and above all keep the border states in the Union by not making the struggle prematurely a war for slave emancipation. Early in the contest Lincoln might not have made emancipation a war aim at all had he been able quickly to broker a reunion of the states on terms guaranteeing that slavery be put back on a course to its "ultimate extinction." Hence, his public statements in the first year and a half of the conflict continually emphasized that it was a war to preserve the Union, not a war to free the slaves. In those early months, nothing could be done or said that might scare Kentucky or Missouri out of the federal camp. Thus, Lincoln quickly overruled the efforts of General John C. Fremont and General David Hunter to free the slaves in their respective military jurisdictions.

Although this action calmed abolitionist fears in the border states, it had the unintended effect of increasing European sympathies for the Confederacy. European support for the Union hinged on framing the struggle as a war to end slavery. If the Lincoln administration formally disavowed freedom as a war aim, what justification could there be for the slaughter? Forcing the South back into the Union with slavery intact seemed a senseless and notorious violation of the people's right of revolution guaranteed in the Declaration of Independence. Lincoln recognized that his domestic strategy of emphasizing the preservation of the Union to keep his wartime coalition of states intact perversely increased the risk of foreign intervention, but in the short run he had no choice but to persist in the policy.

Lincoln's rhetorical leadership encompassed several aspects. It was manifested in his public addresses, in which he justified the war in increasingly apocalyptic terms. It also was revealed in his numerous letters to high-profile newspaper editors, giving him a platform to address the public as a cagey interlocutor whose Delphic pronouncements could be given multiple meanings. Lincoln also exerted his rhetorical leadership in personal conversations, where he presented a warm and witty personage given to speaking in parable-like stories that often proved more persuasive than formal arguments. Overall, Lincoln's rhetorical skills were decisive in legitimating the conflict both domestically and internationally. The North could not have prevailed without them.

Few could have anticipated the zeal with which Lincoln prosecuted the struggle. Nothing in his background suggested he would be so willing to go to such great lengths to fight the war, although those who knew him well understood that there was an iron will beneath his gentle external demeanor. Before the war began, his former law partner, William Herndon, had privately assured the abolitionist Wendell Phillips that Lincoln would "make a grave yard of the South, if rebellion or treason lifts its head; he will execute the laws, as against Treason and Rebellion." Illinois newspaperman and longtime Lincoln observer Horace White remarked, "He intended to preserve the integrity of the Union if it costs enough blood to fill Charleston harbor."[25]

Once hostilities commenced, Lincoln personally oversaw much of the war effort. The telegraph office became a second home as he anxiously awaited reports from the front and micromanaged troop movements via telegraph. As president, Lincoln visited the troops eleven times, spending a total of forty-two days at the front and at times placing his own life in jeopardy. He directed an unprecedented mobilization of human and material resources. His calls for hundreds of thousands of soldiers led to the first American conscription act. To prevent draft evasion, he banned foreign travel for young men of draft age for the duration of the war. The war also saw the first imposition of an income tax and the first U.S. paper currency, in the form of greenbacks. The fiscal-military state first imagined by Hamilton reached full flower under Lincoln, harnessing the potential power of the Union in the service of a massive war effort. Yet, like the military force that it created, the fiscal-military state receded after the war's end, ready to reemerge later in times of national crisis.

The prosecution of the war did not spell the compete cessation of the western expansionist process. With Southerners removed from Congress, a distinctly Northern scheme of expansion accelerated. Nevada, its vast silver reserves beckoning as a means to pay for the war, entered the Union in 1864 before it had attained the minimum population of sixty thousand called for in the Constitution. Lincoln explained, "The immense mineral resources of these territories ought

[25] Burlingame, *Lincoln: A Life*, 1:754, 1:685.

to be developed as rapidly as possible. Every step in that direction would have the tendency to improve the revenue of the government and diminish the burdens on the people."[26] Colorado, also rich with mineral resources, entered the Union in 1864. The Homestead Act of 1862, long blocked by slave state opposition, opened the lands of the West to free occupation by American settlers. West of the Mississippi, the War on Native America continued but with far fewer federal troops, which were preoccupied with the Confederacy. This reduced military presence made the Sioux uprising in Minnesota in 1862 far more serious than otherwise might have been the case. In the so-called Dakota War, hundreds of Minnesotans lost their lives before that rebellion against U.S. authority was quashed and thirty-eight of its ringleaders publicly executed, the largest mass execution in American history.

A TOTAL WAR IN THE NAME OF FREEDOM

As the struggle entered its second year, Lincoln continued to insist that the preservation of the Union comprised the sole purpose of the war. Beneath these assertions, he blazed a clearly discernible path to abolition. Although he had very publicly rescinded Fremont's and Hunter's emancipationist decrees both as a usurpation of presidential power and as damaging to his still tenuous hold on the border states, that was not the whole story. Rejecting the premature emancipation of the slaves as impolitic, he nonetheless embraced General Benjamin Butler's policy of treating fleeing and captured slaves as a species of "contraband" of great material worth to the Confederacy and therefore subject to seizure. In 1862, the administration extended diplomatic recognition to Haiti and sent a minister there, an implicit boost to the idea of black freedom. In that same year, Lincoln made a pact with Great Britain to cooperate fully on the suppression of the African slave trade. Lincoln's moves to abolish slavery in Washington, D.C., and the western territories, and his ultimately unsuccessful efforts to craft a compensation plan to end slavery in the border states, are underestimated in their importance. These actions generated tremendous support in the free black abolitionist community and further encouraged its sense that, whatever policy tack circumstances required him to take, in the end

[26] Richardson, ed., *Messages and Papers of the Presidents*, 6:129.

Lincoln was on the side of abolition. Frederick Douglass, himself at times skeptical of Lincoln's political bobbing and weaving, ultimately affirmed, "A blind man can see where the President's heart is."[27] Lincoln proved a master at saying different things to different constituencies in the name of holding his fragile coalition together, and yet his deepest commitment from the start of the crisis was to freedom. Of all the political players at that time, blacks grasped that commitment most acutely. Their widespread understanding of him as the Great Emancipator was both accurate and prescient.

Deeply committed in principle to freedom, in practice Lincoln wrestled with what that meant, both to himself and to American society as a whole. On the one hand, Lincoln would never have consented to any agreement with the South that did not put slavery back on a course to its ultimate extinction, and in that sense the war was never "a limited war with the limited goal of restoring the status quo antebellum," as James McPherson recently has suggested.[28] Even at the outset, Lincoln would not have agreed to a plan for reunion that did not codify the principle of nonextension, the original point of contention. In the first months of the conflict, he had not glimpsed what the status of freed blacks might be after the war. His own limited dealings with African Americans precluded him for a time from having strong opinions regarding their capacity for full civil equality. As the war progressed, so did Lincoln's understanding of its implications. Beginning as a war for freedom disguised as a war for the Union, by its end the struggle had revealed itself to be a war for freedom, equality, and Union, chiefly as a result of the blood sacrifice made by the tens of thousands of freedmen serving in the Union armies and navies. Circumstances pushed the purpose of the war toward freedom. The abolitionist spring of 1862 saw members of this formerly despised community increasingly lauded as principled and farsighted critics of the now-palpable menace of the slave South. Even more important, tens of thousands of slaves now began to self-emancipate, fleeing to the Union lines, where their status as contraband mattered less than the fact that they had freed themselves from bondage. As newly liberated blacks began to clamor to be

---

[27] Manisha Sinha, "Allies for Emancipation? Lincoln and Black Abolitionists," in Foner, ed., *Our Lincoln: New Perspectives*, 179.
[28] James McPherson, *Abraham Lincoln and the Second American Revolution* (New York, 1990), 31.

allowed to fight for the freedom of those left behind, Lincoln had both an opportunity and a dilemma.

In July 1862, Lincoln announced his intention to begin to enlist black troops in the Union armies as a "military necessity," hoping this most expedient of reasons would overshadow the objections (both at home and abroad) to the idea of racializing the war by arming free blacks. It proved to be one of the most important decisions he made as president, for the approximately 200,000 free blacks that did serve decisively tilted the balance of forces in the direction of the Union. The stories of long lines of black troops courageously engaging in desperate, no-quarter combat in the name of freedom, equality, and Union did much to make the idea of full black citizenship plausible in the eyes of at least some white Americans, Lincoln included. To Southerners, in contrast, Lincoln's arming of the slaves constituted their worst nightmare come true: legions of armed blacks on the march against a slave-holding society. Lincoln himself seemed to understand the terror this held for white Southerners when he wrote to then-senator Andrew Johnson, "The bare sight of fifty thousand armed, and drilled black soldiers on the banks of the Mississippi, would end the rebellion at once."[29] It did not turn out to be quite that easy, but there is no doubt that the fact and symbolism of black troops fighting for both freedom and union is one of the most compelling motifs of the struggle, making reenslavement after the war an impossibility.

Having failed to work out a scheme of gradual, compensated abolition acceptable to the border states, by mid-1862 Lincoln had decided to use his emergency war powers under martial law to emancipate the slaves in the states in rebellion. Hoping to give maximum effect to his decree, he waited until Lee's defeat at Antietam in September 1862 boosted the Union cause sufficiently so as not to give emancipation the appearance of a desperate act by the losing side. The Emancipation Proclamation functioned as a sort of second Declaration of Independence, an announcement to the world regarding the nature of the struggle as well as a redefinition of the purpose of the war for Northerners. The Emancipation Proclamation transformed the war from an effort to put slavery on a course to its ultimate extinction to something resembling a form of immediatism, at least in the rebellious states.

[29] Edward C. White, Jr., *A. Lincoln: A Biography* (New York, 2009), 542.

Some at the time and since have criticized the Emancipation Proclamation as freeing only those slaves in the states beyond Lincoln's immediate control. These criticisms are not well founded. In the first place, Lincoln's strict adherence to law and constitutionalism meant that he could legally take executive action against slavery only in those places under federal martial law. He continued to seek other ways to end slavery in the border states, including plans for compensated emancipation and ultimately vigorous support for an amendment banning it outright. In the second place, everyone recognized that if slavery ended in the Deep South, it would soon end everywhere else. Lincoln presented emancipation as a war measure necessary for battlefield success, but it had even greater significance on the rhetorical front, where standing for freedom gave Lincoln and the Union an impregnable position on the moral high ground, both at home and abroad.

In spite of its function as a second Declaration of Independence, the Emancipation Proclamation contains language that is bureaucratic and restrained, especially when one considers the rhetorical capabilities of its author. One historian has described it as having "all the moral grandeur of a bill of lading."[30] Yet it is no surprise that Lincoln should choose to clothe such a transformative document in the plain rhetorical garb of wartime necessity, a lowest-common-denominator approach far more likely to garner a consensus than a soaring manifesto of human freedom that many Northern whites might find threatening. As a master of rhetorical theater, Lincoln knew when to make his words soar and when to make them crouch.

Emancipation also worked to snuff out any lingering disposition by Great Britain to intervene on the side of the Confederacy. Notwithstanding some fleeting concerns that freeing the slaves might precipitate a race war, the move suddenly situated the American conflict in the context of the Age of Emancipation, following as it did on the heels of the implementation of Tsar Alexander's decree freeing the serfs. At the same time, Lincoln sought to reassure those fearful of the consequences of arming freed slaves. He had long opposed radical abolitionists precisely because of their tendency to counsel and encourage indiscriminate acts of violence in the name of freedom that Lincoln

---

[30] Richard Hofstadter, *The American Political Tradition and the Men Who Made It* (New York, 1948), 132.

viewed as both morally wrong and politically counterproductive. Like John Brown, Lincoln planned to arm the slaves, but with a critical difference: His black troops would be bound by orders, their violence aimed only at combatants and not women and children, and then only in the name of liberation and reunion, not vengeance. Yet, aware of persistent and widespread fears that emancipation inevitably would lead to another Sainte Domingue, Lincoln added a cautionary ending to the proclamation: "I hereby enjoin upon the people so declared to be free to abstain from all violence, unless in necessary self-defense; and I recommend to them that, in all cases where it is allowed, they labor faithfully for reasonable wages.... And upon this act, sincerely believed to be an act of justice, warranted by the Constitution upon military necessity, I invoke the considerate judgment of mankind, and the gracious favor of Almighty God."

Richard Hofstadter once characterized Lincoln's movement toward emancipation as "a brilliant strategic retreat toward a policy of freedom."[31] If it was a retreat, it was to a position that, from the start, had been his ultimate goal. Lincoln's genius as president inhered in his ability to lead a largely resistant American people to a place of freedom that was the logical consequence of their nationalist ideology. He did so by placing the present struggle in a larger historical context. In late 1862 he urged Congress to remember "The struggle of to-day is not altogether for to-day; it is for a vast future also. With a reliance on Providence all the more firm and earnest, let us proceed in the great task which events have devolved upon us."[32]

Once the war became a war for freedom and union, Northern armies assumed broad powers to seize or destroy any Southern property they came across. The time for a mutual reconciliation under a partially reconstructed Union had passed; now the Southern wing of the edifice of Union would be demolished and completely reconstructed upon a new plan. Howard Jones notes, "Lincoln appealed to universal principles of right and wrong and concluded that the destruction of the southern government and way of life was necessary for the betterment of the republic."[33] In his second annual message in December 1862,

---

[31] Hofstadter, *The American Political Tradition*, 130.
[32] Richardson, ed., *Messages and Papers of the Presidents*, 6:58.
[33] Jones, *Lincoln and a New Birth of Freedom*, 6.

Lincoln put the issue squarely to the members of Congress: "The dog-mas of the quiet past are inadequate to the stormy present.... As our case is new, so we must think anew and act anew. We must disenthrall ourselves, and then we shall save our country.... Fellow-citizens, *we* cannot escape history. We of this Congress and this Administration will be remembered in spite of ourselves.... In *giving* freedom to the *slave* we *assure* freedom to the *free*.... We shall nobly save or meanly lose the last best hope of earth."[34] These lines reflected the president's increas-ing efforts to reframe the struggle as not only a war to save the Union but rather a war to advance the cause of human freedom everywhere. And even though it is by no means certain that the fate of republican government everywhere rested on the Union cause – the United States was, after all, not the only democratic society in the nineteenth-century world – it is clear that, thanks in no small measure to the president's rhetoric, white Northerners began to perceive the struggle in larger, historic terms. Equally significant, Lincoln's own spiritual convictions steadily deepened as the war progressed, as did his belief that the strug-gle he prosecuted with increasing fury comprised part of a divine plan whose ultimate form and outcome were unknowable.

THE LINCOLN COROLLARY TO THE DECLARATION OF INDEPENDENCE

Lincoln became a lightning rod for the emancipationist energies of the day, a political ground for all the lightning strikes for freedom both at home and abroad. His sense of himself as a tool of fate had grown ever stronger from the time of the Kansas-Nebraska Act. From that time, Lincoln began to speak and to act as a man channeling a higher power, in the service of a fate larger than him alone. Lincoln candidly acknowl-edged his role as a tool of destiny when, while triumphantly touring the ruins of Richmond at the end of the war, he reputedly said to Daniel H. Chamberlain of the U.S. Colored Troops, "I have only been an instru-ment" in the great struggle for emancipation.[35] A letter to a newspa-per editor late in the war in which Lincoln states, "I claim not to have controlled events but confess plainly that events have controlled me"

---

[34] Richardson, ed., *Messages and Papers of the Presidents*, 6:142.
[35] Burlingame, *Lincoln: A Life*, 2:151.

takes on a different aspect when one recognizes how much he saw all of his actions unfolding according to a providential plan not of his making. In the service of that plan Lincoln unleashed a political and military tsunami that he rode to ultimate victory even as it left unparalleled destruction in its wake. In classical terms, Lincoln put on a display of Machiavellian *virtù* in the name of a higher cause that even today leaves many observers unsure of his motives even as they applaud his outcome. Lincoln's key catalytic role in emancipation should not be underestimated. Lincoln, obviously, is not the only one worth remembering in the struggle to end slavery in the United States. But he is the one indispensable figure in the drama, the only person about whom it can be said that but for him the entire story would have been very different.

In April 1863, exactly midway through the war and three and a half months after signing the Emancipation Proclamation, Lincoln began to contemplate the larger implications of his actions. He had unleashed a war for freedom, and yet at the same time, the Confederate claim to affirming the right to revolution in the Declaration of Independence still had not been decisively refuted. Observers on both sides of the Atlantic still wondered why the southern states could not opt to form a separate government of their own choosing, as guaranteed in the Declaration. Such sentiments were widespread in Europe, especially early in the war, when Lincoln refused to make slavery the central issue. As rhetorician in chief, Lincoln, too, found this objection hard to answer. In a moment of reflection, he drafted a resolution on executive stationery that he hoped would serve as an answer to these objections:

> Whereas, while heretofore, States and Nations, have tolerated slavery, recently, for the first time in the world, an attempt has been made to construct a new Nation, upon the basis of, and with the primary and fundamental object to maintain, and perpetuate human slavery, therefore
>
> Resolved, that no such embryo State should be recognized by, or admitted into, the family of Christian and civilized nations; and that all Christian and civilized men everywhere should, by all lawful means resist to the utmost, such recognition or admission.[36]

In essence, Lincoln proposed a corollary to the Declaration of Independence: that the right of revolution does not include the right

---

[36] The text of this undelivered address can be found in White, *A. Lincoln*, 546.

to form a government built on the enslavement of human beings, and that "Christian nations" should resist any efforts to establish such governments. This provocative resolution merely decreed what had been Lincoln's and the Republicans' attitude from the start of the war, but it seemed in need of a more formal statement. Lincoln shared his draft resolution with radical Republican senator Charles Sumner of Massachusetts, who enthusiastically urged that it be published abroad in order to build support for the Union war effort and head off any lingering disposition to aid the Confederacy.

Lincoln never went public with his resolution, however, resisting Sumner's urgings that it be included in his annual message to Congress. Possibly, Lincoln was concerned that its godlike "thou shalt not" tone overstepped even his own expanded definition of constitutional executive authority. Nevertheless, it may be among the most significant statements Lincoln ever made, a crucial modification of the founding principles of American nationalism that, though never formally released, became the de facto policy of American presidents to follow – namely, that one people's freedom can never be built on another people's enslavement. Finally and firmly established as a foundational principle of American nationalism – perhaps best termed the Lincoln Corollary to the Declaration of Independence – it became equally important as a foundational principle of American foreign policy down to the present day.

Placing the war on the moral high ground of freedom served to legitimate the rising levels of violence and suffering the war unleashed. Historian Harry Stout observes that "emancipation decisively furthered the draconian military course he had already set."[37] Emancipation opened the door to a startling escalation of the struggle, in that a war for universal human freedom could be fought with fewer limits than a war for Union. Before the war, the greatest fear of white Southerners was being murdered in their beds by vengeful slaves; this never came to pass in any substantial way, but they could not have imagined the ferocity with which their own race would strike at them in the name of Union and freedom. In the place of compromise the war now proceeded upon the basis of unconditional surrender.

[37] Harry S. Stout, *Upon the Altar of the Nation: A Moral History of the Civil War* (New York, 2006), 168.

No one more symbolized the relentless righteous violence of the war than William Tecumseh Sherman. He, along with Grant, was a relentless practitioner of the strategy of total war, which designated all of the human and material resources of an enemy state as contributors to the war effort and dealt with them accordingly. The strategy of total war against the South drew on the tradition of the exterminating violence characteristic of the Indian wars. "We are not only fighting hostile armies but a hostile people," Sherman wrote. "We cannot change the hearts of those people of the South but we can make war so terrible ... that generations would pass away before they would again appeal to it."[38] His forced removal of all the white residents of Atlanta was preparatory to the near-complete destruction of the city; that campaign was a prelude to Sherman's famous march to Savannah, in which his battle-hardened army scorched a swath of destruction thirty to sixty miles wide against an unresisting populace. This was followed by an even more violent and relentless assault on South Carolina, the epicenter of the secession, whose people and property felt the brutal lash of Sherman's army in an effort to punish them. "The truth is, the whole army is burning with an insatiable desire to wreak vengeance upon South Carolina. I almost tremble at her fate, but feel she deserves all that seems in store for her." Throughout, Sherman remained deaf to calls for mercy: "War is war, and not popularity seeking. If they want peace, they and their relatives must stop war."[39] This chilling logic justified the nearly unlimited application of force in the name of victory.

REDEEMING THE REDEEMER NATION

As the ferocity of the war increased, so did Lincoln's compassion for both sides, a function of his rising awareness that all concerned bore some responsibility for the horrible conflagration. In place of senseless slaughter for no discernible purpose, Lincoln offered a providentially ordained ritual of blood sacrifice and redemption in which neither side stood fully justified. A not especially religious man for most of his life, as the war went on Lincoln relied increasingly on a type of Old Testament Puritanism to justify the slaughter to a weary people. In March 1863, he

[38] James McPherson, *Abraham Lincoln and the Second American Revolution*, 38–9.
[39] Stout, *Upon the Altar of the Nation*, 415, 369.

issued a proclamation designating a national day of prayer and humiliation, casting "the awful calamity of civil war" as "but a punishment inflicted upon us for our presumptuous sins, to the needful end of our reformation as a people.... We have been the recipients of the choicest bounties of Heaven ... But we have forgotten God.... Intoxicated with unbroken success, we have become too self-sufficient to feel the necessity of redeeming and preserving grace, too proud to pray to the God who made us."[40] Along the same lines, that October the president by proclamation designated the third Thursday in November as "a day of thanksgiving and praise to our beneficent Father who dwelleth in the heavens," a collective opportunity to repent for the nation's sins and to pray for an end to the war "as soon as it may be consistent with the divine purposes."

This enlarged spiritual outlook in the service of American nationalism informed Lincoln's two greatest rhetorical victories: the Gettysburg Address, consecrating the battle cemetery there, and the second inaugural address in March 1865. In the tradition of previous landmark documents such as the Declaration of Independence, both operated to explain America to itself even as they explained America to the world.[41] Unlike the Emancipation Proclamation, whose restrained language aimed to accomplish a specific task without provoking much thought, the Gettysburg Address and the second inaugural sought to generate support for the abstractions of freedom and popular government, to inspire the American people as to their future rather than inform them about their present. It was a rhetorical-political alchemy perhaps unrivaled in history and required only in a democracy in which the will of the people must be taken into account. Although the Gettysburg Address and the second inaugural address represent the culmination of Lincoln's rhetorical leadership, the two addresses would not have found the resonance that they did, both at the time and since, without the thematic foundation established by his previous statements.

Speaking at Gettysburg on such a solemn occasion provided Lincoln with an unparalleled platform to impose a narrative on the entire struggle, to make the immense suffering understandable while

[40] Richardson, ed., *Messages and Papers of the Presidents*, 6:165.
[41] On the rhetorical and moral significance of the Gettysburg Address, see Stout, *Upon the Altar of the Nation*, and Garry Wills, *Lincoln at Gettysburg: The Words That Remade America* (New York, 1992).

subtly inflecting the popular view of it. The rapidly proliferating news media, connected by wire and increasingly international in scope, eagerly reported and repeated the president's words, swelling the audience from the few thousand present at the address into the millions. Lincoln's brevity and lucidity made most observers overlook the way in which the address, using the hallowed war dead as an emotional pivot, continued the transformation of the conflict into a struggle to realize the promise of freedom and equality guaranteed by the Declaration of Independence. Audiences greeted Lincoln's remarks enthusiastically, even joyously. The Cincinnati *Gazette* described it as "a perfect thing in every respect"; the Philadelphia *Press* characterized it as "a brief, but immortal speech."[42] Proclaiming "a new birth of freedom," Lincoln made the war into a struggle for black freedom without mentioning the slaves by name, using his matchless rhetorical skill to gain the tacit acquiescence of many to this radical proposition.

Not all were taken in by the president's eloquence. The staunchly Democrat Chicago *Times* argued, "We submit that Lincoln did most foully traduce the motives of the men who were slain at Gettysburg. They gave their lives to maintain ... the old constitution and Union." The *Cheshire Republican* of Keene, New Hampshire, put matters directly: "If it was to establish negro equality that our soldiers lost their lives, Mr. Lincoln should have said so before. These soldiers won the day at Gettysburg under the noble impulse that they were contending for the Constitution and the Union."[43] The motives of the men who fought in the Union armies may have varied, but the president used his position and his eloquence to enlist them all in the cause of freedom and in the redefinition of the Union that was the edifice of that freedom.

Lincoln's second inaugural address completed the rhetorical transformation of the Civil War from its beginnings as a police action to restore federal property into a crusade for human freedom and republican government of historic significance. Continuing the narrative he had been crafting for some time, Lincoln cast the struggle as God's punishment for the sins of all Americans both North and South, even as he unambiguously named slavery as the cause of the war. In the spirit of reconciliation he claimed that "both sides prayed to the same God."

[42] Burlingame, *Lincoln: A Life*, 2:575.
[43] Burlingame, *Lincoln: A Life*, 2:577.

Strictly speaking, this was not true; the Confederate God countenanced the righteousness of slavery, whereas the Union's God did not. In some sense the war had been about this fundamental difference in Christian theology. Nevertheless, Lincoln counseled resigned acceptance to God's plan: "Yet, if God wills that it continue, until all the wealth piled by the bonds-men two hundred and fifty years of unrequited toil shall be sunk, and until every drop of blood drawn with the lash, shall be paid back by another drawn with the sword, as was said three thousand years ago, so it still must be said 'the judgments of the Lord, are true and righteous altogether.'"[44] This startling Old Testament balancing of accounts was worthy of a Puritan elder, but one should not necessarily conclude that it reflected Lincoln's own views on matters. Throughout his life, an acute sense of what the intended audience to his remarks would find plausible informed Lincoln's powers of persuasion. In this case he judged correctly that, in the minds of the American public, the immense sacrifices of the war, to be justified, had first to be sanctified.

Having transformed the war from a narrow struggle to restore the Union into a transcendent payment of a blood debt for a collective national sin, Lincoln essentially absolved both sides of responsibility for its cause and placed its origins and conclusion solely in the hands of God. Expanding his personal notion of the "doctrine of necessity" to the entire society, Lincoln suggested a radical way of conceiving of the struggle that resonated with a preexisting cultural Puritanism, even as he hedged all of his remarks with the conditional "if." Although it is not often seen as such, the second inaugural address is perhaps best understood as the ultimate statement of American Manifest Destiny. Any Jacksonian Democrat of the 1840s could have endorsed its fundamental assumptions that Americans are a chosen people with a divine destiny. Yet Lincoln's calls for charity and forgiveness amid the horrors of the war proved irresistible both at the time and since, seducing even those generally inclined to reject Old Testament explanations for human events.

As was the case with the Gettysburg Address, the second inaugural quickly achieved canonical status. Emerson described it as "likely to outlive anything now in print in the English language." A London newspaper observed, "His unshaken purpose of continuing the war until

---

[44] Richardson, ed., *Messages and Papers of the Presidents,* 6:277.

it ends in victory assumes the form of a resigned submission to the inscrutable decrees of a superior Power." William Gladstone, the British politician who at one point had assumed a Confederate victory as inevitable, now saw greatness in the American president: "The address gives evidence of a moral elevation most rare in a statesman, or indeed in any man."[45]

Because of Lincoln's leadership, the United States, after four years of fiery trial and sacrifice, had reestablished itself as the leading champion of freedom in the modern world. The war ended with the union made permanent, the empire on which it depended made secure, and the idea of America made transcendent. The European powers took note of the awe-inspiring might of the Union forces, a million strong by war's end. Sherman's army alone constituted what was probably the single best fighting force in the world at the time, an achievement made more impressive by the fact that this imposing force had been conjured out of a skeletal prewar military establishment. The marshaling of all the human and natural resources of the Union constituted the first industrial war in history and gave a preview of what the harnessing of the powers of the nation-state could achieve. The foreign policy power of the federal government had completed its inward migration, asserting itself domestically in ways that would have been unimaginable to the framers of the Constitution. Most importantly, the terms of the Union had moved from rational consent to sublime mysticism. The vision of a permanent Union, conceived by Franklin and fought for by Washington, had been finally realized by Lincoln. Destiny had been fulfilled.

Given Lincoln's acute understanding of his own role in precipitating this truly revolutionary conflict, his assassination one week after the war's end on Good Friday seems preordained. For most of the war, Lincoln had paid little attention to his own security, routinely exposing himself to enemy fire and the hostility of average people in a capital city that was, in effect, behind enemy lines. Knowing that he had asked so many to make the ultimate sacrifice, it is small wonder that he would put himself in danger, execution-style, to a massive head wound from short range. Of the many eulogies to a man whose historic significance was already clear, Karl Marx, writing for the *New York Tribune*, provided one of the best. He remembered Lincoln as "[t]he single minded

---

[45] Burlingame, *Lincoln: A Life*, 2:772.

son of the working class" who had led his country "through the match-less struggle for the rescue of an enchained race and the reconstruction of a social world."[46]

Lincoln did not live to see the ambiguous outcome of his war for freedom. His vision of a free-labor republic dedicated to the interests of working people rather than slave owners and capitalists did not come to pass. Instead, the centralizing forces that had been unleashed in the name of winning the war conspired after it to ensure that labor remained subordinated to capital and black remained subordinated to white, albeit in a free-labor context.

The final defeat of the Confederacy marked the end of the first period of the history of the American Empire. Arising from a fear of being hemmed in along the Atlantic seaboard, the embryonic North American Union had risen to hemispheric dominance. Great Britain seemed unlikely to challenge American power so long as Canada, still under nominal British authority, remained a de facto hostage to American goodwill. Spain had been evicted from the continent and mostly from the hemisphere. Its complete exit was only a matter of time and circumstance. French efforts to reestablish its New World Empire in Mexico collapsed in the face of staunch U.S. opposition, revealing the absurdity of Napoleon III's pretensions. Native American resistance, while ongoing, had been so weakened as no longer to constitute a serious threat to American dominance. Finally, the Confederacy, a homegrown would-be rival to the United States, had been crushed, to be kept in a quasi-colonial state of economic underdevelopment for the better part of a century. The United States was made permanent and stood poised to become a major world power, although its formal entry onto that stage would not occur until the century's end.

---

[46] McPherson, *Abraham Lincoln and the Second American Revolution*, 25.

BIBLIOGRAPHIC ESSAY

This book, though grounded in the author's quarter-century of experience as a researcher, bibliographer, and writer on the topics of early American foreign relations and the American Empire, is inextricably tied to a large body of scholarship, both past and present. The most influential books in the creation of the present text are listed here.

INTRODUCTION

Overviews of antebellum American foreign relations include Max Savelle, *The Origins of American Diplomacy: The International History of Anglo-America, 1492–1763* (New York, 1967), a still-valuable comprehensive survey. Bradford Perkins, *The Creation of a Republican Empire, 1776–1865* (Cambridge, 1993), offers a useful framework for conceptualizing antebellum American foreign relations. Walter LaFeber, *The American Age: U.S. Foreign Policy at Home and Abroad 1750 to the Present* (New York, 1994), traces the expansionist roots of American foreign relations. John Lewis Gaddis, *Surprise, Security, and the American Experience* (Cambridge, 2004), argues that contemporary American foreign policy actions are rooted in antebellum precedents. Robert Kagan, *Dangerous Nation: America's Place in the World from Its Earliest Days to the Dawn of the Twentieth Century* (New York, 2006), is a provocative work that connects the nation's pugnacious expansionism with the spread of liberal capitalism. George C. Herring, *From Colony to Superpower: U.S. Foreign Relations Since 1776* (New York, 2008), is a comprehensive survey by an esteemed scholar.

D. W. Meinig's *The Shaping of America: A Geographical Perspective on 500 Years of History*, volume 2, *Continental America, 1800–1867*

(New Haven, 1993), is, along with the other three volumes, a landmark achievement of multidisciplinary scholarly research and historical insight. It is an indispensable tool for understanding the geographic basis of the American Empire. James D. Drake, *The Nation's Nature: How Continental Presumptions Gave Rise to the United States of America* (Charlottesville, 2011), also emphasizes the importance of geography in the conception of the American Empire.

William Appleman Williams and Richard W. Van Alstyne provide starting points for the study of the antebellum American Empire. See Williams, *The Contours of American History* (Cleveland, 1961); and Van Alstyne, *The Rising American Empire* (New York, 1974; first published 1960); *Empire and Independence: The International History of the American Revolution* (New York, 1965); and *Genesis of American Nationalism* (Waltham, Mass., 1970).

Major Wilson, *Space, Time, and Freedom: The Quest for Nationality and the Irrepressible Conflict, 1815–1861* (Westport, Conn., 1974), remains a conceptually valuable contribution.

Books dealing with the topic of empire more generally include Michael W. Doyle, *Empires* (Ithaca, 1986), a perceptive comparative study, and Paul Kennedy, *The Rise and Fall of the Great Powers: Economic Change and Military Conflict from 1500 to 2000* (New York, 1987), which situates the U.S. experience amid the Age of Europe. Marc Engal, *A Mighty Empire: The Origins of the American Revolution* (Ithaca, 1988), provides a detailed account of the expansionist factions in each colony in the years before the revolution. Andrew Bacevich, ed., *The Imperial Tense: Prospects and Problems of American Empire* (Chicago, 2003), contains a range of ideological perspectives on the topic. Craig Calhoun, Frederick Cooper, and in Kevin W. Moore, eds., *Lessons of Empire: Imperial Histories and American Power* (New York, 2006), a distinguished group of scholars assesses American empire from a comparative framework. Charles S. Maier, *Among Empires: American Ascendancy and Its Predecessors* (Cambridge, Mass., 2006), is a sophisticated study by a senior scholar. David Armitage, *The Ideological Origins of the British Empire* (Cambridge, 2000), links U.S. imperial ideology and action to that of Great Britain. Michael Hardt and Antonio Negri, *Empire* (Cambridge, 2000), an important theoretical approach to empire; Amy Kaplan, *The Anarchy of Empire in the Making of U.S. Culture* (Cambridge, 2002), emphasizes the centrifugal aspect of imperial conquests; Niall Ferguson, *Colossus: The Price of America's Empire* (New York, 2004), is vigorously argued if at times problematic in its assumptions and conclusions. Ann Stoler, ed., *Haunted by Empire: Geographies of Intimacies in North American History* (Durham, N.C., 2006), offers a postcolonial view of American Empire. Eric Hobsbawm, *On Empire: America, War, and Global Supremacy* (New York, 2008), features four short essays by a leading British historian. Richard Immerman, *Empire for Liberty* (Princeton, 2010), traces the history of the American Empire through biographical sketches of six of its key architects. Eliga Gould, *Among the Powers of the Earth: The American Revolution and the Making of a New World Empire* (Cambridge, Mass, 2012), situates the rise of the United States as a part of the European imperial struggle for North America.

The American Empire cannot be understood apart from the creation of an American nationalism. Books on that topic include Ernest L. Tuveson, *Redeemer Nation: The Idea of America's Millennial Role* (Chicago, 1968), which traces the origins of redeemer nation ideology, and Conrad Cherry, ed., *God's New Israel: Religious Interpretations of American Destiny*, revised and updated edition (Chapel Hill, 1998; first published, 1971). Carolyn Marvin and David W. Ingle, *Blood Sacrifice and the Nation: Totem Rituals and the American Flag* (New York, 1999), offers a sophisticated analysis of war and patriotism as key bonding agents in the creation of American nationalism. Thomas Bender, ed., *Rethinking American History in a Global Age* (Los Angeles, 2002), is a collection of essays by a diverse group of scholars that places U.S. history in a global context. James A. Morone, *Hellfire Nation: The Politics of Sin in American History* (New Haven, 2003), emphasizes the role of Christianity in the creation of American nationalism. Thomas Bender, *A Nation Among Nations: America's Place in World History* (New York, 2006), is an insightful discussion by a leading authority on American nationalism; and Carroll Smith-Rosenberg, *This Violent Empire: The Birth of an American National Identity* (Chapel Hill, 2010), details the role of violence as a cultural bonding agent.

There is a growing literature that views U.S. continental expansion from a Native American perspective. It includes Richard Drinnon, *Facing West: The Metaphysics of Indian-Hating and Empire-Building* (Minneapolis, 1980); Stuart Banner, *How the Indians Lost Their Land* (Cambridge, Mass., 2003); and Paul Van der Velder, *Savages and Scoundrels: The Untold Story of the American Road to Empire Through Indian Territory* (New Haven, 2009).

I. ORIGINS OF THE AMERICAN EMPIRE AND UNION

Authorities on the Seven Years War include Francis Jennings, *Empire of Fortune: Crown, Colonies & Tribes in the Seven Years War in America* (New York, 1988). Eric Hinderaker, *Elusive Empires: Constructing Colonialism in the Ohio Valley, 1673–1800* (Cambridge, 1997), presents an anthropological-historical analysis of power relations in the Ohio country. Timothy J. Shannon, *Indians and Colonists at the Crossroads of Empire: The Albany Convention of 1754* (Ithaca, 2000), is now the best work to date on an early stop on the way to forging the Union. Fred Anderson has made a major multivolume contribution with *Crucible of War: The Seven Years War and the Fate of Empire in British North America, 1754–1766* (New York, 2000). Fred Anderson, ed., *George Washington Remembers: Reflections on the French and Indian War* (Lanham, Md., 2004) is a marvelously illustrated story of Washington's early career; and Fred Anderson and Andrew Cayton, *Dominion of War: Empire and Liberty in North America, 1500–2000* (New York, 2005), situates U.S. expansionism amid the legacy of previous European imperial efforts, and Gregory E. Dowd, *War Under Heaven: Pontiac, the Indian Nations, and the British Empire* (Baltimore, 2002), offers a fresh, largely sympathetic view of a major "conspirator" for Native American unity. Matthew C. Ward, *Breaking the Backcountry: The Seven Years War in Virginia and Pennsylvania, 1754–1765* (Pittsburgh, 2003), offers an insightful and detailed history of an often neglected front of the French and Indian War. William M. Fowler, Jr., *Empires at War: The French and Indian War and the Struggle for North America, 1754–1763* (New York, 2005) is a readable overview; Andrew R. C. Cayton and Frederika J. Teute, eds., *Contact Points: American Frontiers from the Mohawk Valley to the Mississippi, 1750–1830* (Chapel Hill, 1998) offers a social history of the frontier from top scholars; Andrew Cayton and Stuart D. Heiss, eds., *The Center of a Great Empire: The Ohio Country and the Early Republic* (Athens, Ohio, 2005), offers a comprehensive look at "the first imperial frontier." Richard Middleton, *Pontiac's War: Its Causes, Course, and Consequences* (London, 2007), is another recent text stressing the importance of Native Americans as

276

actors on the imperial stage. Matt Schuman and Karl Schweizer, *The Seven Years War: A Transatlantic History* (London, 2008), places the war in international context.

The rich literature on Benjamin Franklin includes Gerald Stourzh, *Benjamin Franklin and American Foreign Policy* (Chicago, 1954), which remains the best analysis of Franklin's expansionist vision. H. W. Brands, *The First American: The Life and Times of Benjamin Franklin* (New York, 2002) is the best recent full-length biography; Gordon S. Wood, *The Americanization of Benjamin Franklin* (New York, 2004), reveals how Franklin was an expansionist and a speculator before he became "the first American."

George Washington has been reexamined in Richard Norton Smith, *Patriarch: George Washington and the New American Nation* (Boston, 1993), which is especially insightful on Washington's time as president. Joel Achenbach, *The Grand Idea: George Washington's Potomac River and the Race to the West* (New York, 2004), details Washington's life-long interest both as speculator and a visionary in a river route to the West; Francois Furstenberg, *In the Name of the Father: Washington's Legacy, Slavery, and the Making of a Nation* (New York, 2006), provides a detailed if at times questionable analysis of the construction and evolution of the Washington myth, and Ron Chernow, *George Washington* (New York, 2011), is taking its place as a foundational text on Washington.

Important works on the War of Independence include Samuel Flagg Bemis, *The Diplomacy of the American Revolution* (Bloomington, 1957; first published, 1935); the passage of time has not diminished the usefulness of this text by an acknowledged past master in the field. Richard B. Morris, *The Peacemakers: The Great Powers and American Independence* (New York, 1965), frames the Treaty of Paris as an essential first step to the Northwest Ordinance and the Constitution. Gordon Wood, *The Creation of the American Republic* (Chapel Hill, 1969), is a classic text on the first two decades of American political history. Gordon Wood, *The Radicalism of the American Revolution* (New York, 1992), argues that the widespread emergence of a capitalist ethos in America is the revolution's greatest legacy. Alan Taylor, *The Divided Ground: Indians, Settlers, and the Northern Borderlands of the American Revolution* (New York, 2006), is the best study yet on the civil war aspect of the revolution. Simon Schama, *Rough Crossings:*

Britain, the Slaves, and the American Revolution (New York, 2006) vividly recounts the hitherto overlooked role of slaves in the struggle; Douglas R. Egerton, *Death or Liberty: African Americans and Revolutionary America* (New York, 2009), presents the Redcoats as an army of liberation for black slaves.

Robert H. Patton, *Patriot Pirates: The Privateer War for Freedom and Fortune in the American Revolution* (New York, 2008), is a highly readable tale on the key role of private naval forces in the revolution. Leonard J. Sadowsky, *Revolutionary Negotiations: Indians, Empires, and Diplomats in the Founding of America* (Charlottesville, 2009), emphasizes the role of Native Americans as catalytic agents in North American diplomacy. The ongoing war on Native America is covered in Glenn F. Williams, *Year of the Hangman: George Washington's Campaign Against the Iroquois* (Yardley, Pa., 2005), and Barbara Mann, *George Washington's War on Native America* (Westport, Conn., 2005). John Grenier, *The First Way of War: American War Making on the Frontier, 1607–1814* (New York, 2005), argues that the give-no-quarter conflicts with Native Americans served as the initial template of the Anglo-American warmaking tradition.

2. A PERILOUS UNION

Overviews of the era include Eric McKittrick and Stanley Elkins, *The Age of Federalism* (New York, 1993), which is both insightful and encyclopedic in its treatment of the 1790s. Wide ranging, detailed, and insightful, Gordon Wood's opus, *Empire of Liberty: A History of the Early Republic, 1789–1815* (New York, 2009), is a foundational text for the era by a leader in the field. Marie Jeanne Rossignol, *Le Ferment Nationaliste: Aux Origins de la Politique Exterieure des Etats Unis, 1789–1812* (Paris, 1994; English language edition, Columbus, 2004, translated by Lillian A. Parrott), is a valuable work that argues that American nationalism was intimately connected to expansionism. Peter S. Onuf, *Statehood and Union: A History of the Northwest Ordinance* (Bloomington, Ind., 1987), is the best single volume on this critical legacy of the Confederation government; Peter S. Onuf, *Federal Union, Modern World: The Law of Nations in an Age of Revolutions, 1776–1814* (Madison, 1993), is a foundational work by an acknowledged leader in the field.

Arthur Preston Whitaker, *The Spanish-American Frontier, 1783–1815* (Lincoln, 1927), is an older work that remains valuable by an early giant in the field. Thomas P. Slaughter, *The Whiskey Rebellion: Frontier Epilogue to the American Revolution* (New York, 1986), sheds light on this key event from both local and national perspectives.

Frederick W. Marks III, *Independence on Trial: Foreign Affairs and the Making of the Constitution*, 2nd ed. (Wilmington, Del., 1986), casts the impotence of the Confederation government in foreign affairs as a prime motive for creation of the Constitution. Roger H. Brown, *Redeeming the Republic: Federalists, Taxation, and the Origins of the Constitution* (Baltimore, 1993), emphasizes the need for a reliable taxation power as the underlying motive for scrapping the confederation system. Max L. Edling, *A Revolution in Favor of Government: Origins of the U.S. Constitution and the Making of the American State* (New York, 2003), describes the creation of a strong national state in spite of widespread opposition to the idea, and Gary Lawson and Guy Seidman, *The Constitution of Empire: Territorial Expansion and American Legal History* (New Haven, 2004), offers an authoritative account of the imperial dimension of the Constitution. Ralph Ketcham, *The Anti-Federalist Papers and the Constitutional Debates* (New York, 1986, rept. ed., 2003), offers a representative sampling of anti-Federalist thought. Richard Beeman, *Plain, Honest Men: The Making of the American Constitution* (New York, 2009), a lively narrative of the work of the framers, is a bit Whiggish in its assumptions.

In Burton Kaufman, ed., *Washington's Farewell Address: The View from the 20th Century* (New York, 1969), the author's "A Statement of Empire" is especially valuable. Jeffrey L. Pasley, *"The Tyranny of Printers": Newspaper Politics in the Early American Republic* (Charlottesville, 2004), details the emergence of the newspaper culture in the United States. Todd Estes, *The Jay Treaty Debate, Public Opinion, and the Evolution of Early American Political Culture* (Amherst, 2006), establishes the foundational importance of the Jay Treaty ratification fight. Ron Chernow, *Alexander Hamilton* (New York, 2004), is a masterful biography of the preeminent centralizer of the early republic. Stacey Schiff, *A Great Improvisation: Franklin, France, and the Birth of America* (New York, 2005), offers a detailed and gracefully written view of Franklin's diplomacy;

3. EXPANSION, EMBARGO, AND WAR

There is an abundant literature on the Jeffersonians and their policies, including Henry Adams's foundational *The History of the United States of America during the Administrations of Jefferson and Madison,* 9 vols. (New York, 1889–1891). Merrill Peterson, *Thomas Jefferson and the New Nation* (New York, 1970), is the classic one-volume biography. Alexander DeConde, *This Affair of Louisiana* (Baton Rouge, 1976), is a still valuable account of the purchase. In Burton Spivak, *Jefferson's English Crisis: Commerce, Embargo, and the Republican Revolution* (Charlottesville, 1979), the author's meticulous research and measured judgments paint a damning portrait of Jefferson's schemes of "economic coercion." Drew McCoy, *The Elusive Republic* (Chapel Hill, 1980), remains valuable for its understanding of the role of expansionism in republican ideology. Robert W. Tucker and David C. Hendrickson, *Empire of Liberty: The Statecraft of Thomas Jefferson* (New York, 1990), is a foundational text on Jeffersonian expansionist ideology. Peter Onuf, *Jefferson's Empire: The Language of American Nationhood* (Charlottesville, 2000), is useful on the construction of American nationalism; J. C. A. Stagg, *Mr Madison's War: Politics, Diplomacy, and Warfare in the Early American Republic, 1783–1830* (Princeton, 1983), is the first of several valuable studies by the author on James Madison; J. C. A. Stagg, *Borderlines in Borderlands: James Madison and the Spanish-American Frontier, 1776–1821* (New Haven, 2009), examines in detail the border politics of the Gulf Coast in making a defense of Madison's diplomacy.

Michael Golay, *The Tide of Empire: America's March to the Pacific* (Hoboken, 2003), and Walter T. K. Nugent, *Habits of Empire: A History of American Expansion* (New York, 2008), are lively and detailed overviews of antebellum expansionism.

Gregory E. Dowd, *A Spirited Resistance: The North American Indian Struggle for Unity, 1745–1815* (Baltimore, 1992), chronicles Native American efforts to resist U.S. expansion. Frederick C. Leiner, *The End of Barbary Terror: America's 1815 War against the Pirates of North Africa* (New York, 2006), is a well-researched and well-argued account of the last of the "Barbary Wars." Ashli White, *Encountering Revolution: Haiti and the Making of the Early Republic* (Baltimore,

2010), emphasizes the role of the Haitian Revolution as both specter and example to Americans.

4. CLAIMING THE HEMISPHERE

The War of 1812 has gone through a number of historiographical evolutions. Julius Pratt, *Expansionists of 1812* (Baltimore, 1925), first advanced the thesis of expansionism as the primary cause of the war; Roger H. Brown, *The Republic in Peril: 1812* (New York, 1964), frames internal divisions over the war in partisan rather than sectional terms; and Donald A. Hickey, *The War of 1812: A Forgotten Conflict* (Baltimore, 1989), provides a comprehensive and insightful treatment of the war that was perhaps the first step in the direction of a resurgence of scholarly interest in the War of 1812. In Alan Taylor, *The Civil War of 1812: American Citizens, British Subjects, Irish Rebels, and the Indians* (New York, 2010), one of the most accomplished historians of early America recasts the War of 1812 as a multifaceted internal struggle.

On war as a spur to nationalist sentiments, see Steven Watts, *The Republic Reborn: War and the Making of Liberal America, 1790–1820* (Baltimore, 1987). Watts is especially insightful on the role of the War of 1812 in shaping a generational shift in the direction of liberal capitalism. David Waldstreicher, *In the Midst of Perpetual Fetes: The Making of American Nationalism* (Chapel Hill, 1997), and Len Travers, *Celebrating the 4th: Independence Day and the Rites of American Nationalism in the Early Republic* (Amherst, Mass., 1999), take a cultural approach to American nationalism.

The Transcontinental Treaty is examined in Samuel Flagg Bemis, *John Quincy Adams and American Foreign Policy* (New York, 1949), and William Earl Weeks, *John Quincy Adams and American Global Empire* (Lexington, Ky., 1992), examines Adams's life and work through the prism of the Transcontinental Treaty of 1819. Angel Del Rio, *La Mision de Don Luis de Onis in los Estados Unidos, 1809–1819* (New York, 1981), tells the tale of an able diplomat valiantly defending a fading empire.

The abundant body of work on the Monroe Doctrine includes George Dangerfield, *The Era of Good Feelings* (New York, 1952), which remains a classic work valuable both for its style and for its substance. Ernest May, *The Making of the Monroe Doctrine* (Cambridge,

1975), argues that politics, not policy, drove the creation of Monroe's principles. James E. Lewis, Jr., *The American Union and the Problem of Neighborhood: The United States and the Collapse of the Spanish Empire, 1783–1829* (Chapel Hill, 1998), minimizes the significance of Monroe's words. Gretchen Murphy, *Hemispheric Imaginings: The Monroe Doctrine and Narratives of U.S. Empire* (Durham, N.C., 2005), traces the cultural and racial implications of Monroe's ideas; Jay Sexton, *The Monroe Doctrine: Empire and Nation in Nineteenth Century America* (New York, 2011), is a perceptive analysis of the doctrine's origins and political evolution as a foundational principle of American foreign relations.

5. FREEDOM'S EMPIRE, AT HOME AND ABROAD

Daniel Walker Howe, *"What Hath God Wrought?" The Transformation of America, 1815–1848* (New York, 2009), is the best one-volume treatment of a critical moment in U.S. history, dealing extensively with the expansionist dimension. Richard Slotkin, *The Fatal Environment: The Myth of the Frontier in the Age of Industrialization, 1800–1890* (New York, 1985), is extensively researched and bold in its conclusions.

The central importance of the slavery controversy is highlighted in Michael Morrison, *Slavery and the American West: The Eclipse of Manifest Destiny and the Coming of the Civil War* (Chapel Hill, 1997). Don Fehrenbacher, *The Slaveholder Republic* (New York, 2001) also emphasizes the central importance of slavery. Matthew Mason, *Slavery and Politics in the Early American Republic* (Chapel Hill, 2006), details how the controversy over slavery eroded the expansionist consensus. Brian Schoen, *The Fragile Fabric of Union: Cotton, Federal Politics, and the Global Origins of the Civil War* (Philadelphia, 2009), documents the key role of cotton in the emerging global economic system of the first half of the nineteenth century. Robert Pierce Forbes, *The Missouri Compromise and Its Aftermath: Slavery and the Meaning of America* (Chapel Hill, 2007), is the new standard work on a critical, if somewhat neglected, aspect of antebellum history. Elizabeth Varon, *Disunion! The Coming of the Civil War, 1789–1859* (Chapel Hill, 2008), traces the central role of slavery on the long road to the Civil War.

The idea of Manifest Destiny is explored in John Carl Parish, *The Emergence of the Idea of Manifest Destiny* (Los Angeles, 1932), which details how the idea of Manifest Destiny existed long before the term was initially used. Albert Weinberg, *Manifest Destiny: A Study of Nationalist Expansionism in American History* (Baltimore, 1935), is still perhaps the single best book on the topic. Henry Nash Smith, *Virgin Land: The American West as Myth and Symbol* (Cambridge, Mass., 1950), is a classic and still-useful analysis of the expansionist idea. Frederick C. Merk, *Manifest Destiny and Mission in American History* (Cambridge, Mass., 1963), remains valuable in spite of the author's dubious distinction between mission and Manifest Destiny. Reginald Horsman, *Race and Manifest Destiny: The Origins of American Racial Anglo-Saxonism* (Cambridge, Mass., 1981), is a seminal work on Manifest Destiny. Anders Stephanson, *Manifest Destiny: American Expansionism and the Empire of Right* (New York, 1995), constructs Manifest Destiny as an ideology extending back to the Puritans and forward to the 1990s. Amy S. Greenberg, *Manifest Manhood and the Antebellum American Empire* (New York, 2005), is an innovative if not wholly persuasive attempt to use gender theory to explain antebellum expansionism. Mark Rifkin, *Manifesting America: The Imperial Construction of U.S. National Space* (New York, 2009), argues that "impossibility" and "acquiescence" combined to make destiny manifest in the antebellum Empire.

Books on the U.S. penetration of the Asia-Pacific region include Warren Cohen, *America's Response to China: An Interpretative History of Sino-American Relations* (New York, 1971), a foundational text by an eminent East Asian scholar. Peter Booth Wiley, *Yankees in the Lands of the Gods: Commodore Perry and the Opening of Japan* (New York, 1990), is a detailed narrative based on both English and Japanese sources. Jacques M. Downs, *The Golden Ghetto: The American Commercial Community at Canton and the Shaping of American China Policy, 1784–1844* (Bethlehem, Pa., 1997), is a meticulously researched and engaged narrative of U.S. commercial influence in China prior to the Treaty of Wanghia. Sally Engle Merry, *Colonizing Hawai'i: The Cultural Power of Law* (Princeton, 2000), persuasively demonstrates how a legal system can function as a means of imperial control. Jean Heffer, *The United States and the Pacific: A History of a Frontier*, translated by W. Donald Wilson (Notre Dame, English language edition, 2002), offers a pointed overview by a foreign scholar.

Nathaniel Philbrick, *Sea of Glory: America's Voyage of Discovery, The U.S. Exploring Expedition, 1838–1842* (New York, 2003), is the authoritative work on the Wilkes Expedition by a premier maritime historian. Bruce Cumings, *Dominion from Sea to Sea: Pacific Ascendancy and American Power* (New Haven, 2009), emphasizes the trans-Pacific motives behind continental expansionism.

On the economic and technological revolutions essential to the creation of the American Empire, see Douglass C. North, *The Economic Growth of the United States, 1790–1860* (New York, 1966; first published, 1961), a still reliable source on this topic. George Rogers Taylor, *The Transportation Revolution, 1815–1860* (New York, 1968; first published, 1951), an authoritative, detailed, and concise account of an often-overlooked "revolution." Menahem Blondheim, *Over the Wires: The Telegraph and the Flow of Public Information in America, 1844–1897* (Cambridge, 1994), details the information networks that solidified the Union and tied it to the world.

6. EXPANSIONIST VISTAS: CANADA, OREGON, CALIFORNIA, AND TEXAS

On the politics of expansion, see Frederick C. Merk, with Lois B. Merk, *Slavery and the Annexation of Texas* (New York, 1972); Thomas R. Hietala, *Manifest Design: Anxious Aggrandizement in Late Jacksonian America* (Ithaca, 1985); and William H. Freehling, *The Road to Disunion: Secessionists at Bay, 1776–1854* (New York, 1990). Freehling argues for the central importance of the slave issue in antebellum politics. Michael F. Holt, *The Fate of Their Country: Politicians, Slavery Expansion, and the Coming of the Civil War* (New York, 2004), presents the argument over slavery and the territories as the primary cause of the Civil War. Sean Wilentz, *The Rise of American Democracy: Jefferson to Lincoln* (New York, 2005), is a voluminous treatment of the topic. John Belohlavek, *Broken Glass: Caleb Cushing and the Splintering of the Union* (Kent, Ohio, 2005), validates Cushing's importance as an antebellum figure. Edward Crapol, *John Tyler: The Accidental President* (Chapel Hill, 2006), is the best biography yet written of a neglected expansionist president. Joel Silbey, *Storm Over Texas: The Annexation Controversy and the Road to Civil War* (New York, 2006), is a brief yet valuable work on the Texas question.

On the presidency of Andrew Jackson, see John Belohlavek, *"Let the Eagle Soar": The Foreign Policy of Andrew Jackson* (Lincoln, 1985). Amy Derogatis, *Moral Geography: Maps, Missionaries, and the American Frontier* (New York, 2003), perceptively reveals the sometimes subtle mechanisms of imperial conquest.

On California, see Norman Graebner, *Empire on the Pacific: A Study in American Continental Expansion* (New York, 1955); Neal Harlow, *California Conquered: The Annexation of a Mexican Province, 1846–1850* (Berkeley, 1989); George Harwood Phillips, *Indians and Intruders in Central California, 1769–1849* (Norman, Okla., 1993); and Dale L. Walker, *Bear Flag Rising: The Conquest of California, 1846* (New York, 1999).

On whaling, see Margaret Creighton, *Rites and Passage: The Experience of American Whaling, 1830–1870* (New York, 1995); Lance Edwin Davis, Robert E. Gallman, and Karen Gleiter, *In Pursuit of Leviathan: Technology, Institutions, Productivity, and Profits in American Whaling, 1816–1906* (Chicago, 1997); and Eric Jay Dolin, *Leviathan: A History of Whaling in North America* (New York, 2007). Nathaniel Philbrick, *Why Read Moby Dick?* (Kindle, 2011), affirms the continued relevance of Melville and his work.

7. BULLYING BRITAIN, CONQUERING MEXICO, CLAIMING THE CANAL

Linda S. Hudson, *Mistress of Manifest Destiny: A Biography of Jane McManus Storm Cazneau, 1807–1878* (College Station, Tex., 2001), and Tom Chaffin, *The Pathfinder: John Charles Fremont and the Course of American Empire* (New York, 2002), are engagingly told stories of two prominent advocates of Manifest Destiny.

Samuel L. Haynes and Christopher Morris, eds., *Manifest Destiny and Empire: American Antebellum Expansion* (College Station, Tex., 1997), offers a range of insights on various aspects of the expansionist process. Cornelis A. Van Minnen and Sylvia L. Hilton, eds., *Frontiers and Boundaries in U.S. History* (Amsterdam, 2004), presents theoretical approaches to the study of borders by a distinguished group of contributors.

Donald A. Rakestraw, *For Honor or Destiny: The Anglo-American Crisis over the Oregon Territory* (New York, 1995), gives a detailed, closely argued analysis of Anglo-American diplomacy in the 1840s. Sam W. Haynes, *Unfinished Revolution: The Early American Republic in a British World* (Charlottesville, 2010), argues that Anglo-American relations remained predominantly hostile until at least the 1850s.

Gary C. Anderson, *The Conquest of Texas: Ethnic Cleansing in the Promised Land, 1820–1875* (Norman, Okla., 2005), and Pekka Hamalainen, *The Comanche Empire* (New Haven, 2008), are ground-breaking books that illustrate the crucial role of the Comanches in the geopolitics of the Plains.

Allan Nevins, ed., *Polk: The Diary of a President* (London, 1929), remains a key source for understanding American diplomacy in the 1840s. Charles G. Sellers, *James Knox Polk, Continentalist, 1843–1846* (Princeton, 1966), remains the best biography of an important expansionist figure.

David M. Pletcher, *The Diplomacy of Annexation: Texas, Oregon, and the Mexican War* (Columbia, Mo., 1973), remains a classic. Robert W. Johanssen, *To The Halls of the Montezumas: The Mexican War in the American Imagination* (New York, 1985), is a detailed review of the cultural impact of the war on the United States. John S. D. Eisenhower, *So Far From God: The U.S. War with Mexico, 1846–1848* (New York, 1989), is readable and frank in its assessments. Other aspects of the Mexican-American War are covered in Wallace Ohrt, *Defiant Peacemaker: Nicholas Trist in the Mexican War* (College Station, Tex., 1997), and Paul Foos, *A Short, Offhand, Killing Affair: Soldiers and Social Conflict during the Mexican-American War* (Chapel Hill, 2002).

Shelley Streeby, *American Sensations: Class, Empire, and the Production of Popular Culture* (Berkeley, 2002), assesses popular representations of the war to the American public.

Frederick C. Merk, *The Monroe Doctrine and American Expansionism, 1843–1849* (New York, 1966), and Samuel Eliot Morison, Frederick C. Merk, Frank Friedel, *Dissent in Three American Wars* (Cambridge, 1970): Merk's primary sources on opposition to the Mexican War make it still useful.

See also Patricia Nelson Limerick, *The Legacy of Conquest: The Unbroken Past of the American West* (New York, 1987), and Samuel Truett, *Fugitive Landscapes: The Forgotten History of the U.S.-Mexico Borderlands* (New Haven, 2006). Amis MacGuinness, *Path of Empire:*

Panama and the California Gold Rush (Cornell, 2008), offers an interpretation of U.S. isthmian affairs from a Panamanian perspective. T. J. Stiles, *The First Tycoon: The Epic Life of Cornelius Vanderbilt* (New York, 2010), deals in part with Vanderbilt's Central American endeavors.

On the gold rush as an event in international history, see J. S. Holliday, *The World Rushed In: The California Gold Rush Experience* (New York, 1981); Malcolm J. Rohrbough, *Days of Gold: The California Gold Rush and the American Nation* (Berkeley, 1997); and Kenneth Owens, ed., *Riches for All: The California Gold Rush and the World* (Lincoln, 2002).

8. DISUNION

Key works on the period from the end of the Mexican-American War to the beginning of the Civil War include the following.

On the political crisis of the 1850s, see Richard Hofstadter, *The American Political Tradition and the Men Who Made It* (New York, 1948); Glyndon Van Deusen, *Horace Greeley: Nineteenth Century Crusader* (Philadelphia, 1953); Martin Duberman, *Charles Francis Adams, 1807–1886* (Boston, 1961); Eric Foner, *Free Soil, Free Labor, Free Men: The Ideology of the Republican Party before the Civil War* (London, 1971); David M. Potter, *The Impending Crisis, 1848–1861* (New York, 1976); Alexander Saxton, *The Rise and Fall of the White Republic: Class Politics and Mass Culture in Nineteenth Century America* (London, 1990); Robert V. Remini, *Henry Clay, Statesman for the Union* (New York, 1991); James Dunkerly, *Americana: The Americas in the World, Around 1850* (London, 2000); Sean Wilentz, *The Rise of American Democracy: Jefferson to Lincoln* (New York, 2005); Michael F. Holt, *The Rise and Fall of the American Whig Party: Jacksonian Politics and the Onset of the Civil War* (New York, 1999); and William H. Freehling, *The Road to Disunion: Secessionists Triumphant, 1854–1861* (New York, 2007).

Robert E. May, *The Southern Dream of a Caribbean Empire, 1854–1861* (Athens, Ga., 1989), is a detailed, closely argued, authoritative treatment of a sometimes overlooked aspect of U.S. expansionism.

Yonatan Eyal, *The Young America Movement and the Transformation of the Democratic Party, 1828–1861* (Cambridge, 2008), is the best recent work on a key faction in antebellum politics.

On the filibusters, see Harris Gaylord Warren, *The Sword Was Their Passport: A History of American Filibustering in the Mexican Revolution* (Baton Rouge, 1943); Charles H. Brown, *Agents of Manifest Destiny* (Chapel Hill, 1980); and Robert E. May, *Manifest Destiny's Underworld: Filibustering in Antebellum America* (Chapel Hill, 2002). On Cuba, see Tom Chaffin, *Fatal Glory: Narciso Lopez and the First Clandestine U.S. War against Cuba* (Charlottesville, 1996), and Louis Perez, *Cuba and the United States: Ties of Singular Intimacy* (Athens, Ga., 1997).

9. THE IMPERIAL CRISIS

Key books on the foreign relations dimension of the Civil War include the following.

James McPherson, *Battle Cry of Freedom: The Civil War Era* (New York, 1988), remains a foundational work; by the same author, *Abraham Lincoln and the Second American Revolution* (New York, 1990), offers a brief and yet engaging perspective on Lincoln's significance. See also David Herbert Donald, *Lincoln* (New York, 1995); Howard Jones, *Abraham Lincoln and a New Birth of Freedom* (Lincoln, 2003); Edward C. White, Jr., *The Eloquent President: A Portrait of Lincoln Through His Own Words* (New York, 2005); and Edward C. White, Jr., *A. Lincoln: A Biography* (New York, 2009). White argues that Lincoln was more sincere in his religious views than is sometimes thought. Eric Foner, ed., *Our Lincoln: New Perspectives on Lincoln and His World* (New York, 2008); Eric Foner, *The Fiery Trial: Abraham Lincoln and American Slavery* (New York, 2010), argues that the contingencies of war pushed Lincoln in the direction of abolition; Michael Burlingame, *Abraham Lincoln: A Life* (Baltimore, 2008), is a comprehensive biography of Lincoln; Gary Gallagher, *The Union War* (Cambridge, Mass., 2011), contends that a desire to preserve the Union was the primary impetus for the Northern war effort.

Glyndon Van Deusen, *William Henry Seward* (New York, 1967), is a monumental work that is still the definitive biography of one of the most important nineteenth-century architects of American Empire; Lawrence M. Denton, *William Henry Seward and the Secession Crisis: The Effort to Prevent Civil War* (Jefferson, N.C., 2009), argues that Seward's efforts to avert a war deserve more credit than they have traditionally received.

The international dimension of the Civil War is probed in Howard Jones, *Union in Peril: The Crisis Over British Intervention in the Civil War* (Chapel Hill, 1992), and Robert E. May, ed., *The Union, The Confederacy, and the Atlantic Rim* (West Lafayette, Ind., 1995). R. J. M. Blackett, *Divided Hearts: Britain and the American Civil War* (Baton Rouge, 2001), emphasizes that pro-Union sentiment in Great Britain was greater than traditionally thought. Both Edward Bartlett Rugemer, *The Problem of Emancipation: The Caribbean Roots of the American Civil War* (Baton Rouge, 2008), and Amanda Foreman, *A World on Fire: Britain's Crucial Role in the American Civil War* (New York, 2011), situate the Civil War in an international context.

Edmund Wilson, *Patriotic Gore: Studies in the Literature of the American Civil War* (New York, 1962), is a classic analysis of the war from a literary perspective; Garry Wills, *Lincoln at Gettysburg: The Words That Remade America* (New York, 1992), casts Lincoln's rhetorical strategies in a political context. Andrew Preston, *Sword of the Spirit, Shield of Faith: Religion in American War and Diplomacy* (New York, 2012), contains valuable chapters on Manifest Destiny and the Civil War.

On the devastation of the war and the need to justify it, see Charles Royster, *The Destructive War: William Tecumseh Sherman, Stonewall Jackson, and the American People* (New York, 1991). Harry S. Stout, *Upon the Altar of the Nation: A Moral History of the Civil War* (New York, 2006), details how the increasing violence of the war was justified. George C. Rable, *God's Almost Chosen Peoples: A Religious History of the American Civil War* (Chapel Hill, 2011), assesses the role of faith in the justification for the war. Drew G. Faust, *This Republic of Suffering: Death and the American Civil War* (New York, 2008), recounts how Americans dealt with the sudden upsurge in mortality caused by the war. Nina Silber, *Gender and the Sectional Conflict* (Chapel Hill, 2008), suggests that the sectional divide had a strong gender component. Victoria C. Bynum, *The Long Shadow of the Civil War: Southern Dissent and Its Legacies* (Chapel Hill, 2010), is another chapter in the author's ongoing exploration of the divisions within the presumed "solid South."

INDEX

McCoy, Drew, 70
McPherson, James, 229, 232, 239,
   251, 260
Meinig, D. W., 64, 75, 150
Melville, Herman, 134–5, 147, 210
Memoria (Luis de Onis), 99–100
Merk, Frederick, 184
Mermento River, 99–100
Mesabi Range, Minnesota, 154–5
Mexican-American War
   all of Mexico sentiment, 199–202
   causes, 163, 188–9
   conduct of, 193–8
   as dress rehearsal for Civil War,
      194–5
   events leading to, 178–89
   opposition to, 189–93
   peace feelers to Mexico, 198–9
   support for, 192–3
   Wilmot Proviso, 206–9
Mexicans, and U.S. racial nationalism,
   188–9, 201
Mexico, Republic of
   Anglo colonization of Texas, 164–5
   Buchanan and border conflicts,
      224–5
   France's proposal to install Prince
      Maximilian in Mexico, 254–6
   and U.S. expansionism into
      California, 161–3
   and U.S. expansionism
      into Texas, 163–73.
      See also Mexican-American
      War
Miami Indians, 39, 56–7
Middleton, Henry, 158
Milan Decrees, 81
Minnesota, 250, 259
missionary frontier, 135–9, 159, 162.
   See also religion and politics
Mississippi River, 30, 36–9, 61,
   69–70, 99–100
Missouri, 111, 242
Missouri Compromise, 111–14
Missouri Compromise Line, 221, 228,
   244, 245
Missouri Debates, 111–14, 124, 168,
   225

Missouri River, 99–100
Moby-Dick, or the Whale (Melville),
   134–5
The Model Treaty, 22–4, 26–7, 28
Mohawk Valley, 31–3
Monongahela River, 1–2
Monroe, James
   expansionism and Northwest Coast,
      154–5, 157, 158
   foreign policy with Latin
      America, 98
   "hidden hand" presidency, 101–3,
      112–13
   Louisiana Purchase, 73–4,
      98–101
   and Missouri Compromise,
      111–14
   removal policy, 126–7
   second term, 114–20
   and slavery, 110, 112–13, 123
   treaty negotiations with British,
      78–9
Monroe Doctrine, 88–120, 158,
   179, 180, 204–5, 207, 242–3,
   252–3
Monroe-Pinkney Treaty, 78–9
Monterey, California, 149, 162, 163
Montesquieu, 48
Mormon Battalion, 195–6
Mormons, 224
Morocco, 75–7
Morris, Gouverneur, 41–7
Morse, Jedidiah, 35–6, 129–30
Morse, Samuel F.B., 129–30
Mortefontaine, Treaty of, 65–8
Mosquito Coast, Nicaragua, 204
Most Favored Nation Clause, 23
Mountain Meadows Massacre of
   1857, 224
Muhlenberg, Frederick, 60–1
Murray, William Vans, 65–8

Nanking, Treaty of, 144–5
Nantucket Island, 134, 140–3
Napoleon, 65–71, 81, 85–6
Napoleon III, 255–6
nationalism and appeal to
   religion, 19, 34–6